Stories We Need to Know

D1298131

Stories We Need to Know

Allan G. Hunter

FINDHORN PRESS

© Allan G. Hunter 2008

The right of Allan G. Hunter to be identified as the author of this work
has been asserted by him in accordance with the Copyright, Designs and
Patents Act 1998.

First published by Findhorn Press 2008

ISBN: 978-1-84409-123-2

British Library Cataloguing-in-Publication Data.
A catalogue record for this book is available from the British Library.

Edited by Jane Engel
Cover design by Damian Keenan
Layout by e-BookServices.com
Printed and bound in America

1 2 3 4 5 6 7 8 9 10 11 12 13 14 13 12 11 09 08

Published by
Findhorn Press
305A The Park,
Findhorn, Forres
Scotland IV36 3TE

Tel +44(0)1309 690582
Fax +44(0)1309 690036
eMail info@findhornpress.com
www.findhornpress.com

Acknowledgements

Any work such as this stands on the shoulders – if it stands at all – of scholars who have gone before, and so I happily acknowledge the obvious debts to C.G. Jung, John Weir Perry, Paul Radin, Joseph Campbell and others mentioned in this text.

The people who have helped directly with this work have been many and varied, so I'll start with those who offered material help. I could not have completed this project without the help of the Staff at Curry College Library, especially Hedi Ben Aicha and David Miller, nor without the funds supplied by the Faculty Welfare Committee, which in turn allowed Mina Gibb to do such an extraordinarily speedy job of translating my handwriting into text. The Academic Vice-President and Dean, David Fedo, and Dean Susan Pennini likewise were generous enough to grant me a sabbatical in which to do large amounts of the necessary work.

I was also considerably helped by being able to use research resources supplied through the Seth Sprague Educational and Charitable Foundation to the Curry College Honors Program, which is a recipient of a portion of those resources. More particularly I wish to extend a heartfelt personal thank you to Mrs. Arline Greenleaf for her on-going belief in this project, which springs directly out of my work with the Honors Program, and to Mrs. Rebecca Greenleaf-Clapp, her daughter, who has continued that generous support. This project could not have happened without them.

My thanks go to Dr. Ronald Warners, Director of the Honors Program who has been a friend, colleague, and the perfect tactful mentor in all this. Likewise I am grateful to the Peper Harow foundation (UK) for their assistance and guidance. At Curry College the Committee for Excellence in Teaching was generous in awarding me a grant which was used to pursue this project, and has my gratitude, also.

I am deeply grateful to Andrew Wilson for being able to use his translation of Euripides, and to Greg Atwan for his careful guidance through the subtleties of Greek Drama, and for his skills in translation.

Of those who offered me personal guidance no one provided more than Catharine Bennett, who was prepared, tirelessly, to discuss and help redefine the ideas on these pages. A special thank you goes to Robert Atwan, who was also more of a mentor than he perhaps knows, and I value his input enormously.

My readers – Jeanette De Jong, Jeff DiIuglio, Bette Manter, Alan Revering, and Patty Kean – deserve special thanks for their infinite patience and kindness, as does Paula Cabral for her on-going support. Other invaluable guides include Professor John Batchelor (Newcastle University), Professor John Carey (Merton College, Oxford), Laura Svenka Douglas, Dr. Peter Hainer, Rachel Hartstein, Rebecca King, Sensei Koei Kuahara, Paula Ogier, Andrew Peerless, Anna Portnoy, Nick Portnoy, Suzanne Strempek Shea, Professor Tom Shippey (St. Louis University), and Dennis Watlington. To all a heart-felt thank you.

To Thierry Bogliolo I owe deep thanks for his vision and belief in this project, and to Jane Engel I owe my gratitude for her skilful editing. I would also be remiss if I failed to mention Timothy Staveteig whose encouragement arrived just when I needed it most.

Inspiration came, in large measure, from my students who were really my teachers, especially Jane Deering who generously allowed her writing to be discussed in Part 2. To all my students I owe more than it is easy to calculate, since it was through working with them and seeing how literature could change the inner story that they were creating for themselves, that I was able to observe these six archetypal images in action. The largest inspiration came, of course, from the literature itself.

Table of Contents

Part One

Chapter One

The Problem of Soul Starvation

If we do not believe within ourselves this deeply rooted feeling that there is something higher than ourselves, we shall never find the strength to evolve into something higher.

—Rudolf Steiner

There are so many people, many of whom we encounter every day, who seem to be suffering from some sort of soul starvation. Many of us feel this at some point in our lives. Perhaps it surfaces when we find that for some reason we feel bored and discontented and that we don't care much about anything. At times like this nothing seems particularly important, in the sense that we feel no strong engagement with the outside world. Perhaps we slip into feeling that we don't matter very much to ourselves. For consolation we may turn to junk food, or go shopping. We may eat, drink and smoke to excess, or pop pills. Or we sleep a lot and still feel chronically under-rested. Occasionally for some of us this behavior will take a nose-dive into the devastating condition of depression, which is one of the western world's most persistent diseases. In a world that is full of beauty, of daily miracles, how can this happen? Unfortunately, for the person who feels lost nothing is beautiful.

In my work as a counselor I can say that this is the single most frequent reason that clients seek me out. Old or young, nothing much seems to have real meaning, and they are tired even of the obsessions that used to matter. This shouldn't surprise us. An estimated one in four Americans will take prescription medications to deal with depression at some point in their lives, as they try to cushion the distress that accompanies feeling lost.

Thomas Moore put the problem this way in 1992, in words that apply equally well to our century:

> The great malady of the twentieth century, implicated in all of our troubles and affecting us individually and socially, is 'loss of soul'. When soul is neglected, it doesn't just go away; it appears symptomatically in obsessions, addictions, violence, and loss of meaning.

So, how can take time to care for our souls so that we do not remain in this lost and unhappy state? Moore suggests that the individual's pain may, in fact, indicate a desire to find more to life than seems currently available, that it can be a turning point in the growth of the psyche. Obsessions and compulsions become, therefore, a form of poetry in their own right since they articulate a way in which the individual is reaching for a deeper and more vital reality than is currently available.

The situation is made more complex for the soul-starved person because we are routinely made aware by our news media that there are people who really do seem to be fully in the flow of life and who work effortlessly at what they do. Most of us will see this in its most dramatic form when we watch high level sports events, and the sheer physical mastery of those athletes thrills us. And yet the couch potato, living vicariously through TV sports events, is too prevalent a phenomenon for us to ignore; and that longing for a physical expertise that he or she will never achieve is, surely, a cushion against personal inadequacy. Was it just talent, training, and the accident of birth that made those athletes so proficient? How can it be that some people are so good at what they do, and others can't find anything that they want to do?

In fact the phrases routinely used to describe this situation all sound rather daunting, and that doesn't help. Finding 'what we're supposed to do' – our life-work, our true purpose, our direction – these descriptions make it seem as if there is just one thing we are here to do, so we'd better get started and track it down, and fast. But none of this tells us where to begin. Is it any surprise that so many people seem to give up? There are many popular books available that say they can help us: Julia Cameron's *The Artist's Way* and Eric Maisel's *Fearless Creating* are two good ones. But what if we are not particularly artistic? What if we're not naturally writers, sculptors, musicians, or painters? How do we nurture ourselves in that case?

There is an answer – or perhaps even several sets of answers – and this whole situation is made a lot easier if we can recognize that we have available to us a path that has been trodden very thoroughly by the generations before us. They wrestled with these questions too, and they've left us enough pointers so that, if we pay attention, we won't get lost. These pointers have been present in our literature, in our folk tales, and quite possibly in our genetic structure for several thousand years. Our ancestors have, in fact, left us a road-map of sorts, one that needs a little explaining to understand – just as all maps do. In this case we're not looking at roads and rivers, but at characters in the stories, characters who are images or archetypal representations of who we can choose to become at different points in our lives. These representations are clearly present in almost all of the major stories and religious texts that make up our culture, and if we choose to look into the stories and identify them, we can find considerable guidance for ourselves as to where it is our souls will need to travel to over the course of a lifetime.

These writings, myths, legends, and stories suggest that as we go through our lives each of us can expect to encounter six distinct stages of personal development, which always occur in the same order, each of which must be completed successfully if we are to become fully-realized authentic individuals. Each stage is embodied in an archetype recognized in our culture already – once we know what to look for we can see them every day – and each stage leads on to the next in a clear progression. There may be more than six stages; the ones described in these pages are simply the six most important ones. Certainly they are the most observable. The trouble is that most of us don't get much beyond the first two or three stages because we don't know that there is anything else. This is a bit like a traveler going on a road trip and stopping at the first hotel he runs across only to find he doesn't like it much. It doesn't have half the things he wants. But he books a room for the entire vacation anyway because he doesn't know that there are lots of better places just out of sight, barely a few miles ahead. Perhaps our traveler is lazy, or possibly he doesn't truly believe he deserves a place he will like. If he'd had a decent guidebook he could have avoided this mistake. Yet this is exactly how many people seem to run their lives, without any guidebook or roadmap.

My research and teaching over the past thirty years as a professor of literature and as a counselor has led me to identify the six major stages which we seem to need to go through, in the specific order in which they appear here, so we can reach the understanding that will bring us to a place of psychic peace.

Psychologists will probably label these as developmental phases, and they'd be correct. Yet they are also spiritual stages which, if we encounter them honestly and allow ourselves to understand what they're able to tell us, will generate the spiritual growth that all human beings are offered, and which only a few of us seem to be able to take on fully.

Why is this? Well, the world outside frequently seems to have other plans for us that get in the way – plans that don't include time for spiritual or mental growth. I'll illustrate this by giving you a story from my early years as a college teacher. One cold spring morning I was at a parent-teacher conference, a brunch that the college I worked for periodically offered to attract parents and give them the chance to meet the professors. I sat opposite the parents of one of my more promising students. The father wore a neat gray jacket and a silk tie and was clearly afraid of his tall, stately, over-coiffed wife. Suddenly she leaned forward and spoke in a rapid whisper.

"Our Roland does enjoy your classes, you know," she breathed, "but I don't think it's a good idea to have him reading those books. You know. They give him ideas. And we can't have that."

"Ideas?" I said, "Isn't that a good thing?"

"Yes, but he thinks he can be more than he realistically can be."

"I see. I didn't think *Gulliver's Travels* would do that." I answered.

"Well, we want him to get his education, of course, and get a nice job nearby, and settle down. That's what we want." The husband nodded his agreement.

"And that's what Roland wants?" I asked.

"Of course he does. He's twenty-one. We know what's good for him. The trouble is he keeps saying he wants to travel…"

Here was a thoughtful, caring family. And yet they seemed frightened that their son would ask too many questions and wander away from home territory. After all, why should anyone leave a place that is safe and cozy in order to travel? Is it a good enough answer to say that it's what human beings seem to need to do? That we want to explore, even when we're urged not to? I didn't know what to say to Roland's parents that night since they both seemed so afraid of what the future might bring. It was obvious that behind their fear was a huge amount of love for their son, and it caused them to want to keep him near.

Another example springs to mind. I was teaching a course on writing for self-exploration at my local Adult Education Center, and I asked the participants whether they felt the previous four or five class sessions had allowed them to think about writing in a new way.

Iruna, a lady of 92, piped up immediately, fiddling with her hearing aid.

"It's making my writing a lot more difficult," she announced.

"Could you say more?" I ventured, bracing myself for what might come. I'd been hoping for some friendly feedback.

"Well, every week I send a round-robin letter to the whole family, that's 13 in all, and I used to be able to write pages and pages about the garden and the weather, and who'd been doing what. It was a way of making sure we all kept in touch. And it was no trouble at all. But since I've been coming to this class, doing your writing exercises, I've had all these thoughts. And they're rather more complex. I simply can't go back to the old way of writing at all."

"Ah," I said, "so what does that mean for you?"

"Well, I just can't believe I wrote like that for so many years. I've had to re-think, you know, everything."

These two examples, decades apart, are pretty much typical of what can happen when an individual starts on a journey of inquiry, when he or she starts to comprehend that there are other ways of seeing and of being. Things get shaken up. They get complicated. People get offended or afraid. Life gets richer than we'd ever dreamed, and sometimes the people we know seem to want us not to explore this richness. A woman of 23 who recently worked with me would arrive at my office each week in tears, because she routinely encountered a storm of opposition and emotional blackmail from her extensive Italian family whenever she tried to speak about her need to take certain career steps on her own. Things got so bad that she was tempted to give up her plans for a career in radio entirely. She persevered, however, even though for a short period the verbal attacks she had to endure were brutal, unpredictable, and pitiless. By all outward assessments her family was a good, loving group that included uncles, aunts and many cousins – yet they are an example of how any of us can be held back from an exploration of our own abilities by those who profess to love us.

My purpose in these pages is to show how each of us can embark on our own journey, and what to watch out for as we do so, because even the best of intentions can never really compensate for a good map and the necessary background research as we set out. It's a journey that those nearest and dearest to us may find confusing or even illogical – just as Roland's mother did – and it may mean uprooting the habits and expectations of a whole lifetime, just as it did for Iruna at 92.

Joseph Campbell called this the mythic journey of the hero. Jung explored it in his extensive discussion of archetypes, as did his friends and close associates John Weir Perry and Paul Radin. When Perry and Campbell met up at a conference in 1972 they were both delighted to discover that they had spent their lives working on the same material, coming to very similar conclusions, although neither had known of the other's work until that point. These are the writers and thinkers whose explorations led me to the ideas we're looking at here. The story of how I reached this version of the archetypal journey is to be found later in this book, for the idea of the archetypal journey is not by any means new, and I don't claim it as such. It's been in our culture for millennia, and it has been more or less completely buried for the past four hundred years. What I wish to suggest here is that it has not been systematically assessed and understood, nor has it been shown in action in terms we can understand today. It is one of the true deep structures of the human psyche, if we choose to take notice of it.

Joseph Campbell, for example, suggested that the mythic journey is an option open to all of us, at any time after puberty. Working with students in college settings I've seen again and again how they are all, at some point, faced with the invitation to go on this journey. It is a journey that asks them to discover what is true for them, rather than what society at large considers to be true. Not all take up the offer, and some of those who do cannot stay the course. Some get lost; sometimes temporarily, sometimes for good. More than this, however, is that most people I've worked with have almost no idea where they are in their life journey, nor what starting their journey looks like. In fact quite a few of them think they've already started, when they've done nothing of the sort. The engines are racing and the car's in 'neutral'.

It's open to discussion, of course, as to whether life actually is a journey or not. We've no way of knowing for sure. It might turn out to be a pumpkin, say, or a ball of fluff. However, human beings have for a very long time chosen the metaphor of a journey in order to attempt to describe the experience of going through life, and we still do seem to prefer that description. Even a quick glance at the world around us will reassure us that, yes, as far as most people are concerned life is best described as a journey. Right now I have a newspaper on the table beside me with a Citibank ad that proclaims 'life is a journey.' A song on my car radio yesterday told me that 'life is a highway'; Jerry Garcia is famous for having described his life as a 'long, strange trip'; the Beatles' song 'The Long and Winding Road' seems to claim the same thing. We could add examples from other times in which we'd have to note *The Odyssey* as a story that depends upon the main figure completing a journey, and the *The Divine Comedy* which is predicated upon a guided trip through Hell, Purgatory and eventually to Heaven. We'd also have to include John Bunyan's *Pilgrim's Progress* (where 'progress' had the double meaning of moving forward spiritually and of taking a journey) and Chaucer's *Canterbury Tales*. Notice how these examples show the journey as leading towards an explicitly spiritual goal – heaven, or fulfillment, or even enlightenment. We can even find ironic examples of this metaphor, such as John Mortimer's extraordinary evocation of growing up with his blind, overbearing father, which he titled *A Voyage Round my Father*. There are far more examples and we don't need to record all of them here. What we do need to be aware of is that when people attempt to explain life to themselves and others they will tend overwhelmingly to use the metaphor of a journey to describe the experience of being alive. I will continue to use this concept, since it seems to be part of the way we turn experience into understandable language. That's why I refer here to a 'road map' that is waiting for us.

First of all, though, before we can go anywhere we have to know where we are right now. And that means we have to throw away the modern, popularly acclaimed map that got us lost.

The information that can help us – the roadmap for how to grow psychically and spiritually – has been in existence for as long as human beings have been telling stories. It's just that we've tended to forget this, and in the process we've got derailed. In our society we've tended to value the amassing of wealth and prestige above real growth, understanding, and true happiness. This is what the modern road map leads us to believe is important. We've admired fame at the expense of a genuine sense of who or what is important. Just like Esau in the Old Testament, we've traded our future fulfillment, our heritage, for what the Bible calls 'a mess of pottage'. Put in more contemporary terms this suggests that we are more likely to choose the immediate gratifications of right now – that bowl of savory stew when we're hungry, which is exactly what Esau went for – rather than considering the longer demands of responsibility, of dedication, of authenticity, that will lead us to real contentment. A full belly is nice; Esau knew that. It makes us feel contented and sleepy. But the lasting sense of peace that comes from knowing what your life adds up to is worth a few hunger pangs along the way.

We're in a world that doesn't routinely want to wait for real rewards. As a result our world is littered with has-beens, broken people who had their fifteen minutes of fame or notoriety and cannot now accept that they have found nothing else to offer or take from the world. These are the people who fill the pages of our tabloid press, the famous and the glamorous who seem lost in every aspect of their lives except those in which they are repeating the lines others have written for them when they stand before the cameras.

As more and more Americans turn to the solace of drugs and alcohol, or to compulsive activities like promiscuity or shopping or 'collecting', or to the consolations of food (which is one of the reasons the example of Esau feels so poignant to me), we have the right to ask how so many people came to be so lost.

We also have a right to ask how we can find our way forwards.

You see, it all has to do with that journey Joseph Campbell wrote about, and it also has to do with myths and the archetypes contained in them, all of which exist in stories that we need to know.

Notes

1. Steiner, Rudolf. *The Education of the Child*. New York: Anthroposophic Press, 1996, chapter 1.
2. Moore, Thomas. *Care of the Soul*. San Francisco: HarperCollins, 1992, p. xi.
3. Cameron, Julia. *The Artist's Way*. San Francisco:Tarcher, (10th Anniversary Edition) 2002.
4. Maisel, Eric. *Fearless Creating*. San Francisco: Tarcher, 1995.
5. Campbell, Joseph and Kudler, David. *Pathways to Bliss: Mythology and Personal Transformation*. New World Library, 2004. See also *Reflections on the Art of Living: A Joseph Campbell Companion*, ed. Diane K. Osbon, Harper Perennial, 1995.
6. Mortimer, John. *A Voyage Round My Father*. Play, 1970; BBC TV series, 1982.
7. Esau. The story appears in Genesis, 25. 29-34.

Chapter Two

The Six Archetypal Stages: An Overview

Theories of human development outlined by psychologists and other observers of human nature can certainly help us see how we grow as people. From Piaget to Erik Erikson and beyond, there have been many important insights into what happens in the human mind developing towards maturity. The schematic diagram I'm going to sketch out now does not seek to upset these observations. Quite the opposite; yet it may cause us to think about those observations in a new way.

I will outline the six stages now and then explore them later. I think it is helpful to see the way this unfolds as a whole, first. Then with a general idea of what is being proposed, it will be possible to consider each individual phase, or milepost, as part of a continuum. Please bear in mind that the terms used here are not prescriptive. They do not attempt to define people at different points in their lives, since people are all so different. The stages we'll consider correspond to actual, observed, reality and they occur in literature in the west from Homer, to Dickens, to J. K. Rowling. We can relate these stages to what we can see all around us, if we choose to notice it. And since each description is general, we should not attempt to be overly specific, or rigid, in applying them. So, for example, we all know what is meant by the word "dog." Yet there are thousands of breeds and cross breeds that are called "dog" – many of them completely unlike each other. A Pekinese is not like a Schnauzer, but they both share dog characteristics that we recognize right away, and neither is likely to be confused for a cat.

Here, then, are the six stages I wish you to consider:

Innocent
Orphan
Pilgrim
Warrior-Lover
Monarch Pair (the King and Queen)
Magician

These have been called types. I have observed them so often, and feel them to be so pervasive in the human psyche that I am going to refer to them as *archetypes*.

So, what is an archetype? The easiest way to explain this is to compare it to its sisters: the type, and the stereotype, which I see as roughly hierarchical. For example, I can look out of my window at the birdfeeder and see a cardinal flying about in my yard. It is a male, and certainly an individual with individual preferences. One of its preferences seems to be to head for the black walnut tree, which it uses each morning as a place from which to utter its piercing song of territorialism and, at 5:00 a.m., I am not always the most appreciative listener. So, the bird is an individual, yet I "type" it as a male cardinal. As such, it seems to do what most male cardinals do. It is also, however, a land bird – a more general category, certainly, yet a helpful one if one wants to consider its behavior. As a land bird it has "stereotypical" actions that have to do with its land bird status. It doesn't seem to eat fish, visit beaches, or want to settle on water as a gull might. The over-arching category, however, would be as "bird," which differentiates it from fish, bees, flowers, and so on. This could be compared to the way I am using the word archetype.

When I refer to archetypes, as I will do frequently, it will be most helpful if we bear in mind that just as each male cardinal is an individual, it is also part of a species and genus. There are thousands upon thousands of bird species in the world, millions of individuals, all different, yet all share similarities. My task here is to try and identify human archetypes that are similarly possessed of many possible variations. So, "United States Citizens" come from all over the world, and yet there is something about them that, despite 300 million individual quirks, we can often identify as being different from, say Japanese or Ukrainians. Perhaps Japanese-Americans feel themselves to be a separate category, yet they all pay taxes, have the same voting and human rights, are subject to the same laws, and operate within the same systems as everyone else in the U.S.

An archetype, then, is a large category, in which there can be many individual variations. Perhaps another comparison will help. Two hundred passengers get on a plane for Chicago; all of them are different, except that they are all on the way to Chicago. So, for our purposes, an archetype is used to describe the direction in which a person is moving in his or her life trajectory.

In order to understand this idea we'll need first to give an overall, general description of what the archetypal stages are and how they fit together. Only then can we apply that idea back to our cultural ideas (literature is particularly revealing) to see how it works in detail. If we accept the axiom that great, lasting literature endures because it explores human behavior and, as a result, it articulates significant things about how we live – if we accept that premise – then we can refer to some of the great works of literature, see how they mirror the stages, and how the writers understand them.

It's also worth recalling that the idea of stages is an artificial one. Just as a 13-year-old can behave like a 5-year-old one moment and a 35-year-old the next, the stages I will describe are not definitive. We have to learn to be flexible in our thinking in order to understand how this works. Each stage will be described here in its most typical forms. Each stage also has the possibility to be expressed in a number of ways, which can be either active or passive or balanced, and these forms are discussed as part of each main description. We'll also ask what it feels like to live each archetype, since sometimes the best way to identify a stage is by how it feels when one is in it. We all have a notion about what we may be feeling, and when we're in the middle of something this may be easier than trying to reflect upon it in a more detached way.

The archetypes function as follows:

We arrive in the world as **Innocents**, defenseless and undefending. We trust, we accept, we love, and feel ourselves loved. During this vulnerable period we learn lessons that will take us successfully through the rest of our lives, especially our lives in relationship to those closest to us. If we do not learn how to love, trust, and feel safe, we will pay grievously for it in later life, in terms of being unable to make lasting relationships with others. Another valuable attitude we can gain from this stage is the ability to be open and receptive, and it's a quality we can carry with us throughout our lives. As Barbara Sher put it:

> You can learn new things at any time in your life if you're willing to be a beginner. If you actually learn to like being a beginner the whole world opens up to you.

I'm sure we can all think of those times when we've been afraid to ask the question we thought was going to show us as ignorant, and paid the price for it later. The Innocent has no such hesitations and has no fear of mistakes. As a result she is a rapid and even fearless learner.

Sooner or later this Eden-like world is shattered by something that undermines our sense of trust, and at that point we feel abandoned. We may feel as if no one loves us and we are unlovable. At this point we enter the **Orphan** stage, looking for someone to take care of us, or someone to identify with. The teenager's cry of 'you don't understand' is more a statement about her own confusion – that feeling that no one could possibly understand the situation – and less a true assessment of the parents, who may understand only too well. However it comes about, the growing young person feels pushed out of the nest, alone, threatened, misunderstood, and desperate to be understood by someone.

This important stage requires that the child has someone to take care of his or her bodily needs, but that this person can no longer be held close or fully trusted.

Parents note with despair that their teenager no longer seems to respect them or listen to them. Yet that is only half the situation. The other half is that in order for the young person to discover who she might be, she has to begin by rejecting several aspects of the identity she has established within the family structure. Rejecting is what she needs to do while she tries to work out what her psychic needs might be, and therefore who she might be in herself. In this stage we define ourselves by who we are not, because it's easier than trying to find out directly who we are.

After this rebellion against the accepted order of things some young people then attach to a group that they feel defines and expresses who they are. If this group is part of the acknowledged social order then the young person is adopted into it and from there re-assimilates into the social hierarchy. In this case the Orphan has, after a brief foray into the world, chosen to remain happily as an Orphan who is now fully adopted, and sensing the advantages of being part of the regular world, embraces them.

Not all Orphans can do this, however. Some leave the security of the established order and take on the task of questioning, probing, and not settling down as others do. These are the young people who cause their parents the most anguish, since conventional wisdom seems to demand that if one does not have a steady job and career and family prospects by age 25, then there is something radically wrong somewhere. In fact there may not be anything wrong at all; it may be more a case of the individual taking the time to find out who he or she might be outside the accepted social order.

At this point the young person is about to embark on the **Pilgrim** stage. She is asking herself who she might be apart from peers and parents and social expectations. It may require that she leave the adopted home, the peer group, the parents she already feels so alienated from, even the country she lives in, so she can find herself. Previously her rebellion was about rejecting whatever it was that was offered. Now it's about accepting some segments, and building a sense of identity from the fragments. The Pilgrim is trying to find out what her capabilities are.

The pilgrim of ancient times set out on a deliberate journey, heading towards a shrine. Along the way were various smaller shrines that had to be honored, and the time spent on the journey was to be passed in thinking about the nature of the spiritual journey, and what one expected to find at its end. The outer journey was supposed to be a physical expression of the inner explorations. The great cathedrals of Europe were (and still are) the destinations for these pilgrims. Chaucer's *Canterbury Tales* is in some ways a humorous version of this, since the pilgrims spend a lot of time telling tales that offend each other, and they seem to think of God very little. It's a splendid example of how easy it is to forget the real nature of the spiritual quest.

When the Pilgrim does find a reliable sense of self, one that feels true, then the challenge is whether or not the individual is going to want to use that information to do anything useful. After all, one can decide that one is a drone, and live that way. But the Pilgrim who knows who she is, and what possibilities that holds, becomes ready to take on a real attachment to life. This marks the transition into the **Warrior-Lover** stage. Just as the Warrior can only fight for what she loves, and can only love what is worth fighting for, so this stage is one that is filled with passionate commitment. This commitment may be to a person or to a cause, or most natural of all, to the family one creates. In each case it asks that the person declare who she is, what she loves, and that she will fight for those values. Alas, some people drift into matrimony and parenthood with no real attachment to spouse or children. These are the people who have somehow failed to identify who they are, and what they want, while in Pilgrim stage. Failure at any stage causes us to slip back to the previous stage. We get to do the lesson over until we get it right. Some people never do get it right, of course, but the opportunities are always there for each and every one of us.

As the Warrior-Lover fights for the well-being of others, she can become overly identified with this heroic struggle and self-dramatize in a way that merely inflates her sense of self-importance. If the Warrior-Lover can see this danger and not give in to it she can begin to perceive that as a parent, as a champion of others' rights as well as her own she is, in fact, a sort of servant to a cause. This is when the Warrior-Lover is ready to merge a sense of pride with an awareness of humility and so move into the stage of the **Monarch Pair** – one who serves and protects something larger than her immediate turf, symbolized here as a whole kingdom.

The Monarch Pair is definitely not the one-person powerhouse that the Warrior-Lover tends to be. The Monarch pair, or Monarch, as we shall be referring to this twinned figure, represents the fusion of the gentle female attributes symbolized by the Queen, and the stern male attributes of the King. This is the figure who is in command but enlists help from others. So the parent who is determined to bring up her child properly now softens, and becomes the person who wants to work with the child and with the community so they all can have the life they need. If the Warrior-Lover's life is about sacrifice, even to the point of death, the Monarch is about getting the job done with everyone's harmonious participation, and with a nudge to the child to make sure she pulls her own weight, too. The Warrior-Lover might run the show single handedly – as many single parents do – but the Monarch is more likely to step back and ask the children to be part of solving life's daily challenges. Notice that the Monarch is still the one who carries responsibility, and a Monarch who truly can delegate, who can trust and take responsibility, can seem to work miracles when others struggle. This is the sort of every day magic that brings us to the next stage.

The **Magician** is more like a grandparent, or an adviser who lives outside the daily confusions of the young people growing up. This person can say just the right words, at just the right moment, and change the situation for the better. For example, a man once reported to me that he had been to see the most marvelous therapist. He'd been talking with this therapist for several weeks he said, talks in which he barely let the therapist say anything, as he poured out his woes about whether he should leave his wife and go off with another woman, and which of the two was really the right person for him, and how it would hurt someone either way. He had been going in circles with this for some time. Eventually the therapist simply said: "You know, it's not an either/or situation. Perhaps neither one is right for you." And that, the man claimed, hit him like a blaze of sunshine. It changed his whole way of looking at his life. It's not how much the Magician says, or even whether he or she is necessarily right. It is, instead, that words which can change the situation can be heard when they come from this person. At a more ordinary level, this is Grandma, who can calm the baby when Mother is at her wits' end. This is Grandpa, who can say two words to rebellious Jimmy that will make him see another side to the problem, and make him capable of greater compassion. How do they do it? You could call it Magic. You could also say that this figure has contacted the real wisdom that comes from being in alignment with the positive energy of the divine.

This, in a brief sketch, is what we'll be looking at.

Note

1. Barbara Sher, motivational speaker, quoted in www.brainyquote/quotes/b/bar-barashe173969.html

Chapter Three

The Innocent

Whenever we start something new we have the chance to approach it as an Innocent, because we haven't done it before. And we have at least three choices in the way we act as Innocents. I'll refer to these as incarnations. For example, a newborn, or a young child, is likely to show herself as one of several things: the child can be totally compliant, or totally difficult. Mostly, children become something between the two. In terms of feeding, there are children who settle down and accept being fed right away and are very easy, whereas other children seem to be difficult – for whatever reason. Most children fall somewhere between the two extremes, at different times. Now, translate this back to something like a new office employee. When he or she first arrives in the workplace, that person may be a true Innocent – gullible and easily ordered around – or the exact opposite, someone who uses the status of Innocent in order to get away with doing less. The gullible employee gets set up for abuse, while the difficult employee radiates an attitude that signals: "I don't know anything, so you'll have to do it for me," and "You can't expect me to do anything because I'm new." Obviously, neither attitude is very helpful if one actually wants to get any work done and most of us choose a middle way. We look out for those who may want to mislead us for their own ends, and we also try to do the best we can so we can stay employed. Getting the balance right is the real challenge. If we want to describe this in other terms, we could say there is a passive affect incarnation (helpful and unsuspecting to a fault); an active affect incarnation (unhelpful and rejecting in an overly defensive mode); and a balanced incarnation (trusting, but not dumb or manipulative).

I'm sure we have all seen examples of this at work. I have seen co-workers who have claimed to be unable to operate the copy machines and the computers and have had others make copies for them and send out their emails – for fifteen years. A colleague told me of an episode in his army career when an officer, who was disliked, failed to give an order that would normally have seemed routine, and the entire platoon decided to play dumb. Their defense? "We weren't given the order…" In each case, these people are not relating to each other in a mature, productive way. This is the realm of the passive-aggressive personality.

Another example would be the old Soviet workers' idea of: "We pretend to work and they pretend to pay us." Every parent is familiar with this. The child asks for "help" with homework when what she means is, "Do it for me"; or the grown child who refuses to take control of her life because the parent is always there to do the rescuing. It takes two to get into this mess, of course, but I think you can see the point. Some people find it convenient to be stuck in this phase. Other people are silly enough to aid and abet this "stuck" individual when it is clear that the stuck person has no desire to take charge. That's a pretty good description of co-dependence.

Of course, there are some things that we realize we'll never be good at, and so we have to hand over our power to someone else. We may decide to take our car to a mechanic because we just don't do well with mechanical things. And yet, which of us doesn't first check out the reliability of the garage? Most of us may be "Innocent" about our cars or computers, but we're not innocent about money. Perhaps we'll ask that garage mechanic for an estimate first. We'll try to choose a garage that seems reliable because someone we trust has recommended it, or it has a Goodwrench sign, or a Triple A listing. We don't hand over our car and keys to the first grease-smeared 19-year-old we see. This is the wise, balanced Innocent. We trust, but we do not trust blindly.

What does it feel like to be an Innocent?

The Innocent is often very content, happy with those around him or her, and extremely accepting of others. The Innocent also feels a wonderful optimism, since all things can come right if one only tries the right options.

The Innocent's greatest strength is to be wholly loving and trusting, for when we trust others without reservation they are given the opportunity to honor that feeling and return it – which brings about some of the deepest connections that can exist between people. The bond between parent and child is unlike any other. Some adults are transformed by the experience of being totally loved and trusted by their children and become deeper, more feeling-based as a direct result. The friendships shared by children in their very early years are frequently able to weather more changes than friendships formed at other times. Both examples are enduring testimony to the power of those first time experiences in our lives. The same situation is echoed, to a lesser extent, in later years. Many people have a special fondness for friends made in the first year of college, or the people who went through basic training for the military with them. Going into new situations they were all Innocents, and the quality of those friendships has a special depth provided by the shared new experiences.

Yet this enviable situation will not last. The Innocent has at some point to recognize the first challenge that will face her: who can I trust and whom ought I to distrust? The Innocent, therefore, is likely to feel secure following established routines and will accept what authorities say for the most part, since these are sources of information that seem to have universal approval. Yet if the Innocent is unsuspecting and unquestioning in this way then sooner or later there is going to be a time when deception surfaces. Then the Innocent will be deeply outraged by what has happened. There will be a yell of anger that anyone could dare to do this. At this point the hurt is hard to exaggerate, since the Innocent's world-view has been attacked at its root. The person who at one point thought the President could never do anything ethically questionable may become, overnight, the person who yells for his blood. How dare he betray the Nation in that way! This is the Active Innocent, and anger will allow this person to redefine who he or she is in this altered, strange world. Ultimately the Active Innocent may choose to expose the wrongdoer and seek to punish him, and then may decide that since the threat has been destroyed it will be safe to return to the familiar ways of the Innocent's life. This sort of crusading spirit is necessary and can be effective in confronting wrongdoing, yet it is essentially naïve.

By contrast the Passive Innocent may slump into a depression that says, in effect, we can't trust anyone and we're all victims, and it's not fair. This sort of woundedness, if permitted to develop into depression, can be devastating to the individual. Life really does seem pointless under these circumstances and trust, once betrayed, is hard to rebuild.

What the Innocent learns is where and when to trust, and how to do so in a way that is not based in blind, unquestioning faith. Since trust is one of the cornerstones of any functioning society and of every healthy relationship it is important that we all nurture the positive aspects of the Innocent within us, and yet at the same time we have to learn the balance that is necessary so that we do not become victims. We know that there are unprincipled people out there, but we all want to fall in love anyway. And so we have to decide where to place our trust.

The Innocent has been recognized and described in some particularly poignant ways throughout the ages. William Blake's *Songs of Innocence* (1783) contains poems that are evocations of the pure unblemished viewpoints of children. They are close to nursery rhymes in their simplicity, and when compared to the more somber *Songs of Experience* they have the capacity to remind us of that straightforwardness that was lost for all of us when we began to see life as more unsettled. Compare the following two poems. The first is called 'Infant Joy' and is an imagined dialogue between a parent and a two-day-old child. The child speaks first.

> "I have no name
> I am but two days old."
> What shall I call thee?
> "I happy am,
> Joy is my name."
> Sweet joy befall thee.

The sense of calm delight is evident, and even more so when we read its counterpart called, ominously enough, 'Infant Sorrow':

> My mother groaned, my father wept
> Into the dangerous world I leapt;
> Helpless naked, piping loud
> Like a fiend hid in a cloud.

These lines are filled with far more foreboding; a child like a 'fiend hid in a cloud'! We can just picture the infant yelling in such distress that we cannot calm him. And what parent hasn't had a difficult child and a difficult life at some point? Blake is making a basic contrast for us; his aim is to show the state of the Innocent as that blessed, undisturbed state of unity with creation – and it is something that cannot last.

This unity with creation is important since it conveys a sense of the child simply being itself. Emerson, in his famous essay *Self-Reliance* (1841) draws his memorable parallel to adults watching a baby, enthralled that the baby feels free to be exactly who he or she is, without reservation. This powerful centeredness is, for him, the secret of personal authenticity. Wordsworth, in 'We Are Seven' and in the 1799 version of *The Prelude*, makes the same point. Children grow in innocence, at one with the vital forces of God and Nature, and it is only in growing up that they become estranged from this primary unity. Thereafter, we all yearn to get back to that stage which, at the time, we did not even know we were in. Wordsworth spent his whole life trying to recapture that early, magical experience because he felt it to be the moment at which he was closest to the eternal God-force in the universe, and it was where his creative energies had sprung from. Artists I have worked with have often echoed this when they have spoken about seeing things with new eyes, or getting back to their essential self. Even the enigmatic Bob Dylan has some wisdom for us here. In the 2005 documentary *No Direction Home* he is filmed addressing a gathering of English businessmen, telling them that they are all old, and that he has been trying very hard to "Get young." They haven't a clue what he's talking about, and it shows.

The realm of the Innocent can be a powerful source of personal energy, if we choose to use it. Perhaps this is why we have Jesus' words in which he urges his followers to be 'as little children.' It may not be practical advice for dealing with the world of politics, but then Jesus wasn't giving that sort of guidance. He was giving spiritual advice about how to get back in touch with the essential nature of who each of us is, so that we can become ourselves as fully as possible – not just versions of what everyone else wants us to be. The Innocent can teach us a great deal about how to operate in our souls, our inner world, but less about how to navigate the world of work and money.

Most of us can look back to the early years of our lives and recall the total devotion we may have had to friends and loved ones. Sometimes we can recall how we felt when we were first fully in love. Experience often takes away even the memory of that feeling, especially if the love relationship went sour later. And yet we all yearn for that feeling again. The large numbers of romantic movies churned out by Hollywood encourage us to believe in this sort of pure and idealistic love, even when we know that most of us will not feel that emotion again unspoiled by the cold edge of learned experience. Yet if we are to function in our world and be happy then we have to be able to love and forgive as fully as young children do every time they show love to their parents – no matter if the parent has been bad-tempered a short time before. In the same fashion, parents find themselves loving their children no matter what the child's behavior – and the wise parent also knows how to set a few limits. The parent's greater experience will have changed the way the love is shown, but not the essential quality of that love.

We have to leave the Innocent stage as we grow, but we also need to retain the value of that experience of trust and love. The child who has been loved and has felt trusted will tend to grow into an adult who can love and trust fully. This works at the very highest levels, too. Nelson Mandela could have been part of destroying South Africa as revenge after his long and brutal imprisonment. Instead he chose to work with love and trust with the then South African government, and he wrought a deeper, more lasting change than any bloodbath rebellion could have achieved. Whatever we may think of the effectiveness of his Truth and Reconciliation Commission, it was not about punishment, but about trusting people to acknowledge the dreadful errors of past so they could work together to achieve harmony in the future.

As children we are naturally, unceasingly creative. Anything can be a treasure, a source of imaginative delight. If we lose sight of this playful creativity we have lost contact with the real energy that can fuel a life of fulfillment. The Innocent has direct access to this fountain of self-renewal. Working with clients I have sometimes found it most helpful for them to be able to recall their early creativity and re-activate it through play. It can allow them to reach back directly to a true part of themselves that has something to tell them.

Some people have told me that they did not begin to feel this aspect of their lives until they had children themselves, when they found themselves playing, enthralled, with the child and sharing that world for the first time. Wordsworth knew this, too. He was devoted to his sister Dorothy, who seems to have suffered from some mild form of mental retardation; it kept her in a state that Wordsworth believed was the same as the Innocent's phase. He delighted in seeing things as far as possible through her eyes. The much-anthologized poem 'Daffodils' was almost certainly written as a response to an experience *she* had while walking in the Lake District, which she recorded in her journal. She then talked about it with him and his poem captures the spirit of that joyous moment, some two years earlier. Thinking of it caused him to recapture feelings of innocent delight: 'And then my heart with pleasure fills/ And dances with the daffodils'. What a wonderful image – the middle-aged poet's heart actually dancing, just as a small child might jump for joy upon seeing something beautiful!

If we're prepared to pay attention we can all recapture the Innocent's riches that many of us have ignored for so long.

For most of us the Innocent phase is just that: a phase that one looks forward to growing out of at some point so that we can deal with the outer world more effectively. But how does one achieve this? The trouble is that the next option doesn't always look that attractive. In fact, it can even look like the disillusion- ment and anger suffered by the Active Innocent who does not return to the view that the world is a safe place after the challenge has been met. It is the Orphan stage.

Notes

1. Blake, William in *The Norton Anthology of English Literature*, 6th ed. vol. 2. Ed. Abrams et alia. New York, Norton: 1993. p.33, p.40
2. Emerson, Ralph Waldo. *Self-Reliance*.(1841) "Infancy conforms to nobody; all conform to it; so that one babe commonly makes four or five out of the adults who prattle and pray to it." Paragraph 4.
3. Dylan, Bob in Martin Scorsese's *No Direction Home*, 2005.
4. Jesus: in Matthew 18. 1-6: "except ye become as little children".
5. William Wordsworth's 'Daffodils', otherwise known as 'Poems of the Imagina- tion: XII'. In *Wordsworth, The Poetical Works*, Ed. Thomas Hutchinson, OUP, Oxford, 1973, p.149.

Chapter Four

The Orphan

First and foremost, the Orphan knows that she is an Orphan. She can't go home and be a baby any more and she knows it. She's on her own, but she has either been forced out of that comfortable role or has chosen to move away from it. The Orphan is, on the whole, looking for adoption. Just as the new arrival in the office may well look around and then decide who to latch on to as a mentor, similarly the Orphan looks around for someone to be the adoptive parent while she grows in competence.

The negative incarnation of the Orphan will tend to be passive and grab on to some figure perceived as being important. She will then become a limpet, a sidekick, or a dependent. This version of the Orphan is using the Innocent's sense of trust and, despite knowing that blind trust is a risky proposition, will seek to meld with someone else's power. As such, this type of Orphan may choose to use the protective figure as a cover behind which he or she can hide, coming out only to try and tyrannize over others, using the adoptive parent as a figure in power manipulation. This is an aggressive aspect of what is essentially a passive figure, who is eager to comply with whatever standards of conduct are current. There are many examples of this. The office bully is one version. This is the person who either overtly or covertly suggests that if you do as she wishes, the boss will be pleased – and you *know* how tight she is with the boss, don't you? To some extent, many people working within repressive regimes function in this way, rushing about doing their leader's bidding, hiding behind a power structure, but making sure they benefit themselves first and foremost. This is the crooked policeman, hiding behind his uniform; or the corporate yes-man who will do anything to get ahead, including backstabbing, manipulation of data, and ethically questionable dealings.

It's a situation that we are familiar with, even amongst our highest ranking politicians, which should warn us that this is not about education or class, but about the lack of the soul's development. The rush to invade Iraq can be seen as a sad lesson in the way Orphans think since so many otherwise intelligent people were only too ready to leap on a questionable bandwagon and even to manipulate data to suit their needs. Wall Street has its share of those figures too, and we've seen them in the news. This is the most dangerous incarnation of the Orphan, since such people have, as passive Orphans, no hesitation in sacrificing those who are close to them. These are Orphans masquerading as brave individuals, and they may even believe themselves to be courageous. In fact, courage cannot emerge truly until the individual is on his or her own, facing threats without any available back-up, and this cannot happen until Warrior phase. Totalitarian regimes, extreme political dogmas, and religious cults foster this aspect of the Orphan in people, forcing them to be subservient to a creed or system that 'adopts' them. It gives an illusion of heroic purpose to those who have not already managed to think clearly for themselves.

There are many, and chilling, examples of Orphans who thought they were heroic. I'll pick out a couple of extreme examples to consider, since this is potentially a very dangerous phase. Reinhard Heydrich, who was Hitler's deputy until he was assassinated, had no hesitation in rounding up Jews and homosexuals, while suppressing his own dishonorable discharge from the navy and possible homosexual activities, as well as his Jewish background. He preferred to hide his true nature from himself and accept a ready-made ideology. As Hitler's successor presumptive he had been well and truly "adopted" – and because of course he knew this was not his real parent, there is probably some truth to the rumor that he wished to destroy Hitler and take his place as an even more repellent tyrant. In part, that is why the allies put together a team that assassinated him. In the wider sense also, Hitler's regime appealed at first to the many Germans who felt their country had been reduced to helplessness by the demands of the victors of the First World War for reparation payments. This was, to some extent, a nation that felt fatherless. This is an extreme example, but then the deeds perpetrated in Hitler's name were extreme, and we can't help noticing that he stressed concepts such as 'the Fatherland,' which were tailor-made to attract Orphans. A whole nation, and later on most of Europe, was taken over and told (sometimes at gunpoint) to accept lunatic beliefs. What is even sadder is that so many did so and so many went out to fight and die for those beliefs. The passive Orphans of our world can be easily exploited, and this has almost nothing to do with education, or religious background, or intelligence. It has primarily to do with a level of psychological and spiritual awareness. Whether we are talking about homeless boys adopted into gangs, mafia recruits brought into 'the family', or religious fanatics trained as terrorists, we are dealing with the dangerous incarnation of the vulnerable Orphan. Such Orphans, either on their own or when led by someone who is frequently no better than they are in terms of spiritual development, produce most of the violent acts of the world, and the world has seen far too much of this. We can change it any time we choose if we are aware of how the problem comes into being.

In the classroom, I have seen a different aspect of the Orphan emerge with some frequency, and it is another version of the passive Orphan. This might be the student who wants to be spoon-fed the information and who doesn't want to have to think for himself. "Will it be on the final?" is the question of someone who wants to be told what to do, and who has no interest in exploring the topic any further. In fact, such a question can also be a frightened or angry response to being asked to think. Fear can cause the Passive Orphan to become the Active Orphan, angrily rejecting everything. This is the student who seems to convey the sentiment of, "I'll turn up, I'll memorize the material, but you'll never get me to think."

It's worth exploring this further, since the Orphan stage of development is the point at which most people stall and give up. The growing numbers of our electorate who wish to reduce complex issues to sound-bites are saying, in effect, that they don't want to have to listen, think, and assess. They want someone plausible to tell them the answers. Such people are easily led, easily exploited, and yet they believe they truly have all the answers. When they do this, they become pseudo-Warriors. For these angry Orphans it's easier and more profitable to accept the party line. If we can learn anything at all from the last century, it ought to be just how easy it is to lure human beings into this version of the Orphan. Hitler, Hirohito, Mussolini, Lenin, Stalin, Mao Tse Tung, and Pol Pot – all manipulated vast numbers of their citizens into accepting them as the one trustworthy voice they should follow. Don't think: just follow orders! And millions did. The tactic was simple in its broad outlines – make people feel unsafe so they want to be protected, and then offer them total protection if only they will stop thinking for themselves and follow 'doctrine.'

What does this look like in everyday life? The most clear examples are to be seen with adolescents, many of whom feel alienated from their parents and are so desperate to belong to some group or clique that teen and pre-teen peer pressure is all but impossible for them to resist. The constant phone calls that middle-school children seem to find essential are very often about checking on what everyone else is doing. Who's friends with whom and who has fallen out of favor – it is all vital information since this is the world that provides a sense of belonging, of identity, for them. Wise parents tend to try and interest their children in sports or hobbies that will provide a sense of productive purpose and camaraderie while the child works out who he or she might be. There is no doubt that this can be an agonizing stage for many young people, and the relief with which they welcome their acceptance to a clique, and the anxiety with which they sometimes attempt to stay within that group, can be heartbreaking. This is the Orphan's struggle. Being left out is, literally, like being left wandering in the wilderness. And sometimes young people within those peer groups try to act tough or take risks in order to demonstrate their independence and strength. This is partly why this is such a dangerous time for this age group. Drugs, sexual experimentation, weapons, all of these are designed to impress the peer group with the understanding that even though the individual needs to be in the group, he or she is sufficiently worldly-wise not to seem to need their support. Their struggle to be better or more daring than the peer group simply emphasizes how dependent they are upon its opinions. One young man I worked with saw that his older brother was with a group that would hot-rod their cars and sometimes race cars they had stolen. They had an aura of glamour and excitement. Girls watched the races. So, at the age of 14, this young man wanted desperately to be part of the group that viewed him as too young for their attention. In fact he didn't just want to equal them, he wanted to prove himself better than they were. So he began stealing high-speed cars. Small even by the standards of a 14-year old, he had to bring extra clothing to sit on so he could see over the steering wheel of his latest 'hot-box'. The next step was that he'd drive down to the local police station and lean on the horn until the cruisers came out to chase him. Then he'd race all over town until he'd made fools of the police in their more mildly tuned vehicles. Once the fun was over he'd dump the car and return to the group as one who now had a right to be with them and was also beyond their usual reach. He thought he was a real hero, and he was treated as one. Actually he was acting out a version of the Orphan stage. My long-dead Swiss grandfather had a word for people who acted this way. He called them *halb-stark* – 'half strong.' The word makes the point neatly. One cannot take shortcuts in this realm of psychological and spiritual development any more than one can cheat on a diet or an exercise program. The Orphan has to find a home, or build that home, while working from a place of self-knowledge rather than ignorance.

Interestingly, one of the greatest epics of all time deals with exactly this dilemma. *The Odyssey* begins with Odysseus on Calypso's island, a prisoner, and an Orphan. Calypso offers him a shortcut – he can become her consort, a king, and a demi-god if he'll stay with her. He's already a hero in many people's eyes, so this would be the logical progression for him. Except for one thing: he's only a hero in the sense of having served in the Trojan War. Moreover, if he stays with Calypso he must desert his duty to his wife, his kingdom, his men, and his son – all the things that link him to his true heritage. This hardly makes him heroic or even halfway honest. He is, in actuality, an Orphan who needs to learn about himself before he can return to Ithaca, Penelope, and his kingdom, and live there successfully as a responsible ruler.

And that is what the rest of the epic poem explores. Odysseus may spend much of the tale wandering around the Mediterranean, seeming to be a bold adventurer, but most of the time he is merely lost. When he arrives back at Ithaca and sees how the young suitors are treating Penelope and his kingdom, he bubbles with righteous indignation. Greeted by his faithful dog and his old nurse he immediately receives a lesson in what fidelity means, and he learns that his connection to his kingdom is visceral and eternal. He knows what he has to do and he prepares to fight against formidable odds for what and whom he truly loves. The point seems clear. It is not until we have rejected shortcuts, turned away from easy options, and decided what it is we are really prepared to fight for that we can leave the Orphan behind and take our true place in the world.

The Active Orphan is a very different individual, and is best characterized as a figure who feels that he or she doesn't really fit, and who therefore decides that life means being an outsider forever. This may translate into the gifted person who learns skills in order to establish an identity based on rejecting the accepted status quo. So the computer enthusiast who works out ever more sophisticated ways of hacking into supposedly secure systems might be an example, or the person who takes a malicious glee in creating and spreading computer viruses. This is the angry outsider, the loner who has an agenda that seems bizarre to most of us. Ted Kaczynski, the Unabomber who lived in a cabin in the woods, decided that the world of academia was corrupt and so he began to send parcel bombs to those he deemed dangerous. Academically brilliant himself, a hermit by choice, he also chose a moral code that few of us could sympathize with. A still more recent example is Eric Rudolph, the elusive Olympic Park bomber who also destroyed several women's clinics. Also a recluse, he saw the government as too supportive of minorities. His logic for bombing women's health clinics was that most abortions were performed on white women, which meant that minority women would have more children that the government would then have to support. This would in turn threaten the political position of the 'white races'. There is logic to this thinking, but it is a bizarre, angry, logic. Perhaps the Columbine school shooters were in a similar situation; rejected, angry, and seeing no place for themselves to fit back into the world they knew, they elected to destroy it and themselves instead.

Yet another example confronted me when I worked in a maximum-security prison in Massachusetts. I came across a man who freely confessed to me that the crime that had brought him to jail was based in a similar impulse. He told me that he had deliberately chosen to sell cocaine to middle class youngsters because he felt that the middle classes were to blame for his own deprived childhood, and this was therefore the best form of social activism he could devote himself to. The way forward to rehabilitation for him was to recognize that the twisted logic he had used was primarily a product of a difficult upbringing in which he felt he had literally no home. He had invented a purpose for himself based on prejudice and unexamined anger.

The distinction between active and passive Orphan may seem to be blurred here, so I'll clarify things by pointing out that the passive incarnation can be seen as likely to attach to an already existing, socially established organization, and be very loyal to its rules. By contrast, the active Orphan will be the one who goes off and forms an army of one that reacts against social organizations.

Passive Orphans tend to want to join established groups. Many people join the armed services or the police force in just this spirit, so it is not necessarily a bad thing. Active Orphans may well be believers in conspiracy theories or doctrines which show an active distrust in most of the rest of the world.

The most healthily balanced version of the Orphan archetype is perhaps described as the person who goes looking for a mentor and a guru – knowing that no mentor is ever perfect, and that all of them have feet of clay. The Orphan, eyes wide open, can then learn from the adopted parent and yet not be constrained in the way a biological child might be, with feelings of duty or fear. At this point the Orphan can be almost a sort of apprentice – learning but choosing what to accept and reject, until graduation approaches. It is important to notice here that the Orphan has to leave home, even be expelled from it, as Adam and Eve were from Eden before they could discover what loyalty and obedience were. In fact the old term for a tradesman (such as a plumber or carpenter) who was learning his skills was a 'journeyman apprentice,' which seems to sum up a psychological situation rather neatly, because this process of exploring a personal identity and learning what one can do can lead directly to the next stage, the Pilgrim, where the Pilgrim is truly seen to be on a journey.

What does it feel like to be an Orphan?

A lot of the time it feels as if one is a vulnerable alien in a strange land, just like the exiled Adam and Eve. The Orphan may at first feel fear as a primary, recurrent sense of dread. What if I am all alone and unprotected? What if there is no God, no purpose, no meaning to anything? The Orphan's task is, one could say, not just fear management but the rather more demanding goal of making friends with that fear without being crippled by it. It is a time of coming to accept uncertainty. The Orphan may well seem at times to be almost random in her search for a sense of belonging. This sense of desperation can be so strong that the Orphan can be misled into attachments that seem to offer shelter or identity. High school cliques can be loved and hated, at the same time, for this very reason. Sometimes, in trying to avoid the trap of the clique, the Orphan may instead go into hiding. It can seem safer just to pretend to get along with others, to survive for now, until the possibility for real exploration arrives.

The true balanced Orphan may also be the one who raises awkward questions in the way that only the outsider can do. Why do we do things this way? Is this the only way? Such questions can irritate others, especially those who have chosen the safe option of not questioning in order to 'belong' more fully, and the Orphan may therefore be faced with more rejection. This in turn can lead to depression. Depression which is not due to physiological or chemical imbalances is frequently caused by the Orphan's sense of helplessness and homelessness. In this the Orphan can be seen to be slipping back towards the despair felt by the Innocent who has been betrayed. Since this depression can also be a time of deep reassessment its value should not be under-estimated. The Orphan has to face this alone-ness and depression and realize that it's simply about being temporarily lost. It's not a necessary life condition. Some Orphans are able to remain entirely cheerful as they face their situation, but these are the rare ones. Sometimes they go on to be great comedians, cheerfully pointing out the absurdity of the things they see. These are the exceptions. Mostly the feeling of well being does not return until the individual moves towards the next phase, which offers the possibility of greater self-definition.

At this point, the Orphan decides to leave the protection of the adoptive father and mother, whether these are actual parents or the more symbolic parental shelter of a 'safe' but undemanding job or way of life. This decision takes courage, and one might say that part of the Orphan's struggle is to allow that sense of personal courage to emerge and to be guided by it. This is sometimes characterized by the feeling that even though the Orphan doesn't know what's out there, it's time to take a look anyhow because staying put is just too exhausting. As one therapist I worked with put it, "Most people don't change until they just can't stand being where they are anymore." When that happens the Orphan progresses to the next stage: the Pilgrim.

It's vital to remember that the Orphan may in fact not emerge to feel the full restlessness of Orphanhood until she hits mid-life. Orphans are good at suppressing how they feel so that they don't upset the status quo. So-called mid-life crises are frequently about the re-eruption of the questioning self and an increasing dissatisfaction with the life one has settled into, and this can propel us into becoming Pilgrims.

What are relationships like for the Orphan?

For the child there is a strong desire to reject the parents, coupled to rage that it's often not possible to reject those on whom one depends. Most teenagers go through a phase when they imagine they were adopted and this is their way of trying to figure out how they ever came to deserve parents who are so different, so square, so clueless compared to their own norms. This is the stage when the child who cannot yet drive asks the parents drop her off round the corner from where she is going, so there will be no taint of association. The parents are too dull, the family car is too ordinary, the family home too tedious; and while these things are needed, they are not always appreciated. Paradoxically, when the youngster sees that wealth does not always solve all problems, he or she is likely to be hugely grateful for the 'ordinary' upbringing and background she has had. This is especially true after teenagers have stayed at summer camp or gone to foreign countries that are less wealthy. Suddenly the home comforts are seen anew through the eyes of someone who has been an Orphan in fact, if only temporarily.

The main thing to consider is that children at the Orphan stage are going to be unappreciative and consider themselves misunderstood by parents and older people. Their peer groups become very important, and the 'best friend' – the one rock of solidity in a stormy world – becomes important to a degree unsuspected by parents. The friend, the beloved sports team, or the favorite band – all are raised to iconic status as befits the symbolic value they have now taken on. For the Orphan this may also mean that emotions are felt as overwhelming. One either loves a certain group of people, band, place, or situation, or one hates it, and being deprived of these preferred things is really felt to be the end of the world. "I'll just die if I can't…" may seem like a figure of speech, but the emotions are engaged in a way that is often hard for parents to comprehend, since for the Orphan this is a question of identity, and not being present at the specific event is felt as a dangerous diminishing of that identity. The teenager who cuts school and drives all night with a car full of friends just to see a favorite band perform in another city is acting perfectly reasonably according to the value-systems of the Orphan, especially if there are parental objections. Parents who do not honor the child's need to reject them and renegotiate the understandings that exist between them may well find that their grown children harbor intense feelings of antagonism. Parents who are themselves Orphans may well be most unsympathetic towards their Orphan child's rebellions. These parents have survived by accepting a series of social structures that they feel shelter them, and they will have a lot invested in this so they are likely to pressure their own children to make similar decisions. And they will be relentless in doing so. Fearful themselves, they cannot rest until they have made their own children conform. This can be a situation that is tailor-made for misery.

Shakespeare describes the situation of the Orphan beautifully in *Romeo and Juliet*. At ages fifteen and thirteen respectively they are both expected to conform to 'family' expectations – and neither wants to. When they fall in love, which they do with that startling rapidity so characteristic of teenagers, their emotions are so thoroughly engaged that they are quite prepared to die for the love that redefines each of their relationships to their families. Their new sense of selfhood is directly dependent upon their love, so of course they are prepared to die for it! And as we all know, they do.

Some adult Orphans may tend to have large families as a way to compensate for their feeling of being disconnected from their birth families. Of course, the larger the family, the more pressing is the need to earn money to supply their wants – and so the Orphan sometimes attaches himself to a career, and instead of real contact and love shows affection by supplying the money. The workaholic dad is a version of this; it's a way of belonging.

Although the picture of the Orphan that emerges is of a lost person, eventually most Orphans will settle into conformity as the most acceptable form of living. Families can function perfectly well with parents who are Orphans, and they have done so for generations. The slight disadvantage is that Orphan-generated families tend to produce a powerful coercive pressure to conform, and this can be shattered by internal refusals and rebellions against parental orders. Orphan parents tend to link together out of a sense of fragility. Often people have said to me that they married the 'safe' option, the person they 'knew would never leave', the predictable, reliable breadwinner, or the woman who they felt would be a 'good mother' rather than a scintillating companion. Because of this desire for safety many societies have insisted that their daughters be virgins at marriage, and have discriminated against those left single because of divorce or death. An older man, who has sown many wild oats, matched to an inexperienced girl is thought to make a good marriage because the man will not wish to stray any more and the woman will not know how to. Safety and conformity are very important to Orphans who have given up the struggle to move beyond this phase.

By now it should be evident that there are certain patterns we can point out. Each archetype has an active and a passive version. The task for those on a spiritual path is to be aware of both aspects and then to choose the balanced way forward. If he or she chooses the passive course of action there is a great tendency to slip back to the previous level. So the Orphan who elects to be passive and submit to another's will becomes, in a sense, a passive version of the Innocent, blithely unquestioning, and in this case deciding not to recognize what is truly happening. This is a possibility that will repeat itself in every stage, as we shall see. The passive version of each stage has the tendency to regression while the active version has the tendency to isolation.

An Orphan tends to want to receive, while the motivation to give back to others tends to be the mark of an emerging higher awareness. Think of the 'trust-fund baby' as a figure of our times – the person who has had everything handed to him. Some settle into a resentful acceptance of the money that supports them, and do very little. By contrast others take the opportunity of the regular income and use this situation to explore their world. Or think of the unemployed person drawing welfare. Some people wait passively for a job that suits them, while others who are more active might choose to retrain and develop more skills. Another example might help, here. During the 1960s and 1970s in England and Europe, many traveling theater companies came into being simply because the actors were unable to find work and were reduced to drawing unemployment benefit. With their basic needs provided for these actors then set about putting on low-cost productions of all kinds aimed specifically at those who normally would never have been able to afford theater tickets. Some of the finest 'fringe' theater of those years started simply because the actors and playwrights were unemployed and so had to create something to do and some way to explore what it was they wanted to say. The Orphan may have to find a roof to shelter under while she considers her next move. And a reliable home is a good place from which to look into Pilgrim stage, and that is exactly what those actors were able to do.

Chapter Five

The Pilgrim

The Pilgrim can be seen anywhere young people with backpacks congregate to take flights to other countries. These are people who are perhaps literally wandering the globe. The question we need to ask for this stage is *why* do people choose to wander?

Some people wander away simply because they are in the process of defining themselves through rejection. They leave home, in a teenager's snit, because whatever their parents want they want the opposite. This is reactive, and is a moving away rather than a moving towards something productive. Although this may look at first glance like Pilgrim mode, in fact it can often slip backwards into Orphan mode, because such people are looking for some place better to call home. This phase, which is an example of the Passive Pilgrim, is characterized by somewhat aimless wandering and the expectation that someone will 'find' them, and give them what they want. When this happens, runaway youngsters may join a gang, or become prostitutes, or use drugs and alcohol, since an addiction is also a "home" and a pimp is not going to let his young charges become independent. One can belong to a drug quite easily. Prison can also be a home of sorts, and criminality as a philosophy of life will tell the criminal exactly what to do under what circumstances. By attaching to a group that is on the borders of acceptability and legality the individual is neither fully an adopted Orphan, nor fully free to be an exploratory Pilgrim.

The Active Pilgrim is different, since he or she is looking for meaning. Some people then spend many years traveling, always rejecting any place, or any person they seem to be about to settle with. The wandering itself can become more important than any sense of purposeful activity. "I just can't seem to settle down," is one refrain. "This job isn't quite right for me" might be another. For such a person, the grass is always better, greener, more lush, someplace else. This active aspect of the Pilgrim can be seen in the person who attends eight different colleges in six semesters, and always has a good reason for moving on.

Another way to describe this version of the Pilgrim is the dabbler. This could be the person who wanders from job to job, or sexual partner to sexual partner.

In its most aggressive form this can become compulsive – addictive, even. The wandering becomes an end in itself as the individual racks up conquests, or "experience" – with no idea of what it all may mean. The only consolation seems to be that movement equates to progress for this person. And we know this is not always true. This Pilgrim accepts whatever is offered that looks appealing and has no intention of paying for any of it, let alone offering anything back. And so the Pilgrim may well feel the world owes him something and become bitter when it is not miraculously delivered, or, if something good arrives, then she is likely to question it with a view to rejecting it later. This incarnation of the Pilgrim is searching relentlessly but has no idea how to value anything she finds. So the search must go on, and on.

In myth and legend this aspect of the Pilgrim is usually presented as a ghost or spirit condemned to walk the earth forever alone. The Flying Dutchman, condemned to sail for eternity because of its captain's dying vow to round Cape Horn no matter what, seems a fitting symbol for one who will not alter his greedy desire for a successful voyage. Or there is Bluebeard, locked in a pattern in which he must wed and kill his brides. The test he sets each of his wives is clearly a trap, since he gives them keys to the whole house only to forbid them access to one room – thus ensuring their curiosity and disobedience. Like Adam and Eve they are bound to stray into forbidden territory. Interestingly, in this myth we are told in several versions that Bluebeard has no heirs – which indicates that he can never remain close enough to someone he can trust in order to create a family. The hint is that the Pilgrim has to be able to take the risk and trust, make a commitment to life not to an abstract notion, or be stuck in a repeated pattern.

Other myths are varied, but follow a similar theme. For example, Dracula is unable to die and unable to live as a human. To live eternally he must feed on the blood of others, usually the women in whose quasi-erotic embrace he is suckled (like a baby) back to life, and who then in turn become undead. The suggestion is that the active Pilgrim, living outside the bounds of normal human contact, can lose his soul by fixating on his restless pursuits, and that those who devote themselves to him are in danger of losing their own souls also. They are, literally and metaphorically, sucked dry. If this sounds bizarre, I'd point out that there are many relationships observable around us every day in which one partner seems to take and take while the other gives and gives until there is nothing left. One of my clients struggled unsuccessfully in just such a relationship for years, devoting more patience, understanding and money to it than he could easily spare in a fruitless attempt to alter the dynamic. In this case the Pilgrim had become the parasite, and the relationship faded and died.

If we return to literature we have only to think of Dr. Victor Frankenstein, turning away from his lover to embrace the hellish studies that will haunt him forever in the shape of his vengeful monster. Interestingly, the monster is looking for acceptance and cannot find it, so it chooses a pilgrimage of its own in pursuing Dr. Frankenstein. These are extremes, of course, but then that is how myths make their points. They exemplify the problem neatly: the Pilgrim who chooses merely to keep on seeking without any sense of what it is that is important or what the goal may be is, indeed, a lost soul. As we will recall, Dr. Frankenstein does not realize what he has done until his creature comes to life, when he discovers, to his horror, that he hasn't even begun to think about what that might mean or what the next step is.

The Pilgrim must recognize that seeking is only ever a role, one that must eventually be relinquished. There is a difference between being in a stage and remaining stuck.

What this indicates is that ego-development for the Pilgrim is crucial. The Orphan's task is, in some ways, to find out what the ego is; the Pilgrim's task is to use that ego in a controlled way. Bluebeard must keep his secret room locked so no one can discover who he really is, yet he clearly wants a bride he can trust – why else would he give each woman in turn the keys? The captain of the Flying Dutchman must keep on rounding the Horn so he can finish a successful voyage and be fabulously rich; Dr. Frankenstein is determined to do great things, to defy the laws of nature and cause his assembly of dead body parts to spring to life. In each case the ego focuses on a magical future when all will be perfect, miraculous and full of pleasure – remember that Bluebeard and Dr. Frankenstein are both looking forward to enjoying their brides, the unquestioning, docile providers of sexual pleasure. The ship's captain likewise has dreams of fabulous wealth when he reaches port. In each case this is a delusion. These figures may seem romantic or heroic in their determination, but we should not be deceived. None of them have any real sense of what they are doing apart from gratifying their own egos. None have thought through the consequences of their life choices. The figure of Bluebeard is particularly poignant, since there are many people, particularly men, who start relationships into which they have already placed some sort of booby trap for the other to fall into; this then gives an excuse to reject the lover and go back to the established pattern of tracking down someone new. An example of this might be the man who expects his wife to mirror all his interests, follow his favorite sports teams, be glamorous and sexy and raise five children, and who then expresses dismay when a dozen years into the marriage she's no longer wearing lacy lingerie to excite him or reading the books he likes. In his eyes she's failed to be all she could be; but any sensible observer would say that he's been unable to recognize her as a complete human being because he's reduced her to a laundry list of his expectations.

The healthiest incarnation of the Pilgrim is the explorer, or the Pilgrim-after-truth. This person realizes that rejecting is what one has to do at times, but the aim is to accept things as well, gradually piecing together a concept of what one's role in life is. It may be necessary to roam freely and turn aside from those who wish to pin the individual down, but that is done in the spirit of finding the best match for what one needs, or for what one feels drawn to be. Of course, this stage can be infinitely prolonged. Some people spend decades wandering in the wilderness and still they don't find what feels right; other people never progress from this stage and it is, in some ways, one of the loneliest phases.

How does this manifest itself? Curiously enough we can understand this by looking back to the Orphan. Just as the continuing passive Orphan is likely to experience being abandoned by those who consider him or her too needy (and I can think of several acquaintances and counselees who fit this category, almost all of them women, almost all of whom are waiting to be rescued), so the continuing Pilgrim is likely to be placed in the awkward situation of being a repeat rejecter of others, who often cannot understand why their rescuer has now abandoned them. The Pilgrim would clearly like to be out of this stage, and picking up a stray may make him feel temporarily as if he has found a cause to attach to. These are the fragile marriages and homes created, conjured up, out of neediness on both sides, and doomed because of inequality in the roles.

Imagine the marriage of an Orphan and a Pilgrim. The Orphan cannot change and become a Pilgrim because that may threaten her status as someone who needs a home and stability. Yet if she remains dependent, unevolved, the Pilgrim partner quickly realizes he has nothing to learn from her, and yet is expected to give every-thing – which is exactly contrary to the true nature of a Pilgrim, who prefers to pick up small items here and there, wherever convenient. So for a while the Pilgrim gets the ego gratification of being necessary to someone who is weaker and wants to be rescued and taken care of, but it soon wears thin. The Orphan of this pair has no desire to become a Pilgrim, since he or she has now found a home of sorts. Mean-while the Pilgrim will eventually feel trapped and want to leave. This phenomenon is not new. The cycle of the rescuer/abandoner is a sad cliché of our times. It seems clear that this cycle exists because very often the stages of development involved are unequal, and they are unequal because the attraction on each side is based in an attempt to avoid completing the necessary psychic development each needs to achieve. It's really another short-cut, exactly as we saw with Odysseus.

This is a powerful pattern, for the Pilgrim is likely to feel lost and alone at times, and who understands that better than the Orphan? The Pilgrim can, if he or she is not careful, mistake the shelter the Orphan can offer for a permanent home. Dylan's poignant song, "Shelter from the Storm" articulates this beautifully. Sometimes on our searches, we need a place to pause, to rest, to refuel. The song's narrator speaks of being one who 'came in from the wilderness, a creature void of form' – which sounds like a wandering Pilgrim trying to find self definition – when he meets the woman; 'Come in, she said, I'll give you shelter from the storm'. It may seem like the journey's end when it is really only a staging post.

If we return to the legend of Bluebeard for a moment we can see that it describes this situation with some elegance. Bluebeard gives his new bride the keys to the castle when he leaves, which seems like a gesture of absolute trust, except that he tells her not to look in one room. The only person who would fail to want to take a look would be an absolutely subservient, incurious, Innocent or passive Orphan. He requires a wife who is little better than an object while he shows all the signs of being a Pilgrim, since he goes off on a journey leaving her alone. The test that he sets each of his wives – which ensures each woman's doom – looks like nothing less than a situation engineered to ensure he has a reason to kill each new bride and so he never has to establish the close love-tie that could change the horrible pattern. Like an addict who is more in love with the drug than anything else, Bluebeard is more in love with his pattern of sexual exploitation and rejection than with any real woman. He looks like a Pilgrim, but he behaves as an Orphan.

When the wife discovers the bodies of her predecessors in the forbidden locked chamber she experiences fear and revulsion. If she was an Innocent when she married Bluebeard, and an unsuspecting passive Orphan when she was taken into her new home, she's just been shoved rudely into full Orphan phase, since she knows she can't stay at the castle any longer.

Her emotional reaction now brings her ethical values to the forefront – which is exactly what the Pilgrim has to discover inside herself. She can only choose to reject the life Bluebeard represents, which is based on concealment, lies, and murder. The only way anyone could have accepted this bogus Monarch-like status (for she is in charge of the castle and lands while Bluebeard is away) is by not looking into the reality of the situation, not looking into the locked room. The existence of so many other corpses in that room seems to indicate how impossible that is for normal, healthy people. We all want to know who our spouse is, after all. Solipsism – the failure to look into things – is always a possibility, however. In case we think otherwise, I have only to point to those relationships in which one partner refuses to admit that the other has a drug or alcohol problem, or to those women I have encountered who will not accept the fact that their male partner is seeing other women.

In her revulsion for what Bluebeard has done the bride is establishing a basic moral code of what is right and wrong. She shows herself as a healthy incarnation of the Pilgrim and therefore a direct challenge to Bluebeard's perversion of Pilgrim status. The legend then spells out an important detail – the young woman sends for help and her brothers arrive. She is, in this case, no longer in any way an Orphan, since she has reliable family to call upon, and they do in fact help her to save herself. Asking for help, and accepting it, is the balanced Pilgrim's way.

This is an important point, since so many couples, particularly married couples, do not feel they can ask for help when one partner really needs it. Perhaps this is because of pride, or embarrassment, or shame. Whatever the reason it has more to do with protecting the ego and avoiding shame than with a real desire to confront difficulties and solve them.

Bluebeard may not be able to link meaningfully to others, but his new wife obviously can. The implication is that we can only get away from the repeated treadmill of the unhealthy Pilgrim's fixation by attaching fully to others who represent values we endorse. The male family members are to be seen as the male aspects of herself that the bride has left behind, since siblings can represent those possibilities for oneself that one has chosen to leave undeveloped. The brothers help her to take action – the siblings work together. In at least one version of the legend, the bride's brothers are a soldier and a lawyer – and are therefore symbolic of the desire to fight for what we see is right (if we can equate right and the law) and save our own lives in the process. The bride is now equipped with ethical beliefs she's prepared to act upon and is connected to the male attributes of courage and justice, so she is well on the way to achieving Warrior status. She could run away, in which case she would not be able to defeat Bluebeard and inherit his castle, and she would be an Orphan with no place to call home. The implication is that if we run away from the challenges, if we cannot access our courage, then we will end up in a far worse place than before. As an unmarried woman she at least had a home with her parents, after all.

This legend has been interpreted in many ways: as an injunction to women to make sure they get family support when they have abusive husbands, and as a statement about the nature of male sexuality, amongst other things. It is deeply ironic that the tale is named after Bluebeard, since he is the one figure who does not grow or develop at all. It would be much more relevant to name it after the bride, who grows from unsuspecting Orphan to someone who, in uniting with the male strengths of her brothers, looks as if she has many of the attributes of the Monarch – especially as she gets to inherit the lands and castle. It would not be pushing the evidence too far to suggest that the bride has revalued the worth of the male world, has balanced that aspect of herself with her natural female tendencies, and is now far wiser than she was before. She is in many ways a good example of what is expected of a Monarch. She has progressed from a situation in which the pseudo-Monarch archetype is polarized into each person (she is innocent and loving, Bluebeard is experienced and a tyrant), and has moderated and integrated those aspects within herself in a reasonable, balanced fashion; she is, in fact, the true Monarch.

As we have seen it is a cautionary tale about how one can become stuck in sexual fixation, while at the same time it suggests the direction in which one needs to develop in order to break out of this. It is also that rare item, a legend that helps explain how women develop.

At this point, it should become clear that we are exploring these terms as *images*. There is no one specific definition of Innocent, Orphan and Pilgrim. These labels are outlines from which we can begin to make deductions about human behavior patterns. If we pay attention to what they can show us they can be used as information to tell us where we are on our personal spiritual journey. This is, however, a point at which we need to use caution, for we can be at one stage in one aspect of our lives – perhaps in our professional realm – and at quite another in terms of our personal lives. For example, the man who lives across the street from me seems to defy easy description. He has a steady job, which he likes well enough, but which does not inspire him. He has a family. As the child of a service family, he traveled a great deal. Now he prefers his home comforts; he's a couch potato, really. So where does he fit into this schema? He's obviously not a Pilgrim, as he stays close to home in every sense of the word – at least as far as I can see. Perhaps we could look at him as an Orphan figure who has found a "parent" in the large corporation that employs him. And now he has been adopted, he has no desire to change the status quo. He's very comfortable. He seems to be a reasonable parent, and family is important. His home is full of his and other people's children, perhaps because a former Orphan always knows how to welcome others. But please remember: this is only one aspect of his life. When he gets to his office, he may indeed be a different person – eclectic, eccentric, inventive, a real Pilgrim. So what is he? This is where we have to be flexible and alert. We all can think of examples of people who are magnificently capable at work (perhaps even Monarchs in terms of their mastery of the tasks) who then return home and are clueless about familial and emotional matters. The lawyer who can win cases, bully witnesses, and wow juries may not be able to make meaningful contact with her husband and daughter. This is a cliché of our times – Monarch at work, Orphan in the home. We are quite capable – all of us – of living similarly unbalanced lives. The vocabulary of these stages may perhaps help us to understand what is happening to us and what we need to do. But it is not prescriptive; it's up to us to decide what feels true for each of us. And ultimately, it also defines the challenge we face, which is to be as fully developed as possible in all aspects of life.

So what obstacles does the Pilgrim face? Well, there's always the temptation to slip back into the earlier stage, as the Orphan who has found a temporary resting-place with a benevolent person or organization. Perhaps this will be a college, which is a little like a home, but not a real home. But the true Pilgrim doesn't stay, can't really settle, not yet. The next idea might be the one that she's been looking for, the next possibility; and she's off. It's not an easy life, because so many people tend to want to give advice to the Pilgrim. "What you ought to do is …" And not much of it seems to fit.

In the end, it's easier for men to remain as Pilgrims than women. The deep desire of many women to have children tends to force them into a new role – heroic caregiver. For a while, perhaps decades, the demands of childrearing mean that the would-be Pilgrim literally cannot move on at a moment's notice. And sometimes the deep attachment they desire comes from the connection to children. This is excellent if the woman finds that motherhood does, in fact, define her fully; many women find this to be true. And then there are many others who find that parenting, rewarding as it is, does not fulfill all their needs. So they go back to school, or take evening classes, or fly to Katmandu to find out what is the truest expression of who they are. The Pilgrim phase does not evaporate. Like all phases, it can seem to be resolved when it is merely masked.

It's important to spell this out because the Pilgrim archetype can be obscured when one of its forms of expression is an archetype of service. Life circumstances mean that many people have to sacrifice their own aims in order to care for others. Yet it is always the case that within those circumstances every one of us has the chance to continue to grow if we so choose. The woman who has to care for a sick parent or a disabled child may not have much opportunity to explore other life possibilities, yet she is not prevented from spiritual growth and may even find that service to others gives more opportunities than a less demanding life. Anyone who has done volunteer work will confirm this.

The Pilgrim's challenge is to find out what it is that he or she needs to do in life that will allow the spirit to grow. This can be literally anything, the only condition being that it has to correspond to the highest possible calling that person is capable of, and this can be a tricky area to come to terms with.

I worked with one man who was in this situation. He was determined he would be a novelist. And so he wrote and wrote. After some years of disappointment he came to the conclusion that what was really true for him was that he was a playwright and songwriter. When he took that route the successes began to accumulate and he found himself having a lot more fun than when he was working on his novels. For a while he couldn't believe that this was something that was important because it didn't seem to be as agonizing, as exhausting as the fiction writing, and progress was supposed to be hard work, wasn't it? Once he noticed that being a playwright came easily to him and that it seemed a good way for him to say what he wanted to say, he began to revise his whole idea of how things were 'supposed' to be. For him that was the turning point; the Pilgrim had found that the talent he'd not taken seriously was the one thing he could use to express himself fully. This holds an important lesson for us: sometimes our image of who we may be is not entirely accurate. We have to explore, experiment, consider, weigh, and assess. This is an on-going process we all need to engage in for ourselves. And we also have to listen to the world's feedback for clues. If that feedback is sufficiently consistent we may want to pay attention to it. This is the Pilgrim's task, and it's not one that can be done by anyone else. I well recall my heartache at finding myself in a job that was way too taxing for me, and that I was not really prepared for. I stuck it out, struggled, gritted my teeth. It wasn't until I became ill with the stress that I realized that my image of myself was at fault. I just wasn't much good at this line of work under these circumstances. So I changed my job and found something that was a better match – truer to who I was, and who I am. This is the Pilgrim's area, finding out what is true for him or her, and to do that we often have to let go of ego-gratification, of that self-image that is based on who we'd like to be rather than on who we are. As an old farmer once said to me, "If you've got a plough horse, don't race it; if you've got a race horse, don't hitch it to the plough. The horse don't know. It's up to you."

What does it feel like to be a Pilgrim?

Being a Pilgrim can be most disconcerting. Most of us have talents that we do not recognize or value because we've always had them, and we may have the idea that life should be more of a struggle. The Pilgrim's task is to be able to assess with candor what abilities she does have, value them, and consider how to put them to meaningful use. Perhaps the single most important thing any of us can do is ask the basic question: what am I here on earth to do with this talent? If I develop it what will that mean? This is important. Everywhere one looks there are people who will say, sure, I used to be pretty good at that, but I never did anything with it. Whether it's welding or wedding planning makes no difference.

In my work I'm often surprised at how many people really do not believe they have any talents, or anything to say, or that there is anything they can do. This kind of self-inflicted helplessness probably works well if we want passive low-paid workers, but it's not much use for those who are hoping to maximize human potential. Sometimes the very act of saying that one has no talents is the starting place that is needed, for a person who says that is clearly one who feels that she or he ought to have some sort of potential. Perhaps the best thing one can do is to listen to these people and then reflect back to them that even if they haven't got the answers yet, it's clear they are pilgrims after some sort of personal truth. In rephrasing the problem we move closer to the next step. One has to think not in terms of money or success but in terms of what makes the individual feel alive. To reduce the problem to money-making is to slip into the Orphan's consolation.

If this sounds far-fetched I'd point out that when I worked at an Adult Education Center I'd see many students arrive who had signed up for a class out of mild curiosity, only to find that at the end of six weeks they had a whole new direction in life. And that was exactly why they'd come in the first place. They were Pilgrims but they didn't quite know it when they signed up; they just knew that this was something they wanted to try. The courses would very often alert them to what they could explore further. Then it was up to them what, if anything, they were going to do about that. The process starts with us recognizing what we're good at or, quite simply, what we enjoy. Then as we explore that we have to ask the next question, which is to consider where this will lead to that has meaning for us. So the man who discovers he enjoys cooking may also begin to notice that he prefers using organic foods, for example, and that he likes to use specific herbs. He cooks for his friends. They like his food and his ideas. Soon more people are asking about what he does and they end up cooking this way too. Perhaps it leads to more people eating healthier food – and that can make a profound difference. A friend of mine felt this way about his own culinary skills and wound up quitting his job in order to open a restaurant, to which he brought real genius and joy.

Examples like this may not seem like much until we reflect that it was just this sort of local action that led, in England, to the founding of CAMRA, the real ale movement, which changed the entire hospitality industry in a few short years as people began to demand better beer and higher quality food. The very nature of what made for a 'good pub' was completely redefined in that time. Those who campaigned for their 'real' beer saw themselves as working to protect Britain's heritage from the chemical cocktails that were marketed as beer and were popularly nicknamed 'Eurofizz'. It may have looked on the surface like a casual preference for one beer over another, but in fact it was a complex battle over history and values, as well as over the sort of environment people wanted to socialize in. It was a moral struggle against chemically treated, factory-produced bland beverages, and one-size-fits-all marketing. It all started, though, from that place of genuine enjoyment. When we enjoy doing something we bring in vast amounts of energy that can be mobilized no other way. Enjoyment engenders real power.

It's not hard to add other examples. The organic food chain *Bread and Circus* sprang out of just such impulses about quality, and has helped to change the way food is marketed and sold throughout New England. The resulting adjustment in the general public's attitudes has been described as a food revolution, and the shift to organic produce shows no signs of slowing down.

And here lies the next major point. In identifying what we like and care about we are inevitably giving some expression to our ethical values – values that we may have been unaware we had until we attempted to articulate them. Many of those people I observed at the Adult Education Center – perhaps the greatest proportion – were those who had raised their children and were now looking for something, some new direction in life. Some of them said openly that they'd felt unable to explore what they wanted to until the children had left home. Their Pilgrim phase had been temporarily eclipsed, and now it was back.

Finding what we care about, and what we feel to be our talents, can be a bit like winning a modest sum on the lottery. $20 million would ensure an easy retirement to the Bahamas, or wherever, and we all have private fantasies about that, I'm sure. The meteoric rise to stardom is, alas, the stuff of Hollywood dreams, and less likely to happen than we may imagine. But what about a win of $20,000? That asks a different question. One can't retire and buy one's mother a new house with that. We can choose to throw the money, our talents, away if we wish, or we can strategize how to use it the most productive way. We owe it to ourselves to make use of our talents, and to do that we have to risk looking foolish, we have to risk failure. For our purposes the word 'talent' could be more accurately described as our intelligence, our insight, our compassion, and our wise impulses about what we feel to be important. It is where our energy and passion lie. The Pilgrim's task is to take the chance and not care what anyone else thinks as she explores it. This takes courage, and it takes a specific sort of faith. For the Pilgrim will come in for a surprising amount of criticism from those who have already staked out a recognizable career. In part this is because the Pilgrim has to be able to explore without feeling confined. To many outside observers this looks as if the Pilgrim is merely playing around, when what is happening is that ideas and intuitions have to be given free play. Notice how the word 'play' can be both negative and positive, depending upon who is judging. A true Pilgrim has to be able to play with possibilities without pre-judging them or rejecting them too soon. The diaries of Thomas Edison are an excellent example of what looks, at times, like madcap foolery. While researching possible filaments for the future light bulb, Edison and his research team recorded all kinds of bizarre actions, and when they went to the lunchroom for a break they even seized on different food items as likely prospects. Bacon rind was a promising prospect for a brief period. Eventually they hit upon a material that worked, and the 'play' was forgotten about by the world at large, which wanted a serious inventor to look up to.

One of the greatest gifts the Pilgrim has to offer, and which it is the task of us all to remember, is this ability and willingness to play with possibilities. Being a visionary is wonderful, of course, but one achieves that by engaging in constructive, uninhibited play. The Wright brothers, experimenting out there on the sands of Kitty Hawk, were thought of as eccentric in the extreme. They should have been back in town, looking after the profits from their bicycle shop! Didn't they know any better? Only those with private fortunes could expect to be able to have the leisure to mess about with flying machines, which in 1903 were seen as an extravagant waste of time. After all, they didn't seem to fly very far, let alone have any practical applications. And so the brothers were left to play. Thank goodness.

The Pilgrim will always find a slew of people who will give advice. Some of this advice may actually be good. Some may be based in the advice-giver's need to feel important. And some advice givers just want to calm their own anxieties and see the Pilgrim settled, no matter where, as long as they don't have to worry any more. In ancient folk tales and legends this advice-giver is known as a 'Shape-shifter' – one who looks like one thing but may actually be another. Sometimes they are also called 'threshold guardians' because they have the power to turn the Pilgrim away from the real path. As the traveler negotiates her route through the tale this path is often described as leading into a dark forest – a symbol of the path on which there are no reassuring social reminders of one's assigned role in the world. The traveler has to be true to her own sense of self in order not to be led astray by the shape-shifter. Listen to all advice, question it all, and take only that which feels true – that seems to be the message in all these tales.

For one young woman the shape-shifter was her father, who kept urging her to get a job at the telephone company. It was a safe job, he said, and there were opportunities for advancement. Yet she felt herself to be an artist and a filmmaker. Years later, after she had indeed become an artist and a filmmaker, she could see that her father's advice had come from a loving heart: he just wanted his daughter to have a good job and a steady life so he wouldn't have to worry about her. The advice was well meant and it was even good advice, as she reflected how much easier things might have been with a steady income. It just happened to be the wrong advice. It came from his need for her rather than her own needs for herself. This is perhaps the central tension for Pilgrims – their clueless loving parents and friends continue to want them to conform. The Pilgrims can see that this is a form of caring, and yet they may have to reject it.

Being a Pilgrim is therefore risky. People really do want to force their solutions to problems on those who are still considering what the problem might be. They can be as insistent and as irritating as my aunt Mary offering her fruit cake to visitors who really don't want any. So the Pilgrim has to learn how to refuse inappropriate offers, and to deal with others being offended no matter how graciously one turns them down.

Being the only person who sees things a certain way can be tiring. Consequently we can hunger for friends at this stage, and we can even be relatively happy with friends who are also Pilgrims but who may be on an entirely different path. Occasionally this can break out into bitter arguments between those who seemed to be best friends. If we find this happening to us it may be helpful to realize that it is not always the other person who is wrong or irrational, it is the situation itself that is difficult. Actually the situation is impossible. The Pilgrim, by nature, has to be alone. When one is working out one's identity at this deep level it is rarely possible to be fully present to another and his struggle. Examples of this can be seen in any of the well-documented disputes that existed between the great artists of the Impressionist period and later. Picasso and Braque, arguing passionately about different approaches to art, and disagreeing violently, were in fact far closer in overall aim than anyone else, and yet, those shades of difference threatened to cloud the vision each had and was devoted to honoring. To remain true to their searches they had to reject each other.

In folk tales the Pilgrim is often seen as a simpleton, as one who lives by standards others do not share, and who is pure at heart – and this person is almost always alone. Yet this simpleton is on a quest, a task that may seem impossible, and to which he is always faithful. Far from being an object of scorn, this is a figure to inspire us.

The Pilgrim has to find out who she is, and what she has to say.

In my work with counseling clients I have found it useful to ask them what they like to do, and care about, as a way to begin to find out where their Pilgrim archetype might be concealed. One man responded flippantly that all he liked doing was drinking tea. When asked about this he was able to say that he really did care about tea, its flavors and varieties. In fact he cared passionately about it. His task was therefore to use his passion actively. Rather than traveling miles to his favorite tiny stores and buying exotic brands only for his own consumption he decided to start marketing teas so everyone could taste them. This is what I mean by using our talents actively.

A couple I came across loved Central American ethnic products. They'd go on vacations to the remote villages of Ecuador and Mexico and return each time with a carload of rugs and carvings, having spent all their money. They filled their home with these gorgeous items. And their friends saw these things, praised them, and kept offering to buy them. Since they wanted the money so they could go on more trips they started to sell some of their ornaments. Eventually they went into business 'for their friends' and thirty years later are still having as much fun as before – and as their customer base has grown they've materially benefited many villages that had been poverty stricken until they could find a market for their goods. Perhaps best of all is that this couple can see how they have truly brought joy to the many people who now own the items they have brought back from distant villages, and that a marginal interest that had been labeled as 'folk art' has been helped to grow into a cultural awareness of some of our poorest, least-considered geographical neighbors. They're doing their bit to support tolerance, understanding, and cultural diversity, even though they'd probably never lay claim to such inflated terms.

Notes

1. Dylan, Bob. 'Shelter from the Storm', from *Blood on the Tracks*. Columbia records 1975.
2. The legend of Bluebeard was first recorded by Charles Perrault and published in 1697, and seems to have been very ancient even then. Perrault made a career out of rewriting various fairy tales and folk legends. It is possible the story dates back to the sixth century legends about St. Gildas.

Chapter Six

The Warrior-Lover

When this itinerant figure of the Pilgrim does make a choice of one consistent course of action – and that can be precipitated by family demands such as having children, as we have noticed – we have another role. It's called the Warrior-Lover, because when we choose something to fight for, we do so because we believe in our actions. We fight for what, or who, we love. Many of us become Warrior-Lovers when we find a significant love relationship. That is when we stop being Pilgrims after something to care about, because in finding love, and deciding that this person, and no other, is the one we want to be with we make a commitment. Given that there are billions of people in the world, many of whom we could possibly find attractive, settling on one demands an act of imagination and a leap of faith. Some people who have no significant others become Warrior-Lovers when they choose to raise their children alone. They make a choice, based in love, as to what and who comes first.

Clearly one can fight for one's family or for a cause, and one can be a real Warrior-Lover, without being in any way violent. One merely has to think of Gandhi's stand against the racism of Imperial British Rule. His "fight" was non-violent, but it was a struggle nonetheless. Martin Luther King jr. was another exponent of non-violence and a valiant campaigner, always upholding non-violence even in the face of considerable opposition. Similarly, those who march and protest for Peace or Justice are engaged in a struggle, but usually they do not wish to hurt others.

Naturally, we all know of supposedly peaceful demonstrations that have turned violent. I'd suggest that this might well be because the Warrior has several incarnations. Some people join a cause and fight for it because they are angry at what they see as injustices and they want to fight, to smash, to destroy. This is the aggressive version of the Warrior and it is more correctly described as the pseudo-Warrior. Such people are to be found everywhere. They truly may believe in revolution, or whatever their creed is, but they thirst for the fight for its own sake. And yet, think of the other options. Perhaps one could therefore see the Warrior-Lover as best represented in the image of the traditional Samurai or in King Arthur's Knights.

These were peaceable, religious men who fought for justice when required to, and died for a noble cause rather than allowing evil to flourish. Such men were devoted to ideals of justice and correct conduct rather than to the demands of class loyalty. For example, in *King Lear* Shakespeare gives us the example of the Duke of Kent who challenges his own king when he sees that what Lear is doing is a threat to the stability of the kingdom. "Be Kent unmannerly/When Lear is mad," he bursts out. "My life I never held but as a pawn/To wage against thine enemies, nor fear to lose it, /Thy safety being motive" (*Lear* 1.1 145-6; 156-8). He has always been loyal to Lear, but not blindly so. He is, instead, dedicated to justice. This is the sort of almost foolhardy courage Shakespeare allows us to witness, and the Duke of Kent, sixty years old, is banished for his honesty. Everyone watching that play in an era when kings could be horrifyingly despotic would have trembled at Kent's courage.

A different example might be the name of Greenpeace's campaign boat, 'The Rainbow Warrior'. This is certainly not a warship in any sense, and yet it is used by very brave people under extremely trying circumstances as they attempt to challenge environmentally destructive practices. Sailing into a nuclear testing zone before a scheduled blast requires total commitment to the cause of disarmament; yet it is not a violent act.

We can also include intellectual Warriors in this group, since there are researchers after truth – journalists, academics of all kinds, teachers – all of whom choose a path and stick to it with devotion, believing in the enduring human value of what they strive for. Notice, though, that the end value has to be for the good of mankind. The person who campaigns tirelessly to promote schemes that will not ultimately benefit mankind, and may in fact hurt others, is accessing the Warrior aspect of this stage but not the Lover. So the executive who works to maximize corporate profits while ignoring the long term polluting his company perpetuates is not, clearly, using both aspects to advantage. An example of this might be the heroic efforts put forward in a tainted cause by such organizations as cigarette manufacturers, who attempted for decades to cover up the true effects of smoking. Or consider those large mining companies that tried to disguise the pollution their methods caused. This is the Warrior without the Lover, or the pseudo-warrior. Whenever this happens we have a person who, for one reason or another, is not fully open to the truth of what is happening. A person who ignores the truth is one who has failed to complete the Pilgrim's search for what is authentic, and so despite acting like a Warrior this individual is in fact an Orphan, hiding behind the company's orthodoxy and failing to take responsibility for her own belief systems. Such a person can be good at what she does, highly successful, and well paid, but she's spiritually still an Orphan.

Similarly, those people who just love fighting are not true Warriors in the sense we are discussing here. The man who has no fear is not brave. Show me a man who has no fear and I'll show you someone who either is stupid or has no soul. Real courage involves knowing what fear is and not giving in to it. The bully knows fear but disguises it and hides it in various ways. Again, such a person may seem like a Warrior, but falls far short of the ideal we are talking about. This may be hard for us to see, since our culture surrounds us with images of the fighter – not all of which are helpful or even sane. The *Rocky* movies give us the illusion of the plucky fighter who wins through, except that if we look closer we see that Rocky seems to work from rather crude motivations such as revenge, anger, pride, and a desire to punish. Nothing lasting and good can come out of that. Perhaps Hollywood made a lot of money in promoting *Rocky* and *Rambo* and other movies of that sort; it did so by offering us an image that is a perversion of this most helpful image of the Warrior.

In folk tales the Warrior-Lover is often defined in his higher motivations by being pitted against a similar figure who has only base ambitions. So, in the fourteenth century poem named after him, Sir Gawain rides out to meet the Green Knight knowing he has no chance of winning, but determined to be loyal to his religiously-founded beliefs and codes of right conduct. In the *Song of Roland*, Roland fights to the death against the Saracens for the sake of his religious beliefs and his devotion to his fellow crusaders. King Arthur has to fight his wicked half-brother Mordred, not because he wants to but because it is the only way right can prevail. This method of contrast helps to bring out the qualities of the Warrior-Lover who is the focus of each tale so that the reader (or listener in the case of the earlier tales) can see the difference between high and base motivation. The true Warrior-Lover is not a bruiser, but someone who has a cause beyond his immediate personal needs or family loyalties. He also has a thorough awareness of the value of human life and what is at stake when he risks it, and this is symbolized in his relative weakness before his opponent.

Perhaps this is what lies behind the Old Testament story of David and Goliath. David is going to do what he has to do, even though he must be scared, and even though the fight looks impossible. He becomes a symbol for all heroic acts undertaken in a spirit of faith, which is probably why the legend has had such a grip on our imaginations for so many years. In Renaissance Italy it became a favorite subject for sculpture, from Donatello, to Michelangelo and Bernini. It articulated the need of the individual and of the state to believe in itself, and to act without fear. No wonder the statues are inspiring. No wonder Michelangelo's *David* was first placed in the Piazza Signoria in Florence, the main square of one of the greatest of the Italian city-states, where it acted as a declaration of the worth of courageous, purposeful, selfless action. The original has since been moved to the shelter of the Academia, but the Florentines felt so strongly about their statue's value as an expression of civic pride that a copy was commissioned and stands in the Piazza to this day. They didn't do this because they simply wanted to fill the empty space. They did it because it reminded them of important spiritual values that they wanted to be able to honor every day they saw it.

So what are those values? Anyone who has ever spoken with real, professional, military personnel knows that the true Warrior in that context is a person who respects the lives of those he or she serves with or who are under his or her command. The task is not just to kill, but rather to achieve significant objectives while preserving the lives of one's own troops as far as possible. Now, consider for a moment what happened during the Vietnam War. Many people served with great valor, believing fully in the worth of what they did. Many chose to go even though they knew full well what the Peace protesters had to say, and what the Presidency was attempting to do. As such they made conscious moral decisions about their actions. If we focus on the individuals' decisions, and not the outcome of the war itself, we can see some of these servicemen and women as truly in the tradition of the Warrior-Lover, acting out of love for their country. Their journey has full integrity. Yet I'd also suggest that on their return from their tours of duty these Warriors met another challenge, which was to be able to face social criticism and even ridicule. Many Vietnam vets could not manage both struggles.

Some of the critics of the Vietnam War, of course, were hardly much better than scared Orphans who found a home in the Peace Movement. Some were conspicuously brave, and they faced a different struggle. The question here is not what action a person took, but did that person bring integrity to that action?

Perhaps a comparison will work here. There is a famous poem by e e cummings which begins:

> i sing of Olaf glad and big
> whose warmest heart recoiled at war
> a conscientious object-or . . .

In the poem Olaf experiences horrible victimization at the hands of his fellow recruits and officers, and broken in body but not in spirit, he eventually dies in jail. The poem concludes:

> Christ (of His mercy infinite)
> i pray to see, and Olaf, too
> preponderatingly because
> unless statistics lie he was
> more brave than me: more blond than you

This poem, written by a man who had served as an ambulance driver in World War I, delivers the simple point that some of those who were conscientious objectors persisted in their beliefs even though it meant persecution and death. There are, it seems, many ways to be a Warrior-Lover, and they have very little to do with which side eventually triumphs.

How might this translate into everyday life? Well, all parents have to be Warrior-Lovers at some point. They have to go above and beyond usual levels of devotion because they love their children. They have to do what they have to do, and if that means going without much sleep for several months and still hanging on to a job, while junior fights off whatever childhood ailment he has, then that's what the parent does. The parent may also have to lay down a few rules from time to time – rules that are not popular with the children – and may have to enforce some of them. For without a few ground rules, most of us would not survive into adulthood. The loving parent is prepared to face the truths, deal with the necessary disputes, advocate for the child … and so on. These are all struggles, all fights, but without fisticuffs – we hope. They are for the best interests of the child, and they are done as acts of loving-kindness. The parent who gives in to the child all the time in the hope that the child will love him is living in a fool's world. So we all have to "do what's right" and we all have to know which battles to fight: when to insist, when to back down, and when to listen. Is the child being difficult? Does that merit an immediate punishment? A rule has been broken, after all. Yet there may be reasons we know nothing about, and the child's tantrum may be about something entirely different, which we'd do well to investigate. The teenager who cuts school may be acting out a rebellion; she may also be afraid of something that is going on at the school, such as bullying. The Warrior, because he is also a Lover, has to balance the executive power to punish with the right amount of understanding, compassion, and kindness. And as a Warrior the parent has to intervene where necessary.

It's a difficult task to be in Warrior-Lover mode successfully. The Warrior sometimes has to remember that it's not possible or even desirable to win every battle. It's the larger campaign that matters. Is there any point in having a tremendous struggle to assert one's will over a child about some small detail, and in so doing losing vital amounts of good will, or even damaging the relationship fundamentally? The battle is won, but the war may well be lost. Think of the number of family tensions that can cluster around something as silly as broccoli. Junior will not die of malnutrition if he doesn't eat his broccoli or beans, but unless the struggle is approached with care he may carry a lifetime of resentments that everyone could do without. Sometimes a strategic retreat is, in fact, far more effective than a swingeing victory. I can think of at least one case where the family dog, who would eat anything, was enlisted to help break this sort of deadlock. The father would insist that the children had to eat what was on their plates, and would then turn a blind eye as various items were smuggled to the ever-grateful dog. Father's point was made, no one suffered, and the children thought they were oh-so-smart – little suspecting that father had seen his limits and had backed down. The father had years of experience working in industry, and he knew that sometimes we all have to pretend we haven't seen small infractions because if we try and run things by the book it just causes resentment.

Sometimes things become a little more tense. When the child yells, "Get out! I'm going to do this my way!" several choices are available. One can insist on staying put and getting things done one's own way with the child, and incur the lasting annoyance of all concerned. And sometimes one can step back, leaving the child to deal with things on her own. The child soon perceives that she did not want to be left entirely alone, as she had said. What she wanted was merely some elbowroom. That is the point at which the whole situation can be renegotiated – the parent gets some input, and the child gets to exercise some control. Both learn in this new process.

Sometimes it seems that the best thing a parent can do in a difficult situation with a child is have the courage to ask the basic questions, and to be able to listen to the child's answer. How often have we seen on our TV screens, or read about, or witnessed parents who are afraid of asking their children what's happening in their lives? In fact, part of the reason we have, and need, therapists is because families sometimes have trouble talking directly to each other about what isn't working. Without that resource we would all be far poorer. The Warrior-Lover has to be able to access the courage to look the other person in the eye and ask what it is she needs to talk about, whether the conversation is taking place between a parent and a child, or an employee and a boss, or between a married couple. For without those conversations the distress and upset can only emerge in ways that are inappropriate or destructive. The employee who does not feel heard by the boss will be angry, unproductive, and even a saboteur of the best interests of the company he works for. To reverse this tendency is very straightforward, but it takes work and patience. The employee has first to make sure that she has been able to access her Warrior-Lover's skills. Did she approach the boss with courage, without aggression, with an open mind? Notice how different this seems from the popular idea of what a Warrior could do. Was the discussion able to proceed in mutual respect? Just because one's boss is senior does not mean that he or she necessarily has better skills. Sometimes the Warrior-Lover's task is to educate the opponent.

In the Grail legends – those tales written about King Arthur's knights who went searching for the cup used at Jesus' Last Supper, which was called the Holy

Grail – the task that awaited the knights was to find the sick Fisher King whose illness had made the whole kingdom barren, and to ask him the simple question: 'What ails you?' It was a question that everyone else had avoided asking because, after all, he was the king, and they were all afraid of offending him by suggesting that he might not be in excellent health. Only Sir Galahad, who was the purest of the Knights, asked the question and so found the Grail. Honesty, openness, and courage are the virtues that are obviously important, but there is more.

It takes a special sort of courage to be able to talk with others this way, especially if there is a history of conflict or awkwardness. And that is the whole point. It really is more than blurting out a question, because the whole success in asking it depends upon the questioner being able to gain the trust of the other, making sure the one who is suffering knows that this is a truly caring inquirer who will listen without judging. The relationship has to exist first, and that takes time, love, effort, and courage. In the Grail Legends this is symbolized by Galahad's struggle to find the Fisher King, and the knight's holiness of intent is already vouched for because he's one of the Round Table. The legend is extraordinarily rich in what it can tell us if we focus on the full picture, rather than the 'what happened next' viewpoint. Robert Bly calls this 'thinking mythically.'

The example of Sir Galahad can therefore suggest to us that when we speak to our children, our spouse, our friends, or our employers we have to be able to do so from a place of good faith. They have to trust us – or we won't get a straight answer – and we have to trust them. They need to know we're not going to manipulate, cajole or judge. They have to be assured that no one is trying to make them look silly or attempting to patronize them. So the questions have to be open-ended. In active-service military life (and in war movies, some of which can be highly accurate about the relationships concerned, and which most of us know more intimately) this is demonstrated in the absolute trust soldiers have in each other. This is the inter-reliance of the 'band of brothers'. Unfortunately it is something that has proved hard to translate back to civilian life. And perhaps that is a clue to us about what the Warrior-Lover can teach us. For this is what lies at the heart of Galahad's questions: the courage to be open.

Imagine how different life could be if more people took the time to develop this skill of open questioning. The parent who yells, 'What the heck is *wrong* with you?' at her child may be asking the important question – but what a way to do it! It's already an accusation. Something is 'wrong' with the child, so the child is being put in a situation where she's not only wrong but *she* is the problem, not the situation or the behavior, and she's expected to explain it all, as well! A better way to ask the question might be the far more neutral and more loving, 'What's happening here?' In this version the condemnation is simply not there, although the inquiry is. Imagine how people working out their divorce arrangements could benefit from the sort of measured dealings that Sir Galahad's experience hints at.

This wisdom is what enables the Warrior-Lover to exist between the extremes of the Zealot and the Bully. The Zealot knows he is right, but is intolerant of others and does not hesitate to break rules in the pursuit of his agenda. Moreover he is likely to lecture others on what he perceives their duty to be. Such a figure is going to be coercive, strident, and oppressive. The cause may be a good one, but being overly militant in promoting it will repel many people and ultimately taint the cause. The Zealot has strong, rigid beliefs and attempts to force those upon others. In some ways, the Zealot seems admirable, and has deep, passionately-held beliefs. But the Zealot has really stopped thinking. What is good for him *must* be good for you. One cannot question such a person effectively. The Zealot can really be seen most easily as the Active incarnation of the Warrior-Lover archetype as it slides inexorably towards the unquestioning level of the Orphan.

Some people see Oliver North as an example of this sort of thinking. Colonel North was a brave and dedicated man, but he had no legal or moral authority for diverting money to the Contras, which was an organization bent on overthrowing the elected government of Nicaragua. In congressional hearings he was almost impenetrable. Asked if he thought his actions were right he famously said that he thought his scheme to finance a private war was: "A pretty neat idea". Right and wrong seemed to have evaporated. Questions don't please those who have the terminal disease of certainty.

The mirror image of the Zealot, the Bully, has all the same attributes but is devoid of real belief. This figure is intent only on controlling others as a way to avoid facing his feelings of inadequacy. He may hide behind a belief, but actually he's only out for himself, and seeks consolation in the amassing of wealth, or of toys, and takes pleasure only in power. As we've had cause to notice before, the Bully is really a debased version of the Orphan hiding behind a convenient identity. This is the passive incarnation of the Warrior-Lover archetype.

Both of these figures are drawn, here, as extremes so that the point can be clear. In real life we may have areas of our life in which we are Zealots and areas in which we Bully others, and still other areas where we are truly able to exist as Warrior-Lovers. The challenge is to be that way in all aspects of our lives.

And here is one of the more difficult aspects of the Warrior-Lover's life challenge: the Warrior must be prepared to suffer, be vilified, be disgraced, and even be killed for the good of the cause. The Warrior-Lover, just like a soldier, must be ready for personal defeat and accept it. The Warrior's failure is often the greatest success in the larger context. Jesus, for example, was tortured, disgraced, deserted by his followers, and publicly crucified. Yet, without that crucifixion, I doubt if very many of the Christian-based religions of the world would ever have come about. In becoming a loving martyr his persuasive example remained long after his death on the cross. Martyrdom is today a word sullied by religious fanatics of all sorts, as suicide bombings seem to be a fashionable form of terrorism. But blowing oneself up and killing a marketplace full of ordinary citizens, including women and children, is not the same as dying for one's beliefs, alone, as a protest. A few examples may help.

Wilfred Owen, the poet who served in the trenches of the Western Front, protested against the slaughter of World War I and refused to fight any longer. He was vilified, labeled as "shell-shocked," insane, a coward, despite the medals he had won. Eventually he decided to return to the front lines because he felt that even though the war was wrong, he owed his loyalty to the men in his Company and he would not stand aside as they continued to fight and die. He returned to the Western Front and was killed in action. Yet his example is now enshrined in our imaginations as well as in literature, because of his seemingly suicidal decision. As a result he has helped to change attitudes at all levels concerning wars and who dies in them – usually the poor, ill-educated enlisted men Owen refused to abandon.

Other examples might include the thousands of people who worked for the combined British and American Intelligence Services during World War II, many of whom have never been recognized, rewarded, or praised. Quite a few were not even paid. William Stephenson's extraordinary account of some of these people in his book *A Man Called Intrepid* points out that several of the figures who literally saved the West from fascism, did so while financing intelligence organizations out of their own pockets. Their reward was that tyrants were stopped from taking over the world. Their legacy is that, to this day, their detractors argue about the methods they used. Being a Warrior-Lover means taking unpopular actions on occasions, and taking responsibility. Being a leader is not a popularity contest, served by opinion polls: trimming one's stance to what is accepted by the many can be, in the extreme instance, just another example of lack of principle. Politicians are often accused of this and occasionally with good cause.

In more everyday terms the Warrior-Lover who is a parent will have to know that her children will probably not recognize all that she did for them until many years later when they have their own children – and perhaps not even then. The parent also needs to accept that if she does a good job she will become obsolete when the children leave home. Her task is positively heroic – it is to launch her children with sufficient independence so that they do not need her any more. The Warrior-Lover, just similarly, is fighting until peace is achieved; whereupon she's out of a job. Of course most parents hope that their children will come back and visit and be loving, and yet the truth of the matter is that children need to grow up and cut those apron strings if they are to develop their own meaningful lives. They will have to find their own values to fight for and identify their own people to love, and they won't need the parents nearly as much when they have found those meaningful connections.

The Warrior-Lover parent wants to raise children who are going to take a Warrior's path also, and producing a slew of kids who do not want to leave home is akin to having a family of Innocents and Orphans to deal with. The Warrior-Lover has to be sensitive to this, and allow children – and indeed all the other people in his or her life – to grow at their own rates and in their own ways, and that involves engaging the Lover part of the archetype. For without that nurturing aspect, children cannot hope to grow into true Warrior-Lover status. Without the necessary nurturing those people who want to be the Warrior's friend because they admire what they see as the Warrior's decisive attributes will merely feel inadequate and misunderstood, and this means they are less likely to be able to rise to the spiritual challenge they are invited to take on. The army knows this territory well. Soldiers are trained not by distant University Professor types, but by their own corporals and sergeants, those who will show them how to do the job, take no nonsense, and yet value them absolutely as members of a team. It's never called love in the training manuals, but veterans of all campaigns know that's exactly what it is.

A different version of the Warrior-Lover may be seen in the case of the artist or the scientific researcher who feels a duty to relay the truth no matter how unpopular. Perhaps an example would be William Faulkner, who received the Nobel Prize for literature at a time when many of his books were out of print because of low sales. I doubt we'll see Stephen King taking the Nobel, despite his rocketing sales and vast royalty income. Sometimes the not-so-popular teacher in school may actually be the one that students learn most from, not the easygoing popular young thing who talks in street slang.

It may seem as if I'm stating the obvious here, and I take that risk because it can be very hard to tell the difference between the true Warrior-Lover and the pseudo-warrior. One of the enduring myths of our time is the image of the crazy artist as somehow an admirable figure. The wounded creator, the alcoholic writer, the drug-soaked painter, and the wildly eccentric 'genius' have all been held up, at some time or other, as figures to emulate as they blaze a path of uncompromising daring. The young and impressionable will sometimes take the drugs and mimic the behavior in an attempt to persuade someone, anyone, that they are on a path of great seriousness. This is a very dangerous myth, and the concepts behind it need to be clarified.

While it's true that many great artists have been mentally unstable, we need to look a little closer at what's at issue. Beethoven had a disastrous childhood, went deaf in the prime of his career, and was certainly a magnificent composer; and equally certainly he wasn't easy to get along with since he raged and lashed out at all those who loved him. Van Gogh, cutting off his ear and later shooting himself is a well-loved example. Hemingway shot himself. Almost every day of his later life, Faulkner drank until he passed out. Rimbaud was on a self-destructive course from his teens onwards. And we could add more and more examples; Anne Sexton, Sylvia Plath, the list goes on. Yet I'd like to point out that behind the cliché lies an important truth. These were artists who had produced the best work they knew how, were devoted to their tasks, and who realized that even the very finest they could do was not going to change the world right away, and that the personal cost would be huge. They were, in a very real sense, faced with the limitations of what the Warrior-Lover can do. Beethoven, going deaf, must have been tempted to retire. He was already famous. Yet he held true to his passion, and went on to produce his finest work despite his disability. When Hemingway realized his later work lacked the vitality of his early successes, he knew he was stuck. His private papers show his agony as he realized he was written out and his productive career over. He could have become some sort of grand old man of literature, a spent force making easy money on the lecture circuit. Instead he chose to exit ahead of time with the help of a shotgun. As such he chose not to fight the next stage that faces every Warrior-Lover – the same stage that drove so many other substance-abusing artists to avoid their sorrows. The hardest fight of all is to be a Warrior-Lover and to realize that one's courage fades, one's abilities dim, and yet the fight remains, every day, needing to be faced, alone. This is when many people take refuge in self-destructive acts.

It is only when the Warrior-Lover can face this unpleasant fact as an inevitable part of the spiritual journey that there is a chance to move ahead to the next stage. We are all going to be tested by life; we are all going to hit our personal limits, and this will be immensely distressing. The task is to come to terms with this. If being a Pilgrim is all about finding out what we can do and finding our faith, then being a Warrior-Lover is concerned with testing that faith – until it cracks. Then one has to carry on despite this. Paul Farmer, the gifted doctor described by Tracy Kidder in *Mountains beyond Mountains,* can give us some useful pointers here. Dr. Farmer has pioneered health care in some of the world's poorest places, and yet he describes what he does as 'the long defeat'. Ultimately, he acknowledges that there will always be poor and needy people, and that the problem will never be solved, but this does not mean he will let himself abandon the task and, in his own words he says:

I have fought the long defeat and brought other people in to fight the long defeat, and I'm not going to stop because we keep losing. Now I actually think sometimes we may win…. We *want* to be on the winning team, but at the *risk* of turning our backs on the losers, no it's not worth it. So you fight the long defeat…. I don't care if we lose. I'm going to try to do the right thing. (pp. 288-9)

The story of Jesus again offers some good examples of this. Jesus on the Cross calling out "My God, My God, why hast thou forsaken me?" is a harrowing thought. Yet if we understand it as Jesus the man being tested to the same point to which we all will be tested, then the event becomes an emblem of what is likely to happen to us all. Peter, his disciple, is also tested. After the crucifixion the onlookers question him and he denies he is a follower of Jesus, just as Jesus had predicted. His faith is tested to the breaking point. Yet Peter, despite being very unhappy about his actions, does not fall apart in self-pity. He chooses instead to learn from his limits and then to re-dedicate himself to his beliefs anyway. This is the Warrior-Lover's ultimate challenge.

Mother Theresa is worth quoting on this topic. "We are not here," she said, "to be successful. We are here to be faithful."

Wayne Dyer suggests that we do not go through stages so much as we decide, through the power of our intentions, to raise our "vibrational energy" so that we can engage with the world in the highest, most productive manner. Ideally, we do what we do for the sake of truth (a higher vibration) rather than because we want to appear successful (a lower vibration). This idea has some attractive aspects to it, and we can see it as another way of looking at the questions raised by the stages of development outlined here. It is important to recognize that whenever we start any brand new sequence of actions, we are likely to have to go through some or all of the stages. What is vital is to recognize that there is a difference between approaching life with courage, and approaching it with fear. Fear is a powerful motivator, after all. Yet the fearful person will choose a trajectory that becomes a parody of the healthiest line of action. The fearful Innocent may never leave home, or may make so much fuss about doing so that he or she has to be adopted by someone, and so the Orphan stage never really happens in its fullness. If the adoptive parent should then fail, or die, or leave, we find a terrified individual who is only too ready to attach to anything as a way *not* to be in doubt. Cults thrive on such weak and confused individuals. Addictions become useful ways of shaping lives that are otherwise chaotic, since the addiction gives a compelling reason for action, all the time.

It's also worth remembering that anyone can start off life with courage, and that one's courage can be undermined, lost, and destroyed. The man who devotes huge amounts of time and energy to completing his collection of nineteenth century tram tickets may have the determination and the work ethic of a true Warrior-Lover, but I'd suggest that the input of effort is not worth such a questionable result. I'm not trying to knock detailed scholarship, and I'm not criticizing the hobbies that people have which surely bring them pleasure and engage their creativity. I am questioning whether this is the highest destiny of a human being. It may be that this person prefers this hobby, or obsession, to dealing with the larger situations that life may send. Struggling for world peace is not to everyone's taste or ability; it's easier to collect Hummels, or vintage cars, or salt and peppershakers, just as it's easier to play Bingo seven nights a week. But is this the highest response to the Warrior's call? Is this what we were put on earth to do? I doubt it. Governments everywhere seem to agree. They recognize their citizens for services of all kinds, as long as these can be seen to be in some way beneficial to the greater good of mankind. To be the possessor of the world's most complete collection of samples of barbed wire may be wonderful, but is it really the way to spend one's life? I chose that example because there are collectors who spend a lot of time, energy, and money collecting vintage and historic barbed wire, and who are very knowledgeable on this topic. And some of them choose this kind of task because it is easier than engaging with real life. Their Warrior mode is governed by fear, and the vibrational energy Dr. Dyer talks about is most definitely not as high as it could be. Perhaps they have been tested by life until their courage failed, and now they have chosen a more congenial, more muted existence. They have backed down from the second part of the Warrior-Lover's path.

Notice that Fear and Ego seem to go hand in glove. Here's an example that seems fairly typical: "I have the finest collection of pre-1920s farm tractors in the country." Look at that statement. "I have" is all about ego – my possessions, which give me status. I have noticed that in museums, especially public ones, the staff tend to say, "we have," or "the collection contains…" which is so much softer and more inclusive, and which more accurately reflects the basic reality that individuals don't really own objects. Individuals get to keep objects for a while, then they die and someone else gets to keep them or throw them away. That's much more humbling – and more accurate. Yet by saying "my collection" one is tacitly ignoring one's own mortality. And anyone who pretends death doesn't exist is surely in a state of fear.

So what does it feel like to be a Warrior-Lover?

The Warrior-Lover has taken charge of his or her destiny, and that can mean a powerful sense of being responsible for others, for being the best one can be, and this occasionally leads to inner tension. If the Warrior-Lover is to succeed then she must recognize that this archetype is infinitely variable. As a Warrior she will encounter situations in which she is not certain, and the task is to be able to access the previous levels, especially the Pilgrim, and then to use this information at Warrior level. So, for example, the Warrior-Lover is perhaps an environmentalist by persuasion and follows that ideology. That means, however, that the person has to see that 'environmentalist' is a label and not a definition. It needs to be questioned, explored, and understood on a daily basis. Which environment is being referred to – my neighborhood, my country, my planet? And which one am I going to put my effort into? When I think about pollution do I mean mercury in the water or nuclear proliferation? I can't fight all those battles, so which ones will I choose? And will I be able to bear in mind that my struggle is but a part of the whole? At the same time will I be available for my family and loved ones? For if I win the battle against a major polluter but in the process my family falls apart, then how is that a success? And if I oppose this scheme to build a dam, because it will destroy certain rare plants and animals, but in doing so I ensure that certain other economic benefits cannot happen and families will be threatened with poverty, then how is that good for those people? These are difficult, perhaps impossible, choices. Yet they cannot be shirked. The Warrior-Lover has to be able to become a Pilgrim at times so she can clarify the situation, and then move back into the more developed role and live it accordingly. Equally, the Warrior-Lover will have to try to understand the feelings of those who have not left Orphan stage, and that's a group that makes up much of the world; so the Warrior-Lover will have to exercise considerable compassion. Being a Warrior-Lover is not an excuse to stop thinking; it's an invitation to think more deeply.

What the Warrior-Lover discovers is that the 'enemy' is not always the actual opposition. The other side is made up of people just like any others. Their choices and values may conflict deeply with one's own, and we may hate their decisions. Yet we cannot hate them. For if we do we are over-simplifying. Perhaps the person who opposes us is also a Warrior-Lover, one who has come to his or her beliefs after a considerable amount of thought and introspection. If so, that person must be invited to become part of a dialogue. For if the other really is a Warrior-Lover then she will have a sense of truth and purpose. This person is, therefore, actually an ally on the path to finding truth. The Warrior-Lover's real fight is only ever against the passive Orphans who have sold their souls to easy answers, to quick rewards. These are the slaves of this world; they can be immensely powerful in their sheer numbers but their minds are in chains, and they are not open to discussions, to questions, or to doubts.

An example of this search for truth might be seen in those peace activists who came to this path after having served in the military. Senator John Kerry and author Ron Kovic come to mind. Each has been roundly criticized for inconsistency, for changing sides. Whatever one thinks of these figures for our discussion here it's necessary to focus on their courage – first as serving military men, and then in being able to change their minds and declare that they had done so.

The Warrior-Lover has to stay open at all times. So if she is faced with someone who says something that seems bigoted and stupid, the most helpful response is not to fight that person immediately. That simply forces the other person to harden an attitude that is offensive. The more productive way forward is to ask that person to say more about these attitudes. When prompted to say more most people will do so, and if asked to define what they mean they will sometimes find that their particular attitudes make very little sense even to themselves.

Socrates was famous for doing this – and was eventually sentenced to death by those he had annoyed. His technique was alarmingly simple. He asked people questions, and when they replied he asked them to define what they meant. He continued to reflect back to people the dubious nature of their unexamined concepts, until he had led them to their own inner contradictions. He was dogged in the extreme and said that he was simply trying to make men honest with his inquiries. He certainly made them more thoughtful and reflective. I would argue that his death was in fact a victory, and that his questioning approach is still mightily effective. His accusers, meanwhile, have faded into the ashcan of forgotten history. Skilled therapists will often use a version of his techniques when they mirror a client's statements in order to examine them. Inconsistencies soon become obvious, causing the client to have to consider more thoroughly just what the real issue might be. This is a version of Sir Galahad's question to the sick Fisher King, "What ails you?"

In my work with writing for self-exploration, I have my clients keep their writing and refer back to it, and I ask them to question what they say in the light of earlier statements. Often this surprises them. Did I really think that? they ask themselves. And the proof is on the page in front of them, in their own writing. Proprioceptive writing, pioneered by Linda Trichter Metcalf and Tobin Simon, brings this technique to the fore. When a client writes about 'the situation I'm in,' for instance, the facilitator asks for a clearer definition of what that actually means. One could say that this method asks us to examine the clichés we have created for ourselves, and it challenges those unexamined concepts that we have woven into our lives unthinkingly. It asks us to re-examine the very language that defines the terms upon which we choose to live right now. I give this example in such detail because it seems to describe the Warrior-Lover's task, which is to keep the channels of communication open to the questioning Pilgrim within each of us. For the Orphans of the world are those who have swallowed whole unexamined concepts and clichés, and they need help if they are to move beyond their ready-made belief systems. Through the use of respectful challenges – the Warrior aspect of the archetype challenges, while the Lover aspect respects how difficult this can be for the Orphan – real spiritual growth can be achieved.

If the price of freedom is constant vigilance, then the Warrior-Lover could be seen as the constant questioner, the honest skeptic, or even as the guardian who ensures that we do not enslave our minds. This can be a lonely and exhausting task. It can also be exhilarating, since more and more people seem willing to ask these questions when they are encouraged to do so.

The most important thing a Warrior-Lover has to face is perhaps the most dispiriting. As we have noted already, sooner or later the Warrior will crack. This is not something we like to think about. We tend to assume that our soldiers will go to Iraq, or wherever, and they will fight well, then they will come back and some of them will have some counseling for post traumatic stress disorders or anxiety, and then they will go on as before. The brutal fact is they will never be the same as before. Never. Even those who have chests full of medals will show signs of mental distress later, sometimes much later. Just as war makes cowards of us all, so the Warrior-Lover will eventually collapse. There is an old saying in the secret services, and in covert operations generally, which states quite simply that everyone breaks down under torture. The question is not if it will happen, but how long it will take before it happens. This is true of Warrior-Lovers, also.

In my extensive reading of military histories and biographies one does not see this stressed, but it is quite obviously part of the discussion when non-official historians write the accounts after the fact. A. P. Herbert's classic *The Secret Battle* is perhaps the best instance of this discussion, while A. G. Dudgeon's *Hidden Victory* makes some similarly penetrating observations, and I could give numerous other examples. The Warrior-Lover – if she continues the fight without shirking – will eventually be undermined by it. Perhaps the metaphor that lurks behind the story of Christ's crucifixion is that even the finest hero will be destroyed by the task, but that once that darkness (or the symbolic three days and nights) of defeat has been encountered the individual can 'rise again' to a higher level of awareness. It is this destruction and re-emergence that allows the Warrior-Lover to make it to the next stage.

The Warrior-Lover's fight is frequently characterized in literature in terms of the outer struggle against definite obstacles, yet it will be clear from this discussion that the Warrior-Lover must undertake an internal struggle as well against fears, doubts, and the destructive part of herself that fighters everywhere know they have to keep in check. The inner journey is one in which one faces fear and discovers that it is only fear, and not a total inability to be courageous. Fear is an emotion, and like all emotions it does not need to be acted on without question. Fear exists within us because it helped our species survive. The ancestor who ran away from danger might not have been the most noble of people, but he is much more likely to have survived to reproduce. Fear is therefore an inevitable biological part of who we are. When we feel afraid it is simply information that tells us that our bodies may be in danger. How we react to that information is what is important. Living to fight another day is often much the most sensible option.

Dealing with inner fears, however, can be more challenging. The traumatized person may have to become a Pilgrim for many years in order to find out what he is afraid of. He may then need to seek a mentor or therapist who will help him seek further. Ultimately, though, it is one's own inner dragons that have to be struggled with and this struggle happens alone, and the person one struggles with is oneself. This is the Warrior-Lover's fight. He does not just meet death, but meets his own desire to die, and his wish to give in to the dark urges of the Shadow self. The Warrior meets his opposite, the sense of chaos and madness that he has tried to suppress or ignore in himself. Living in fear of one's inner demons places us firmly back in the realm of the passive Orphan, depressed and fearful. In ancient literature this confrontation with chaos is sometimes symbolized by the hero's descent into the underworld, a place in which one meets the dead, a place that is the opposite of all the values of the upper world.

In the legend of Orpheus, which has existed in many versions across the centuries, Orpheus is a superb musician who must go to the underworld to rescue his beloved wife, Eurydice, who has died. Obviously this is a terrifying quest, and it specifies the Warrior in his role as a Lover. Orpheus manages to free his wife and is allowed to lead her to freedom as long as neither of them looks back. As they come close to the surface again, Orpheus (a bit like Lot's wife in the Bible story) cannot hear Eurydice behind him and in fear he looks back, whereupon she is immediately returned to the land of the dead. In despair Orpheus vows he will never marry again or have anything to do with women. This enrages the Thracian women who tear him to pieces in a bacchanalian revel. This puzzling story exists in many forms ranging from the Greek myth of about the 6th century BC, through medieval literature where it appears as Sir Orfeo, and in operas by Peri, Montiverdi, Haydn, Gluck, and others. It seems to have enduring appeal. This is perhaps because it dramatizes an important aspect of the Warrior-Lover's task.

If we are to be Warriors we do not have to be fighters – we can be musicians or artists like Orpheus – yet we will have to fight in our own ways. Orpheus uses his talents with courage and with love (for what love can exist without courage?) to get what he desires. We can get what we most desire only by facing our most profound personal uncertainties, risking everything, and going into that underworld.

If we are prepared to take that risk we can, it seems, work miracles for ourselves. Orpheus takes his skill to the absolute limit, and he uses his music to persuade the gods of the underworld to release his wife. As he does so, Orpheus is rescuing the other half of himself, the female aspect that will bear his children and therefore allow him to be part of the most wonderful creativity that nature allows. He validates the Lover aspects of himself. Yet when we access the courage to do this the legend tells us we must never look back or long for that negative depressed place, that place of anxiety for what might be about to go wrong, or it will snatch away our possible happiness, love, and creativity and leave us devoid of courage. Love requires courage, which is faith in oneself, as well as faith in the loved one. Orpheus looks back in fear, remember, and that's when his quest falls apart. In part this is a suggestion of sexual fear – Orpheus's action in looking back seems to ask if his spouse is still loyal, and following him. Almost every artist knows this in different terms – it's the fear that comes when one doubts whether one can do work as good as one did in the past. That's the look over the shoulder, the flash of fear. As so many writers know, this is the feeling that is most likely to bring about writer's block. It's the anxiety that makes us cautious, that makes us not go out on a limb creatively. It makes us play safe – and no great art was ever created by playing safe.

The enraged reaction of the Thracian women to Orpheus's desire to withdraw from all contact with them may seem brutal to us, since they end up ripping the poor mourning Orpheus to pieces. Yet we need perhaps to see this as symbolic of his behavior being an outrage against Nature. For any person to lean upon a past trauma as a reason to fail to use a god-given talent (and Orpheus was said to be able to charm animals from the forests and even move rocks with his music) is, in many ways, an outrage. God-given is not a term used idly here. Orpheus was the son of the god Apollo, who was the god of the sun and of poetry – which at the time was always sung to lyre music. Orpheus has inherited his musical talent from the god of music himself. The suggestion here is that such talent is not something that belongs to the individual, but that it is a link to the divine that must be shared. No personal grief can be more important than the need to continue to use our talents. Even if we lose our loved ones, perpetual mourning is not an option. We have to keep on being creatively involved in the world if we are not to fragment hopelessly as human beings. And symbolically, Orpheus being torn to shreds is a mirroring of that.

In this legend we are shown an Orpheus who refuses to re-engage with the world after the loss of Eurydice, and this is presented as a form of self-indulgence. It is important to spell out that most of us won't have a capability as wonderful as Orpheus's musical genius, but we will have our own wisdom, compassion, and sense of connection with the world. We cannot withdraw these from circulation. Our losses will make us wiser, perhaps, and stronger; and if we do not use this awareness to re-engage with life we will, in psychic terms, collapse.

In more twenty-first century terms, when we recover from trauma we get well because we discover our courage to heal, and having done so we always run the risk of slipping into the memory of that sad and desperate time. Like Orpheus we can always look back and get stuck in the fearful mindset. How often have we come across people who have given up on love after an unhappy marriage or affair? These are the people who have agreed to live with only half their lives. To avoid pain they will also refuse joy. One woman I met with had not been on a date with anyone since the age of 20, and she was now close to 60. This refusal to recover from whatever hurt she had once suffered had robbed her of the possibility of a vital, loving life with a partner, and had also soured all her other friendships. This was the Orpheus myth in action. She had chosen to identify only with the pain, and she had stopped being a person who was fully alive as a result. She was an Orphan longing for shelter, and she had made misery her home.

This sort of reaction can happen at a less dramatic level, too. There are many people who have stopped doing whatever creative pursuit they once loved because of a harsh criticism from the wrong quarter. Almost everyone I've ever questioned can recall at least one school teacher or professor who said something like "You'll never get anywhere if you write/draw/think/work like that." Many actually took this seriously, and never attempted the tasks again. The myth specifically tells us that sorrowing after past wounds is not a useful course of action. It will alienate and enrage others, and it leads directly to the fragmentation of the self.

The Orpheus myth is useful from yet another perspective – and myths like this are extraordinarily rich in what they can tell us – because it mirrors a key aspect of the Warrior-Lover's struggle, and that is the relationship with the parents. Just as Orpheus was expected to use the talents he had inherited from his divine parent, and to do so in his own way, so must we. If the Orphan can be seen as at first rejecting parental protection (while secretly hoping for someone else to come along and offer the same sort of shelter), we can view the Pilgrim as rejecting parental authority and choosing to go out on his own. When the Pilgrim finds what it is he or she needs to do she becomes in effect a self-parenting figure. This means that the standards she chooses to live by will be derived from inherited and parental sources to some extent, but will have been made anew. So a woman might rebel against her parents' values, but she will, inevitably, come to realize that she may be more like them than she at first wants to acknowledge. When she does make this connection it can help to heal the relationship to the parents. This has proved to be a turning point for many of my clients. "My mother and I are so much alike, and yet we're so very different" was the way one woman put it recently, and the comment seemed to sum up the whole situation neatly. The Orphan mourns that her parents were so flawed; the Warrior-Lover welcomes their quirkiness and sees it as having contributed to her wisdom and her own way of how she wishes to be, in this present moment.

In the case of Orpheus we could say that when his music failed to ensure his success in reclaiming Eurydice he decided to opt out of life. It's almost childish; if I can't have my way then I won't play. He's a Warrior-Lover; he's come up against his own limits and now he's sulking like a teenager. As we've already suggested, a Warrior has to face the limits of his courage and yet still carry on anyhow.

And this is where the relationship with the parent comes in. For sulking is always about the feeling that the world isn't fair, and someone had better come along and make it fairer, and soon. Even for the son of a god it isn't fair, and moody withdrawal is a way of attempting to coerce parental actions that will set things back the way one wishes them to be. Yet this is the way of the Orphan, not the Warrior. Orpheus's failure is that he does not complete the Warrior-Lover's task. He does not face his failure and have the courage to carry on in life as a fully functioning member of his society. In retreating and blaming he still sees others as able to put everything right for him rather than taking responsibility for himself. He fails to parent himself into adulthood.

If we look back at our parents from the position of the Warrior-Lover, what we will have to recognize is that they did the best they could under the circumstances that made them who they were then, and that, as it happens, they helped to make us who we are – even if it's only the fact that their genetic material is in us and so we look like them, act like them, and perhaps even think like them at times. The short, dark-haired young woman who comes from a family of short, plump people may yearn to look like supermodel Jerry Hall – six foot tall and blonde – but eventually she may have to recognize that this just isn't going to happen. Similarly the Warrior-Lover has to accept that even though she wishes to be different from her parents, she is also very much of the same mold. Only then can she move towards achieving one of the most important milestones any of us ever have to reach – the reconciliation with the parent. The parent is no longer seen as an ideal or the exact opposite, but as a real person, fallible, confused, and loving.

It's hard to over-emphasize the importance of this. The bond with the parent is primarily a love bond. That's what we saw in the Innocent. This relationship comes under strain in the Orphan phase, and may be further stretched by the demands of the Pilgrim phase. Until that bond is healed the Warrior-Lover cannot love fully. And if she cannot love properly then it becomes extremely hard to be a Warrior-Lover at all.

Many of us marry or enter into long-term relationships before that parental bond is healed, but this does not mean the relationship is doomed. If the Orpheus myth teaches us anything it is that passionate love exists even if the parental baggage has not been sorted through yet. More often than not passionate love exists *because* the baggage hasn't been dealt with. People are attracted to those who have been damaged in the same ways they have been. When the loving couple produces children the entire range of experience each of them lived through with their parents is now reactivated in their memories. As almost any parent will confirm, having a child causes us all to think back to our own childhoods, and wonder. It forces us to rethink our pasts. We may decide that we'll do the exact opposite of everything our parents ever did, but that surely means we're thinking about what our own experiences were, and how they formed us. Watching one's parents deal with their grandchildren can be an eye-opening experience, also, and sometimes it gives the grandparents the opportunity to do things in a more relaxed way than they did with their own children. It's a moment when both sets of adults can re-think how they did things, re-define their relationship, and heal any rifts.

For those people who have no children of their own, the road to healing the relationship with a parent can be more demanding, but it is essentially the same. Life gives us almost limitless openings, especially those moments when we can see other people with children and learn from them. If we stay alert we can use these observations of others as a way to re-think our pasts and make the necessary connections. Or we can take our courage in our hands and talk with our parents directly about the experience of growing up and asserting our sense of separateness.

Returning to the story of Sir Galahad, we notice that he does heal the king – a substitute father figure – and so brings life back to the entire realm. As a symbolic representation that the relationship is healed and everything is correctly aligned again with the energy of God, one could hardly ask for a better example. So how does this apply to everyday life? Sometimes it is not the child who can heal the parent-child relationship, but someone entirely different, someone who is pure of heart like Sir Galahad. Sometimes it is the grandchildren who turn out to be the agents who allow family rifts to be mended, with their promise of future happiness. Parents and grandparents get the chance to meet on an almost equal footing as they are now all parents together. If they can all allow the openness of equality and good faith then wonderful things can happen in the relationships. Sir Galahad's example is indeed a useful model for us.

For other people it may seem impossible to mend this relationship, since their parents are not able to be part of this sort of dialogue. This does not mean that all spiritual progress is thwarted, however. For several years I have worked at The Blue Hills Writing Institute at Curry College, which specializes in Memoir writing. To some extent all the people who attend this writing program are essentially doing the same thing: they are looking to understand their relationships with the past, and this includes their parents, with a view to gaining the clarity that will allow them to keep growing. In some cases the parents are already dead and buried. Yet the relationship still needs to be considered and healed even years after it would seem to be over. For others the emphasis is on their own parenting and their need to heal the fissures in the connections to their children. This almost always leads to a discussion of each person's own experiences of being parented. Exploring one's life story is an essential part of what the Warrior-Lover must do. That is the deeper value of the trip to the land of the dead – the land of the past – that Orpheus undertakes.

Stepping back from this discussion for a moment, it's worth observing a couple of things. First of all, anyone can look like a successful Pilgrim or Warrior. There are lots of ways to fake it and sometimes that's the best a person can do just at that moment. And that's fine. But we all know what the real task involves. So let's spell that out now.

One thing that seems to be vitally important for a Warrior-Lover to do is to make some sort of overt statement of belief as to what she cares about. Orpheus does it when he negotiates to get Eurydice back. Odysseus does it, implicitly, when he feels anger at the men who are trying to woo his wife and take over his kingdom. Sir Gawain has a shield with a pentangle on it to remind him of the virtues he believes in, and so on. If one cannot spell out one's beliefs, however imperfectly, one cannot really be sure one has them. This type of codifying of beliefs can take many forms. For example, near my parent's home in England, in Stoke D'Abernon church, there are small crosses gouged into the stone pillars near the altar rail. In the eleventh century knights who were about to go on crusades to the Holy Land had to hold a vigil, kneeling before the altar all night, praying for their purpose. Of course they were in armor, complete with weapons, and some of them used their daggers to make these crosses while they waited for dawn and the blessing that came with communion. This ritual was more than some empty custom. Alone at night the Warrior-to-be was faced with a series of moral questions: Why am I doing this? Am I prepared for what lies ahead? Do I have the faith to continue to do it until the task is done? Would the highest moral authority (in this case the Christian God) approve of what I'm doing? Am I prepared to stay up all night, fasting, examining my motivations, because this one night is just a tiny sampler of what I may have to face in the months ahead? Is this expedition really true to who I am?

The knight was, in a sense, finalizing his personal beliefs, knowing he was expected to act on them. He was also looking deep inside himself.

If we are to be Warriors and Lovers we must do the same – spell out what we believe and what we intend to act on. And then we must act.

Think of those knights with their heraldic crests and their coats of arms. Underneath each family's crest was a statement, a motto, often written in Latin. These were short pithy sentences, about ten words or less, that seemed to sum up what the family valued. Sometimes, as part of my counseling work, I ask my clients to create a crest, complete with a motto, which I call 'words to live by.' These will be their Warrior's action words. I then ask them to think about the words they've chosen and decide whether or not they want to accept them, rewrite them, or start again. Then, I tell them, comes the hard part: to live as if those words matter.

One man I worked with chose his words in the famous pig-Latin phrase 'non illegitimati carborundum' which he happily translated as 'don't let the bastards wear you down.' He knew exactly who 'the bastards' were, and he knew how they could wear one's soul to shreds, yet he was quite prepared to take on his struggle, knowing more clearly now what it was he would face. In contrast, a woman chose the delightful phrase 'Like water', which she explained as referring to the clean, refreshing, life-giving value of this most ordinary of substances, which incidentally would wear away stone in time. Her aim she said was to stay pure in thought, like clear water, to seem yielding, and yet to be persistent while bringing life. Quite a concept to put into just two words! Another man, an artist, came forward with a humorous response: 'Perhaps not right, but never in any doubt'. This seems to me to be absolutely in tune with the Warrior's path. One has to act as if one has no doubts sometimes, pushing a line of action, and then, later, after one has given it one's best try, one may have to admit one was wrong and try again, and laugh at oneself. As such it was both a description of what can happen to anyone, and a reminder of what this particular man had recognized in himself, for he had a tendency at times to be over-confident and he needed to pay attention to that trait.

Anne Tyler, the novelist, in her short piece 'Still Just Writing' describes her life as an over-extended mother who had no time to concentrate on her writing, and who also felt completely exhausted. When asked one day what she was doing in her life she replied, quite simply, knowing she'd hardly had a second to spend on her work, 'Still just writing'. It was an elegant response, because it was at once a promise and an affirmation. Despite every demand upon her time, she hadn't given up; she was storing away material, ready for when her chance would come again. These were words she certainly lived by.

D.H. Lawrence titled one of his books of poems, *Look! We Have Come Through!* Since his marriage to Frieda was in tatters at the time, his finances non-existent, and his health failing, it seemed a strange title. Yet it's clear that it was a declaration of some power. The world and chance had thrown some heavy rocks at him, and yet he was still writing. These were words he was living by, truly.

The words we choose to live by, once again, are not rigid. They are reminders designed to help us recall what we believe when the going gets rough and life become confusing, because we'll all be confused at times, and we'll all need reminders about what we've chosen to do. Moreover it's not necessary to have worked out all our fears and neuroses before we take on this task. In fact, in some ways, no one can ever do that; these things are resolved by doing, not by pondering. A quotation from Jane Goodall, the renowned primatologist, seems to sum up some important aspects of this stage:

> Every individual matters. And every day you live you make an impact on the world around you. We are not in this world to make money and accumulate things. We are looking for meaning in life – like finding ways to make the world a better place.

The Warrior-Lover has a cause, and has also to recognize that no cause is worth pursuing without considering the cost to human beings. No abstract idea is more important than the welfare of people, because every individual matters. That is the balance the Warrior-Lover strives for.

There is one final historical image for this archetype that we can usefully consider. One of the most common depictions of knights in action is almost a cliché. The knight, often St. George, skewers a fearsome dragon and rescues the maiden held captive. Obviously, this is the good Warrior, fearlessly facing evil, rescuing purity and innocence. And it is also far more than this. What we need to know in order to understand this image is that the dragon was not just a symbol of evil, but particularly of greed. The dragon in Anglo-Saxon literature was a creature that guarded the riches buried with dead chieftains. In Eastern thought, however, the belief was quite different – the Chinese dragon was a symbol of wisdom and many other desirable virtues. But in the western tradition the dragon was synonymous with selfishness and greed and power. It couldn't do anything with the wealth it guarded, nor with the maidens it had a habit of abducting. All it could do was breathe fire, terrify, and destroy. Everything about dragons reflects the sterility of unused power or power used only for destruction. The Warrior St. George is pure in heart and courageous, and in killing the dragon he liberates all the wealth it guards, all the creative potential it forbids others to use. This is embodied in the virgin, who is both pure and a representative of the female generative attributes which can be joined to St. George's male, aggressive aspect. The Warrior's task is to redress wrongs so that the world can be a more productive place. In mythic terms this is very similar to the figure of Robin Hood, stealing from the unjust rich and giving that wealth back to the poor. Robin, as we recall, has Maid Marian as a female figure he has to rescue from the greedy Sheriff of Nottingham – a dragon substitute if ever there was one. Marian is clearly intended as a virginal figure – since maid meant virgin or unmarried woman – and even her name suggests the name of the most famous virgin in history, the Virgin Mary. Robin Hood may have become a costume drama for most of us, but it has the same roots and lineage as St. George. And this is the important message of these tales, and all like them: in killing the dragon St. George gains the opportunity to meet with his opposite aspect, the softer 'female' side of his character symbolized in the virgin, and bring that aspect of himself back into the world. It is when these two attributes, male and female, are united that the Warrior-Lover archetype comes to its full power and can make the next step and become the Monarch, or in St. George's case, a saint. Those strange fifteenth century canvases by Paolo Uccello and others may confuse us and amuse us with their unlikely dragons. If, however, we allow ourselves to see them in mythic terms they are, more correctly, a reflection of the saint's transition from the Warrior-Lover to the Monarch stage of life.

Notes

1. *King Lear*. All Shakespeare quotations are taken from *William Shakespeare: The Complete Works*, ed. Peter Alexander. London and Glasgow: Collins, 1970.
2. *Rocky*, directed by John G. Avildsen, 1976.
3. David and Goliath, 1 Samuel, 17.
4. ee cummings. 'I sing of Olaf glad and big' (1931). *The Anthology of American Literature*, 8th. Ed. vol. 2. Ed. G. McMichael et alia. New Jersey: Pearson, 2004. pp. 1187-8.
5. Robert Bly, 'Thinking Mythically' was the term used at the Iron John workshop, *Interface* at the Hosmer School, Watertown, Mass. June 1987.
6. Oliver North, "A pretty neat idea" as reported in *Ronald Reagan: the Power of Conviction and the Success of Presidency*. Peter J. Wallison. Boulder, Colorado: Westview Press, 2004.
7. Stephenson, William. *A Man Called Intrepid*. New York: Ballantine, 1976.
8. Kidder, Tracy. *Mountains Beyond Mountains: The Quest of Dr. Paul Farmer, a Man who would Cure the World*. New York: Random House, 2004.
9. Jesus' statement is recorded in Matthew 27. 46. Some claim that he was quoting Psalm 22, which opens with very similar words. If so, it does not invalidate this point.
10. Peter's rejection of Jesus appears in Matthew 26. 69-75.
11. Mother Teresa's words are recorded in Sinetar, Marsha. *Do What You Love, The Money Will Follow: Discovering your Right Livelihood*. New York: Dell, 1987.
12. Dr Wayne Dyer: Dr. Dyer writes in various places about vibrational energy. *Inspiration: Your Ultimate Calling*, Hay House, 2006, is a good example of his thinking.
13. Metcalf, Linda Trichter and Simon, Tobin. *Writing the Mind Alive: The Proprioceptive Writing Method for Finding your Authentic Voice*. New York: Ballantine, 2002. The best way to find out more is to go to: www.pwriting.org.

14. Herbert, A. P. *The Secret Battle*. Encore Editions, 1983
15. Dudgeon, A. G. *Hidden Victory: The Battle of Habbaniya, May 1941.* Arcadia 2000.
16. The myth of Orpheus can be traced back to c. 530 B.C., and was recorded by Virgil (70 B.C. – 19 B.C.) as well as other writers.
17. Tyler, Ann. 'Still Just Writing', essay, 1978. Reprinted in *The New Millennium Reader* (3rd Edition) ed. Stuart & Terry Hirschberg. New York: Prentice Hall, 2002.
18. Lawrence, D. H. *Look! We Have Come Through: A Cycle of Love Poems*. London: Chatto and Windus, 1917.
19. Jane Goodall has said similar words on several occasions. This particular quotation was recorded in the news release for the University of Southern California following her address there, Oct. 25, 2004. See: Katherine Yungmee Kim, www.usc.edu/schools/college/news/jane_goodall

Chapter Seven

The Monarch

The first thing to point out about the Monarch archetype is that it encompasses both the king and the queen, the male and female aspects we have seen in the example of the legend of St. George. For thousands of years an unmarried monarch was not only a most unusual thing, but also somewhat dangerous, since legitimate children were needed for political marriage alliances and for the succession. The Monarch or Monarch Pair, therefore, is to be seen as a balance of the male and the female working harmoniously together for the good of the realm.

We can see this around us everyday if we look at families. There one will see that parents each take different roles as they raise their children. Whether these roles are divided according to the 'traditional' family arrangement of mother and father or in some other way, one parent is going to be slightly more nurturing and gentle, while the other is more of the executive. Each couple works out its own balance, and when this is done successfully it can be most effective. In fact raising a family is something that seems to require more than just one parent. As single parents the world over report, there comes a time when the children seem to need the guidance and contact of the missing parent or that person's substitute. The damage done by absent fathers is, perhaps, the most obvious and most frequently talked about evidence of this. If both parents are inadequate, then more often than not the child will find someone to be an honorary parent. Of course, a single parent can do a magnificent job in bringing up a child and, ideally, the single parent is able to access both aspects of the Monarch Pair, as appropriate.

We'll need to recap here, for a moment, in order to understand what is at issue. As the Warrior-Lover grows in self-awareness and real courage – for these aspects grow as we begin to exercise them – he or she is no longer simply a supporter of a principle of justice, but also of mercy. In this way the Warrior-Lover develops the awareness of balance that will later be used more fully when the transition is made to the Monarch Pair. The Warrior also has an outer struggle and an inner struggle, for she has to come face to face with her own limits – the place at which courage fails – and accept this. And so the Warrior-Lover learns to fight for beliefs and love others in the outer world, and to take on the inner struggle and come to love herself even when facing the inevitable failures of her spirit. It is the confronting of both struggles that brings the full expression of both Warrior and Lover status. Only when this has happened can the Warrior realize an important fact: it is not necessary to fight every battle oneself. One can in fact be much more useful as an advisor to others, directing their youthful energies wisely as they develop on their own paths. By being attentive to this one can preserve a valuable series of future Warriors who may need to be restrained and advised so they do not go astray, or burn out too soon, or too badly. This is when the Warrior-Lover begins to move into the next phase, the Monarch Pair. The name matters less than the concept.

For the Monarchy is, actually, only a concept. The king does not do any fighting himself, although he may well have been trained and fought as a young man. Neither does the queen fight. Yet the ruler is often likely to be engaged in directing a struggle of some sort. The question here is whether or not the struggle is justifiable. The ruler who is selfish becomes simply a tyrant, one who looks out only for himself and cares nothing about the fate of those who serve him loyally.

The tyrant can be seen as the active incarnation of the Monarch and this perversion of kingship is too common for require spelling it out. History is full of tyrannical kings and scheming queens, and rather than see this as a division according to sex one would do better to see both as examples of how the archetype can go sadly astray. Catherine the Great of Russia was every bit as ruthless as any other male tyrant the world has seen, while Marie Antoinette's intrigues ran France in a thoroughly corrupt fashion that were the equal of any medieval Pope's machinations. More recently, central African states have, of late, suffered more than their fair share of such corrupt rulers. What is truly sad is that some of these rulers have come to power seemingly by popular acclaim, promising reform and a better life for the average citizen. The temptations of high office must be enormous, because so many seem to loot the treasury before being forced into exile. This sort of recurrent governmental disaster benefits no one. The rulers themselves do not seem to be noticeably happier or more fulfilled human beings, and the local inhabitants certainly don't gain much. This is the selfish and aggressive incarnation of the Monarch, which quickly descends to Orphan level.

Parents can be a little like this, also. The overpowering and violent father figure can be a terrifying influence on any family, producing fear and rage in the children. The manipulative and self-involved mother can have a similar effect. These are the cliché figures of our time and we have all seen too much of this sort of behavior.

The situation is compounded because being generous and kind doesn't solve the Monarch's problem. The gentle, passive incarnation of the Monarch tends to become an easy victim of political machinations just as the passive father tends to allow sons and daughters to run wild. Neither selfish nor selfless rulers seem to last long. A balance of the two is essential. The challenge for the ruler is considerable, since it involves being both exalted and yet serving the people one is raised above. Noble servitude is one phrase I have heard used.

The archetype suggests that this sense of balance is achieved when the king and queen work together, but it is important to notice that even as they work together the aim is that each will be able to achieve the necessary internal balance personally, also. Everyone must have seen the family in which mother is always soft and pleading for her children, and father is remote, hard, and unloving. It's not a pretty sight. This polarization is not what the archetype seeks to convey. Each individual must come to a state of equilibrium within him or herself, as well as with her partner, so that a reasonable dialogue can occur and continue.

The Monarch, just like the parent, is often placed in a difficult situation where he or she must do something that may seem brutal but is, actually, done for the best of long-term reasons. The Monarch must be prepared to face criticism from those who do not see things the same way and who may not know the whole story and he must also be prepared to be left without the consolation of a story-book ending. A parent who has to reject her son, even going so far as getting him arrested and imprisoned because of an out-of-control drug habit, this parent is doing more than showing 'tough love'. This parent is going against the personal and perhaps selfish desire to show love by protecting her child, and is instead thinking in terms of the child's long-term survival, even if he never forgives her and remains alienated. It's a heart-wrenching thing to have to do, but the greater love is shown in placing the child's welfare first, and the parent's needs second. Monarchs have to be able to take such decisions and must be prepared to live with the consequences – and to bear the uncertainties.

In this royal pairing the Monarch ideally is both decisive and executive, and tempered by the female principles of mercy and concern for the good of all. This is a balance, just as marriage ideally is a balance allowing both aspects, male and female, Animus and Anima, to step forward. Yin and Yang together make up one whole, and in Eastern thought the male and female energies have to be brought into balance for harmony to arise. So how does this translate for most of us? If we decide to take on the challenges of the Monarch's role, we must, all of us, be prepared to put forward our beliefs, stick to them, and live with the results.

An example may be useful. Gandhi believed in non-violence. His whole movement depended on it. When his wife became ill, she needed an injection that could have saved her. Yet an injection was, for Gandhi, a violent act upon the body. He refused to allow it, and she died. It's not a course of action anyone would like to be faced with, and Gandhi has been criticized for it, as well as for other things. Since he also believed in reincarnation it may be hard for us to place ourselves in his situation. Yet what is clear is that for the Monarch the actions one takes definitely will impact many others. For the Warrior, they tend to impact oneself and one's immediate surroundings. In the belief-system Gandhi was part of, this dilemma represented the most basic test as to whether or not he could live what he preached. His wife's death was doubtless very hard for him. Yet the political ideal lived on – and perhaps saved more lives as a direct and indirect result. 'Right' is a difficult concept under these circumstances.

For the Monarch, "I" ceases to exist. The royal plural "we" is not just an affectation. The Monarch speaks in terms of the whole realm's best interests. The Warrior may well be faced with the dilemma of, "What must I do?" but the Monarch will be more likely to see it as, "What needs to be done?" The ego becomes much less important. The businessman who refuses a promotion in order to spend more time with the family may well be acting as a Monarch, putting the family's cohesion before his own ambitions. As a result he may well be part of a family that does a much better job raising children than would otherwise have been possible.

The Monarch may at times have to use a forceful personality in order to make things happen, but the best use of this energy is not about coercion, rather it's about declaring how things will have to be. On a more mundane level, for example, we trust our doctors to do what is best for us, not for them. They may tell us we need painful surgery, perhaps, but we expect they make these statements knowing they will be for our ultimate good. Unfortunately, there are cases where doctors do what is best for themselves financially, with scant regard for what the patient may actually need. These pseudo-Monarchs do not always fulfill their obligations when money is dangled before them. And yet other doctors will work for free because their sense of humanity demands it. I know which sort I prefer, although I don't expect my doctor to work for nothing!

The Monarch will choose a task that he or she feels needs to be done, and will see that the task is more important than the individual doing it. Ego demands for recognition therefore fade into the background. The trusted doctor into whose hands we place ourselves will, in all likelihood, work as part of a team of caregivers, and this team will take steps to include the patient as part of the process of getting better. The model is of enlisting the patient's cooperation rather than forcing a procedure on him or her. As health insurers are discovering, when the patient is made part of the process wellness is achieved far more quickly and at less expense. This is the Monarch principle at work – there is no doubt as to who is in charge and who is holding the responsibility, but all involved are encouraged to be part of the solution. Patients involved in this way are more likely to do as the doctors recommend, less likely to forget or skip medications, and they will be more alert to any change in their condition that needs to be attended to. It doesn't take a huge leap of the imagination to see that families, businesses, and organizations could also be run in a similar way.

Another example of the Monarch in action might be those writers, journalists and artists who labor hard and devotedly, without thinking about fame or making a lot of money. They do not expect to impress their friends or become public figures. Their mothers will probably never read their words or feel proud, for example. These people work because something that seems to be true needs to be communicated. No doubt their relatives would like them to sell a million copies and become rich and famous. But they are not doing this primarily for their mothers or any family member. They are doing it because they believe it might be helpful to all people. Or as one of them said to me, "To be strictly accurate here, I'm not doing anything. The idea is here, needing expression. It is using me, and perhaps many other people in other ways, as a way to get itself expressed. It's the idea that matters, not me." Now, this doesn't mean this person is necessarily a Monarch; it simply means that she has had some flashes of insight and experience that has let her see what the Monarch's role is like. We *become* the stage of Monarch, or Warrior, or Pilgrim, as we are in the middle of doing what we do.

The Monarch knows how to get things done, and does so effectively. As a leader she will be able to inspire others, and to invite them to join in activities that are of enormous value to the greater good, knowing full well that one volunteer who is motivated will be far more effective than a crowd of conscripts. Some less able Monarchs aren't quite as good at doing this. They may have to become Warriors temporarily in order to get the message across. The difference is not so much in seeing what needs to be done, but it is rather in being able to mobilize the forces to do it. It's often easy to see what we'd like to achieve. It's a lot harder to make it happen. For example, I can watch sports on TV and I can see what my team needs to do – and I can yell encouragement. But I couldn't do the moves as well as they can. The true Monarch in this example might be the coach, who directs the best efforts of the team and brings about the best possible play the team is capable of producing. Sometimes we speak of 'team spirit' as the thing that makes a team truly exceptional – and yet I'm sure we all must be aware that generating this spirit is the coach's job. The coach can be severe, or nurturing, as the instance demands. Applying those 'male' and 'female' parental attributes at the right time is an art. Getting the balance right is everything.

Literature is full of Monarchs. This should not be a surprise, since in novels and plays we have far more access to the precise inner workings of the individual than we do with most people we come across in daily life, and also because it is often easier to see a fictional character than it is a real one. Such figures as Churchill and Franklin Roosevelt, for example, certainly acted as Monarchs much of the time, and yet we have histories that show us their human failings, and these leave us in doubt as to what exactly they were in the terms we are discussing. I think it's safe to say that these two leaders were able to be both executive and decisive, and also that they cared deeply about their people. This in turn led them to make the sorts of decisions that Monarchs have to face. The creation and dropping of the atom bomb was a fearsome responsibility. Historians still argue today about whether or not it was justified – and who can say so one way or another? Yet the Monarch is the one who must take a stand on difficult moral issues, and be prepared to face the aftermath.

In literature the renditions are perhaps clearer and less extreme – which is probably one very good reason why every civilization needs literature. We need it to show us, sometimes in diagrammatic form, what the nature of the human struggle is. An example that springs to mind for the Monarch would be from Jane Austen's *Pride and Prejudice* (1813). In it we see that both Elizabeth and Darcy are proud, in different ways, and inclined to prejudice. It is only when Darcy stops being proud in his behavior that Elizabeth has the chance to look at her own tendency to jump to judgments and recognize her self-satisfaction in doing so; pride by any other name. When they marry, after having gone through stages that are undeniably Pilgrim and Warrior-Lover (each has to fight for the other even when they to think their own hopes for romantic happiness have been destroyed), they achieve the Monarch pair's balance. When they decide to marry they are a fusion of male and female; of cool logic and warm heart; of famous, wealthy aristocrat and semi-disgraced, impoverished gentry on its way to poverty; of lofty ideals and pragmatism. Each is sensitive, alert to others, and also resilient. Jane Austen makes it entirely clear that each is able to bring out the best in the other – and that the families on either side (who remember the way each used to be) can barely be brought to understand why they want to marry! Yet the happy pair knows it is absolutely right. They know the changes they have gone through are important. Both lovers then have to stand up to what their families say against their choices, and go ahead backing their own judgments only. They make an obviously balanced Monarch pairing, and each has achieved balance.

If we are in any doubt about this, Jane Austen gives us several other weddings to compare. Charlotte Lucas and Mr. Collins marry, yet they turn out to be happier when out of each other's company and seem to cope with each other – maintaining an uneasy peace – rather than growing to greater wisdom. Wickham and Lydia Bennet's marriage is based on folly and blackmail, while Jane and Bingley are seen to be amiable but too passive, with Mr. Bennet telling them outright that their servants will cheat them. None of these pairings except for Elizabeth and Darcy seems to have included much spiritual growth. What Jane Austen knew, intuitively, was that her two main figures could balance each other, bringing forward good qualities that needed to be developed and challenging qualities that threatened to become destructive. When they do so they are, at last, fit to be in a place of real power – since they will have enormous say in the lives of literally those hundreds of others who are Mr. Darcy's tenants. A real Monarch Pairing is not just a neat romantic twist but an actually necessary outcome for the prosperity and happiness of the whole estate.

One of the greatest demands made on the Monarch is that, to maintain the balanced aspect of the archetype, he has to be able to listen. This requires patience, empathy, and the ability to hear what is not said as well as what has been said. Perhaps the model we can look for is the law court judge. The judge does not usually decide the innocence or guilt of the accused. Instead the judge will listen to the arguments on both sides and instruct the jury. A practiced judge will assume that both sides have reasons to distort the truth and will act accordingly – understanding that this is the way the law courts function. Witnesses will be unreliable, will be untruthful either out of malice or ignorance, and yet all must be heard in patience. Finally the judge must instruct the jury to make sure they know how to do their job, and then he will pass sentence in such a way as to seek the best result for all. Punishment is not the aim, neither is revenge. The law is to be applied in a way that makes sense to everyone. The sentence passed down will send a message to the individual, to any observers, and ideally it will allow those who are capable of reform to have the chance to change their lives if such resources are available. That is a balance of severity and mercy, surely.

The comparison of the Monarch to a judge is apt because in the not-so-distant past kings were the final judges of appeals in difficult cases. In fact the idea of a 'Court' is specifically derived from the courtyard in which the king and councilors met, the King's court, to decide such cases. A vestige of this power is to be seen in the President of the United States who can still pardon convicts, and in England the Queen can still detain a prisoner 'at Her Majesty's pleasure' if that person seems to be an unusual case who needs special consideration. This is reminiscent of the way a parent will, on occasions, bend the rules when it is in the best interests of everyone. So, for example, the teenager who crumples the fender of the family car and feels agonies of remorse probably needs no further sanctions. He's already punished himself enough and a token reparation may be all that can be expected.

The comparison with a judge can be taken one stage further. Jonathan Swift suggested that the allegorical figure of Justice which adorned most law courts –

the familiar blindfolded woman with a sword in one hand and scales in the other – was indeed apt, since the law was about weighing evidence and punishing with the sword, while remaining impartial, as signified by the blindfold. But would it not be better, he suggested, if the figure of Justice were to have also a bag of gold, with which to reward the good citizens? The Monarch's job (and the parent's job) is to nurture what is good and to reward what is done well.

The Monarch is, of course, always on display. This can be exhausting. She may have many people who are devoted to her, and yet she cannot just accept that approval and behave towards all those people as if they were her equals. Think of this in terms of the family. A parent will try hard to develop a trusting, loving relationship with all her children, and yet this is unlikely to be the same sort of relationship as she has with her true best friend, at least while the children remain small. Even in the most harmonious of families the parents' words still come loaded with extra value, positive and negative, which is derived from the simple fact that the parents have the power of history on their side. This is why a parent's casual comment can sometimes feel so cutting to a child, when to an outsider it would be immediately forgotten. A parent may want to become her child's best friend, yet the actual fact of the matter is that there will always be an imbalance, to some extent. It will never go away, although the relationship may be very close. Similarly for the ruler and the subject the relationship can never be entirely equal. The task here is not for us to bemoan the inequality or to pretend it isn't there. The whole point is to acknowledge it and get on with being as honest as possible with each other even so. For when one allows oneself to be fully conscious of this, one can arrange not to let it get in the way.

If the Monarch's task is to develop a good relationship with the 'other' side of the self, then such growth of the stereotypical opposite functions involves listening to and appreciating other viewpoints. These viewpoints are not just male and female, yin and yang. They also involve listening to the whole kingdom – the Innocents, Orphans, Pilgrims and Warrior-Lovers. In terms of the family this means not just mother and father talking together, but both parents listening to the children as well, at whatever stages they are at, and making decisions based on that knowledge. Monarchs traditionally have an inner circle of trusted advisors to help them with this, called a cabinet, and nurturing such truth-tellers can be a long and rewarding task. Note, though, that these relationships are not going to develop in the usual way we may understand friendships – shared interests, conversations over dinner and so on. Just as a real Monarch has to be trained up to the job, and will eventually inherit not only the throne but the advisors and their administrations, so too, as we grow to Monarch-hood, we'll discover that there are others who will see who we are, recognize our calling, and who are Monarchs in their own rights. One person does not run a kingdom; it takes a whole machinery of understandings and alliances, all working together. The Monarch may well be captain of the side, but he is also the ultimate team player; similarly parents always need to confer with other parents or they risk losing sight of reality.

There is a story told about Britain's King Edward VII on his state visit to France in 1903. The anti-British Parisian crowd heckled and jeered until a nervous aide said to him, "The French don't seem to like us." "Why should they?" replied the king, and continued to wave and bow from his carriage. Edward knew his job was not to worry about slights to his ego. He was there to build alliances, a monarch conferring with other monarchs. As such he had no illusions about how he expected to be treated. In fact one might say he had let go of personal expectations as he pursued the necessary political entente that he hoped would ensure peace. Eleven years later World War One erupted; fortunately most of Europe, and particularly France, was newly aligned with Britain. Edward's work, criticized by many at the time as foreign junketing, had paid off; but by then he was dead.

In the daily world we can see the Monarch in action when an individual is able to work productively with others, no matter what their differences may be. If the Monarch has to listen to the people, just as a parent has to listen to the teenagers in the family, so also he has to listen to his peers, in the same way that parents also have to listen to other parents and be in tune to some extent with what the social order supports. But there is a third factor, and it is that Monarchs have to be able to listen as equals to their own parents or authority figures – even to the point of rejecting the older generation's views. We will often see that the wise grandparent will choose to offer advice only with care, and will step back from interfering. This is not necessarily timidity. In this way the grandparent allows the parent to feel her own power and learn to use it appropriately. This stepping back marks another phase in the relationship to the parents, one that is based on the older person allowing the other to be who he or she is, rather than directing. So the mother who was extremely useful and directive of her daughter at the time of the daughter's first pregnancy will now find she has less to offer the family of teenage grandchildren if she stays in this role. The wise course is to accept this and change the role.

This requires the grandparent to let go of wanting to be at the center of the family's focus at exactly the time when the temptation is to move more into the limelight than ever before. Partly this is what lies behind all those jokes about interfering mothers-in-law. These poor ridiculed figures have made the basic mistake of attempting to give unwanted advice, which is perceived as belittling to the younger person. In such cases the older person's ego need is to be right, or useful, or seen to be wise, and it is this ego desire that the Monarch must move beyond.

Picture for a moment the patriarch of the house, presiding over a long table full of grown up children and their spouses, perhaps at Christmas or on Thanksgiving Day. Familiar as it is, it's actually an image that is frequently encountered of the Monarch archetype that has gone wrong. By seeking to stay in control the patriarch forces the grown offspring back into a child-like subservience, and effectively crushes initiative as well as real dialogue. This aging tyrant needs to learn to step back and honor the emerging Monarch within the now-grown children. Unless he can do so their growth will be prevented, sometimes even stopped entirely, and the likely result is that regression to earlier stages will occur in the resentful children.

Sometimes, in my workshops, I'll ask the participants to explore family meal times, which usually leads into a discussion of the 'formal' meals of holidays and celebrations. Often the memories are happy. Equally often they are filled with resentments about 'feeling like I'm twelve years old again' as a woman of thirty-five phrased it, referring to the way her mother treated her. Exploration of this sort of tension can lead to the uncovering of a large number of causes. In this case the mother was lonely and wanted to bring back the days when her children were small and depended on her for everything. So she acted as if they were all children still. Her ego-need to be useful and at the center of things was what lay behind her behavior. In other instances this sort of behavior can be a defense against the awareness of aging; sometimes it's just a habit in which the children reluctantly collude. Behind all this lies the central fact: in each case it has to do with a real failure of one person or the other to be genuine about who he or she is in the present moment. The Monarch is the person who can bring this relationship back to the place of sane reality.

Strangely enough, in these cases this work often has to be done by the child since the error is most likely to occur because the adult wants to keep the child as a child, and so this task demands courage, determination, tact, and occasionally emotional muscle. For it is always easier to leave things as they are. The Monarch in this case is the one who is prepared to say that she wants a real, equal relationship with the parent, and if that's not possible then she would rather not have any relationship at all. The Monarch will listen to others willingly, learn from them, respect them, but she will not allow anyone to pull rank or try and swing seniority.

A typical scenario might be that the grandparent needs to hold onto this role because he is afraid that without the role he will be neglected, and such thinking represents a regression to Orphan thinking. For it is the Orphan who clings to the outer expressions of status while ignoring what's really happening. As we grow older we all risk being somewhat out of touch, but to use our own failing as an excuse to criticize the younger generations is neither helpful nor healthy. This is merely the action of a pseudo Monarch.

A true Monarch is a person who takes action and causes actions to be set in motion, aiming at a larger result than the merely local. In the example we've just been discussing, the Monarch wants a real relationship with the senior members of the family not because it serves her direct interests, but because such relationships are vital for a sane family dynamic, for everyone. The Monarch looks to the future. The challenge for each of us is to allow ourselves to do this without fear of what may be said about us later. Here is one of my favorite quotations on this topic from one of the architects of this country:

> I must study politics and war and trade that my sons may have liberty to study mathematics and philosophy.

John Adams wrote this, and I still smile as I think of his wisdom. Notice how he points out that what he has to do now is not something he is expert in. He does not have all the answers; he has to study so that he can make reasonable decisions. There is no false dignity here, just a sense of a job of work he has to do so the future can be a better prospect for others. There is even a sense of pride that his sons will actually exceed him in their expertise when their time comes.

Notes

1. Swift, Jonathan. *Gulliver's Travels.* 'The image of Justice with…a bag of gold open in her right hand.' Part I, chapter 6.
2. Edward VII, in Tuchman, Barbara. *The Guns of August.* Presidio, 2004, p. 19.
3. John Adams, in a letter to his wife, 20 May 1780.

Chapter Eight

The Magician

As the Monarch becomes more aware that she is serving the true and the good aspects that exist in this world, a change can occur, and it is one that is fraught with the same dangers as before. If we regard the Monarch as the ultimate manager, an ambassador who can make things happen, then there is perhaps an even more impressive level: the Magician. This stage is not easy to describe because, for one thing, there aren't that many people who get to this level, and for another, they tend to be all but invisible when they do. The true Magician is not the stage figure who pulls rabbits out of hats, or wears a large white robe and sports a shaggy beard. The true Magician is the person who makes things happen while seeming not to do anything much at all. There is a quotation from the Tao Te Ching which seems to express this succinctly:

> When the Master governs, the people
> Are hardly aware that he exists.
> The Master doesn't talk, he acts.
> When his work is done,
> The people say, 'Amazing:
> we did it all by ourselves!'

This is the person who knows how to sow a suggestion so that others seize upon it, take it up as if it were their own, and rise to the occasion. The Magician allows people to become more than they formerly believed themselves capable of being. In this way, miracles can occur. And often, when they do, those who have been part of that miracle believe they did it all themselves. Where the Monarch may have to use force of will and even force of arms, the Magician uses no force at all – but can inspire others.

W. B. Yeats in 'The Long Legged Fly' has a truly wonderful evocation of the way the Magician works, when he describes the great figures of history at decidedly un-great moments. Here he describes Michelangelo:

> There on that scaffolding reclines
> Michael Angelo

With no more sound than the mice make
His hand moves to and fro.
Like a long legged fly upon the stream
His mind moves upon silence.

One of the most famous artists the world has ever known is shown at a moment of thought, and seemingly doing nothing much – except for that small hand movement that is gradually producing the paintings on the ceiling of the Sistine Chapel. Great things happen when at first sight nothing much is to be observed.

Perhaps the Magician is not really a person at all on some occasions, and I'm thinking of those times when people get together and produce a synergy that allows them to transcend the expected bounds of achievement. In our personality-based world, we tend to want to point out people who "made things happen". We may call them Rainmakers, to emphasize their ability to make marvelous events occur, rather than focusing on the more fugitive examples of those in whose footsteps wonderful changes come to pass. I have seen doctors, healers, social workers, all of them flawed and human, contradictory and ornery on occasion – all of whom have worked with individuals whose recoveries have been, at times, miraculous. Did these professionals make it happen? Not really; but they did provide the space, the opportunity, and the support that allowed the individuals who were suffering to generate their own salvation. That's a form of magic, too.

Principally this stage involves a reduction of the ego expectations we so often live by. So, for example, one comes across writers, painters, and creative artists generally who talk about "the writing" rather than themselves doing the writing, or "the light" rather than about themselves seeing the light that they feel moved to paint. Michelangelo's famous statement about the sculpture already existing in the marble, and his task being to release it, always strikes me as the comment of the Magician who knows he is the servant of the task, not the "doer." The cathedral builders of medieval Europe left only their first names on their work, when they left any name at all – they knew the work was more important than they were. An echo of this is heard in another seventeenth century building, also a cathedral. The architect Sir Christopher Wren is buried in his masterpiece, St. Paul's Cathedral in London. On his plain slab of a tomb is engraved his name and the Latin words "Si monumentum requiris, circumspice". This translates as "If you require a monument, look around you." What more needs to be said?

Often the task of creating can be tortuous, and yet still have a miraculous quality. Bono's comment about a song U2 put together is worth quoting. "We worked on the song for about three years and it wasn't happening. Then one day it all just came right, and it was like the song had always been there, waiting." Sometimes discipline, hard work and faith are needed so the magic can work itself and then the creation arrives when the time is ripe. William Faulkner, when asked why he chose to live in and write about Oxford, Mississippi, when he could have been living in London or Paris, replied that he knew he had enough stories in "my own little postage stamp of native soil" to keep him writing for the rest of his life. The stories were already there. He didn't have to hunt for them.

This sense that the individual is doing something greater than himself is a very ancient one, and it exists in the Greek idea that a God or Goddess of creativity called a muse would descend on the artist and give the necessary inspiration. Creation happens *through* the individual, not because the individual wants it. Most of us have experienced something like this at some point. Think of the idea that just arrived and was too good to miss; the words that seemed to speak themselves before we knew it, and were exactly the right words. The poet and essayist Rebecca McLanahan refers frequently to the muse as a divine something that directs her work, and she admits it is more powerful than she is. The Magician is, in the mystic sense, the channel of divine wisdom. And we all have sparks of that. Swami Satchidananda, the Hindu mystic, put it like this: "I know that something or someone is handling me, and I am just the instrument." The Magician knows that God-energy, or the energy of the universe, or something, by whatever name one wishes to call it, is happening, and the best thing one can do is not to impede it by using one's ego. The Swami goes on to say this in many ways, and one more example stands out. He, the great Hindu teacher, has no trouble in declaring what is going on when he teaches: "The real teacher is the teachings."

A fine example of this appeared in my daily paper, the Boston *Sunday Globe*, recently. Bob Blair, a postal carrier, decided to put up poster boards that gave the name, rank, and regiment of each US soldier killed in Iraq and Afghanistan, one board per telephone post in his town. He started doing this on Memorial Day 2003, and then did it again the following year, and the year after that. This year his posters stretched over 34 miles of road – roughly equidistantly spread on all eight main roads leading out of Holliston town center. It is an intensely moving sight, and absolutely unforgettable. Blair's comments are worth noting, also. "People ask me how I got the idea – it was just kind of there," he says. The elegant simplicity of an idea that is just 'there' – that's what the Magician can do when we allow that archetype to emerge. Now when the posters go up it's not just Blair with his staple gun, it's people from the whole community. People who have lost sons and daughters, those whose relatives are still serving, veterans, republicans, democrats, all of them work together for this. Blair himself refuses to say anything about his opinion of the war. He has no wish to be a political spokesperson. And in keeping his silence he allows everyone else to come to their own conclusions in their own ways about what all these combat casualties mean. The message is more important than the man who delivers it.

If we are alert we can see examples like this all around us. A young man I know works in a day care center. He is astonishingly good at what he does and children adore him. When I asked him how he did it, he looked bemused and mumbled something about it being just something that the children brought out of him, he guessed.... Or consider the teacher who can make a roomful of rowdy teenagers into a learning community, almost without their realizing it. In the recently broadcast PBS documentary 'The Hobart Shakespeareans' teacher Rafe Esquith is shown working with a class of fifth grade immigrant children, many of whom speak little English, as he introduces them to Shakespeare and gets them to put on a performance of *Hamlet*. The interviewer asks the teacher at one point if he could have found a better job, and he replies. "I couldn't have found a better job. I could be better paid..." The reply typifies the Magician in action. The worth of the job is that it has to be done and done well, not in the ways it's rewarded. Teachers I have met have often had an admirable sense that Education is something that needs to happen, and it needs to be done with dedication for the long term good of everyone, not just because it will make for a career, a raise, or a promotion.

History has many examples of leaders who have been able to get fractured organizations to work together – the list of Nobel Peace Prize winners being perhaps the most impressive testimony to this. Unfortunately, peace is often fragile and many of those who received the award have subsequently seen the strife renewed. Such is the nature of our times. But this does not mean the Magician failed. Nelson Mandela was able to facilitate a transition of power in South Africa in a situation that most people expected would be a bloodbath – given the corrupt and angry figures on all sides of the discussion. Before the transition of power many white South Africans left their homeland because they feared the civil war that they saw as inevitable. It didn't happen. Now South Africa has plenty of challenges ahead, and it's not exactly the Promised Land yet, but we should marvel at what one man was able to help bring about. That's the Magician, and the magic, at work.

Another way to look at this is to ask what the magic is in its purest form. I suspect the answer may be that the real magic is love. Out of love comes devotion, honesty, faith, belief, courage ... you name it. I can't think of any positive attribute that is not somehow rooted in love. Mandela may not have loved his jailers, but he didn't pursue vengeance against them. He didn't give in to hate, and in doing so he loved mankind more. The artists and writers I have named are showing love, also, in the way their messages about the truths they perceive are offered to everyone, as a gift.

In every day terms we have Magicians all around us, if we care to look. Many of them are grandparents, although not all grandparents are Magicians by any means. How often have we witnessed a child who will not listen to her parents solemnly taking in just a couple of words said by a grandparent and then changing her attitude? Now, one may say that is just because the relationship is different; and that's exactly why the grandparent can be so effective. The grandparent is rarely as fit or as agile at the actual parent, so the child could easily evade this figure. There is, often, a special persuasive power that resides in the individual who is not caught up in every detail of the day-to-day aspects of child raising, or who may have a slightly different perspective on what goes on. Why is it that a child will fuss when mother wants her to do something but will cheerfully do almost anything for grandma, even when there's no bribe or reward? I don't want to idealize the role of grandparents, I just want to remind you that often there is magic in that relationship, and that we are using it here as a model for how the Magician's actions can be seen to work.

The Magician faces temptations, too. In fact, some people think they have become Magicians when they are merely manipulators. One may be very gifted and use those gifts for less than decent purposes. It doesn't take much effort to recall the names of gifted and charismatic politicians who have turned out to be shallow opportunists. Or think of the number of Wall Street insider trading scam artists in the past few decades who thought they were gods but turned out to be just rather shabby crooks. And that is the whole point of these six stages. If we want to fool ourselves into thinking we are a Monarch or a Magician, we can. It's a free world and we're always free to delude ourselves. The point is that we have to be honest and even a little self-critical in applying these archetypes to our total life situation. Whenever we fool ourselves, we slip down to a lower level – at least one level. The six stages are not Boy Scout badges that, once achieved, are never taken off the sash. We have to remind ourselves each day what our responsibilities are and what we may need to work on if we're going to be the best human beings we can be.

There is an ancient Sufi story, fairly widely known, that may illustrate what is meant. Once upon a time, the story goes, there was a very saintly, holy man, and the angels were so impressed by him that they decided to appear before him and ask if he'd like to come to heaven. So they appeared before the sage and he politely declined their request because he felt he still had work to do on earth helping people. This impressed the angels even more, and they resolved that they had to offer him a gift, since he was such a holy and selfless man. The sage thought about this and eventually he replied that he would accept a gift. He said he would like to be able to do immense good and bring peace and happiness wherever he went, but with one condition. What's that? Asked the angels. The sage replied that was that he should never know the good he did. The angels were only too glad to grant his wish, and marveled at his holiness and selflessness. And so the sage went about his business, and the story tells us, in his footsteps flowers and trees appeared in the desert sand.

This beautiful tale sums up much of what we've been considering. The Magician does not look for rewards or recognition for himself since the ego is not in need of such soothing. The story also tells us that the results of what we do may not be obvious to us, but that doesn't mean we should not do what we feel is important. Gandhi said it differently, but the sentiment is the same: "What you do may seem insignificant, but it is vitally important that you do it." Think of those parents, grandparents, teachers of all kinds who have had an impact on the many lives they have touched, and yet probably those they affected did not know it for years.

The Magician is visible, very often, in another unusual form. When aging parents become less capable they offer their grown children a remarkable opportunity for the next step in their relationship. This is the chance to become the parent to one's parent. Old people are seen by some as merely a nuisance, an inconvenience to be humored. Yet it is worth noticing that there is a chance here, if one wishes to acknowledge it, for the adult to move into a different relationship with the aging parent, one that in fact reverses the previous early-childhood power balance. Now it is the old person who needs the support. As the old person loses agility, mental alertness, and struggles to understand new technology, he or she will also tend to shed a large portion of the earlier identity based on achievement, competence, and worldly advancement. Like an aging athlete who no longer has the skills or physique that once defined her life, the parent will have to reassess who she is in the world and with the grown child. This gives the child the opening to show love in a different way, and for the old person to accept it. The mark of the older person who is a true Magician is to know this is happening, and encourage it so the adult child can get what he or she needs from this realigned relationship. Some old people just fall into selfishness – wanting to be looked after – and in this they regress to Orphan stage. The wise Magician will try and give the adult child the chance to explore this new relationship and to find the essential core of love behind all the differences and resentments that tend to spring up over a lifetime. This demands that the older person shows considerable courage since the task may involve the digging up of old grievances in order to reconcile them. When this happens the relationship between the two can be healed and completed. The old person will eventually die and be missed of course, but there will not be uncontrolled floods of tears at the funeral from those who did the necessary work in coming to a loving place with the deceased.

This has been called anticipatory mourning; the knowledge that the loved person will soon die has allowed those close to him or her to say goodbye and make their peace. 'Anticipatory mourning', however, is not a term that even begins to describe the process under consideration here. At this point the child receives the great gift of being allowed to show love in the same fashion as the old person, when newly a parent, was able to show love to the baby and growing young person. This is a love that is not conditional upon the older person retaining his or her abilities or status. People who have spoken about nursing their aging parents through final illnesses have often related the sense of profound satisfaction that came from being able to be with their parents at that time. Conversely, those who have denied their illnesses and shut loved ones out of their dying process, which is always messy, have perhaps out of pride failed to allow others to come close. In such a situation everyone feels slightly cheated.

An example of this in action would be Geoffrey Wolff's biography of his father, *The Duke of Deception*. In writing the story of his father the confidence trickster and criminal, Wolff comes close to understanding his dead father – but the miraculous part is that he was able to re-establish his relationship with his mother, and that she spoke with absolute candor and precision about her life to a son who had been, to a large extent, estranged from her until then. "Neither of us, I think, trusted the other's love," he wrote. Then he spells out the process they went through together.

> Between the ages of twelve and fifteen I saw my mother three times, for a total of about ten days. Between the ages of fifteen and twenty-six I never saw her. [...] When my mother agreed to help me with this book, when she put her life in my hands, I decided to interview her with a tape recorder [...] It wasn't until I transcribed her words, twelve hours of talk, that I appreciated the full force of her gift to me [...] When I asked a hard question, my mother paused, and tried hard to answer it. If I didn't know what to ask, my mother asked for me. [...] What my mother told me of our history brought us together again." (p 48, 49, 50)

His mother's scrupulous desire to be accurate was a truly loving act, especially considering the deceptions his father had woven for so many years. This honesty was far more important to her than any desire to appear in a favorable light to her son, her family, or to the greater public who would read the book. Her great gift was to trust that her son would use the information for understanding, and not for condemnation. In allowing her son to take control, to write the book which risked exposing her even further, she showed considerable courage and even more love. The healing that her son needed couldn't have happened if she'd stood on her dignity and concealed the painful truth of her less-than successful life. Like a true Magician, she helped to bring about psychic healing for a man who already had sons of his own, and whose futures would be shaped by their father's ability to come to a place of peace with his past, and with his ability to love.

Nothing else matters as much as allowing another to love and be loved. Few things can be as powerful, or as vital to our spiritual growth, as to be with someone as she moves towards death, and to be invited to be part of that letting go. At such a time the only thing we remember is love. The Magician's final task is to bring that last great lesson forward.

Notes

1. *Tao Te Ching*, translated Stephen Mitchell. Pocket Editions, Harper Perennial, 1992, #17.
2. W.B. Yeats, 'The Long Legged Fly'. In *W.B. Yeats, Selected Poetry*. Ed. A. Norman Jeffares. London: Macmillan, 1970. Pp.197-198.
3. Michelangelo: in Taterkiewicz, Wladyslaw. *History of Aesthetics*. 1962. English edition by Continuum International Publishers, 2005, p.146.
4. Bono, U2. DVD documentary with *How To Dismantle an Atomic Bomb*, filmed 9-10 June 2004, Universal Music International.
5. William Faulkner, widely repeated quotation from *Sartoris*, found in: http://web.csustan.edu/english/reuben/pal/chap7/faulkner.html
6. *To Know Your Self: The Essential Teachings of Swami Satchidananda*, ed. Philip Mandelkorn, Integral Yoga Publications, Virginia, 2003, p.ix, and p.xi.
7. 'One Man's Memorial', Lisa Kocian *Boston Sunday Globe*, May 29, 2005, W1 and W13.
8. PBS tapes, *The Hobart Shakespeareans*.
9. Mohandas Gandhi, quoted in www.featherstudios.com/Pages/Primary/wisdom.html.
10. The Sufi tale is attributed to Mullah Nasrudin, the legendary Turkish sage.
11. Wolff, Geoffrey. *The Duke of Deception: Memories of My Father*. New York: Vintage, 1990, p.48; 49; 50.

Chapter Nine

The Road to Magician level

In some ways one can say that the whole point of all the stages so far described is to direct the individual to the Magician's level of awareness. Not everyone will get there of course, yet we all can, if we choose to apply ourselves to this. Here is a schematic chart that may help to show the route to Magician status and the challenges it involves.

Stage and lesson to learn	Passive/Accepting	Active/Rejecting	Balanced
Innocent [Identity and love]	"Do it for me! I can't do anything for myself." No spine.	"You can't make me do it." Complainer, angry.	"I may have something new to contribute."
Orphan [Attachment & Independence]	"Save me. It's not my fault I'm in this mess." Helpless.	"Go away. Everything's my fault." Angry/depressive.	"Where can I find reliable directions?" Ego sense is established.
Pilgrim [Learning & Direction]	"This isn't quite right for me somehow …" Too many directions; accepting; vague.	"This is all wrong and you are all fools." No direction/angry.	"What can you teach me?" Ego rising.
Warrior-Lover [Faces life/death issues]	Bully. "Let me hide behind something and terrorize others." No principles; angry.	Zealot. "You have to do it my way." Rigid principles.	"What is right, and how can I do it?" Ego diminishes.
Monarch [Service to others]	Too gentle. Tries to nurture others without discrimination. "I want you to love me". Not enough ego.	Tyrant. Judges others. "I don't care what you think of me". Too much ego.	"What must we do?" Letting go of ego gratification.
Magician [inclusion of others]	Aloof from the world; Reclusive.	Arrogance.	'How can we find ways to create harmony and love?"

You may notice that the Balanced column, the healthy one, is the one in which questions are asked whereas in the other columns statements are made. The individual who chooses to progress will find that asking open-ended, productive questions is the most satisfying way forward, because such questions reflect an open mind and invite honest answers. We become open and shake off prejudice by taking care that we ask open questions. By contrast the other incarnations are closer to set attitudes or fixed positions, and fixed positions are like fortresses; they are really hard to leave without a great deal of courage.

Notice also the number of times "I", "me", and "You" appear in these questions. They are there because of the emphasis the individual seems to make upon where real effectiveness lies. So the passive/accepting figure may use any number of ways to describe that he or she is at the receiving end of things, a person who is helpless in what you, or they, do to her. The victim always has 'them' to blame, or 'you', but rarely takes the stance of accepting the responsibility that would move him or her out of victim-hood. Just similarly the rejecting figure may tend to be equally self-involved, but will express it in terms of what he or she is – or is not – prepared to do. If the victim speaks in terms of "what they've done to me,' the rejecter speaks in terms of what "I" will do given half a chance. Notice how the Balanced column slowly moves from "I" to the more neutral "we" and from there to "How", "Where", and "What" type questions. The ego, once established in Orphan phase, becomes less important with each new stage achieved.

The chart above is perhaps helpful in another way, since we can begin to see it as a progression away from the parent and a rearranging of that relationship. The Innocent and the Orphan both need parents or their substitutes. But the Orphan becomes ready to graduate to Pilgrim stage when he or she no longer needs a specifically parental figure. The Pilgrim is interested in learning and in growing, but not in being tied to a specific dependent relationship. In fact, one might say that the Pilgrim is moving towards the stage at which one is offered the chance to parent oneself and when this happens the individual makes the change to Warrior-Lover status. Parenting oneself is not the same as ignoring or neglecting one's parents. It is a development in which one answers to one's personal sense of a higher authority (traditionally parental in some form or another) and decides which moral code has to be internalized, and when it is to be applied. Sometimes this means being able to take a reasoned and calm stand that is the exact opposite of one's parents' views. C.G. Jung's rift with Sigmund Freud could be seen as just such a growth point. Jung's refusal to take on the role as Freud's chosen heir to his psychological theories was probably not just a re-run of childish ideas of rebellion. It was an important move so he could express his own truth about what he saw. At that point he refused to be an Orphan because his desire to explore as a

Pilgrim drove him to become his own "parent". This allowed him to develop his own sense of authority – which is an essential for exploring and assessing one's chosen sphere of expertise. After rejecting Freud, Jung went on to formulate some of his most ambitious and far-reaching theories, theories he could not have even begun to nurture had he stayed within the orthodoxy of the Freudian school. And so he went his own way at Warrior-Lover level and continued to develop along with his ideas. If he had passively accepted the role as Freud's heir he might well have slipped back to Orphan status.

As we have already seen, the Warrior-Lover has to heal the relationship with the parents that was fractured during those early fights for self-definition, so that as a Monarch she can greet them anew as equals. When we reach Magician level we have to realize that the relationship with the parent may well be one in which we seem to have become superior to our parents in the sense of worldly competence. This happens naturally as the aging parent becomes, sometimes, less interested in keeping up to date with some aspects of life. Yet, as I have pointed out, this can also happen because the wise parent has chosen to step back and allow the adult child to be in charge.

The nub of the matter here is that we have to learn that the way we treat our parents (or the memory of them, if they are already dead) at this stage is a mirror of the way we treat the universe. And as we treat it, so will it treat us.

If we choose to harbor resentments about parents and others, this will be reflected back to us in everything we do, and we will tend to resent anyone who stands in authority in a re-run of those old aggrieved emotions. If we are able to remember the love our parents and those who may have been parent substitutes showed us, then we will feel that love, project it out into the world, and find it coming back to us. The poet Goethe can help us here when he says: "Treat people as if they were what they ought to be and you help them to become what they are capable of being." It's good advice, and so obviously true that it should surprise us that we so often don't follow it. Treat people with trust and they will, very often, more than repay that trust. Treat them with contempt and they will do the same to us. When running workshops and groups I have found again and again that one person who takes the risk of being open, honest, and trusting can transform a whole room into a place of genuine respect and trust. Once one person has spoken up, others find the courage to be authentic, to reveal themselves to the group. Suddenly we find ourselves talking in an entirely different way. And of course when that happens the things that can be discussed and resolved are almost limitless.

The Magician knows this, and facilitates it.

Perhaps we can refer back to Jesus when we think of the Magician, for whatever one's religious beliefs, Jesus was a remarkable teacher. He suggested that when we have 'faith' we can work miracles – move mountains, in fact. Wayne Dyer writes in response to this that we need a powerful sense of 'Intention' and then we can achieve in the same way. Emmet Fox makes it quite clear we need to attune ourselves to the Jesus teachings so that we can 'demonstrate' our full potential in the world. I have already written about artists, writers, and ordinary people who have been able to move to a place of 'flow' where they feel the muse has taken them over, and good things are allowed to come through them. I want to spend a little more time on this.

In my work I have come across examples of people who have wanted something very much, and some have achieved it. Others have failed. Some achieved their goals through sheer hard work – saving hard for that new house or expensive car. I am not really interested in those examples, because I want us to focus on those people who became fully themselves, rather than those who collected luxuries and toys. Those who achieved this level of full actualization shared one main attribute, it seems to me: they had no doubt about what they were supposed to do. They did not deflect their aim to easier targets, more readily available rewards. They knew who they were, first; then they set about putting those qualities in motion. I think this is what is meant by 'intention' and 'faith'. Many of these people have spoken about how their particular life direction was not something they had to choose, but rather that it was something that seemed to choose them. They didn't decide to be blues musicians, for example, because that seemed particularly glamorous or profitable. They did it because they knew that's who they actually were in their hearts. This was their way of expressing their truth. Their direction was not about ego but about a deep caring for the work as a way of expressing something they felt could only be expressed this way. These people were the lucky ones. They knew from comparatively early on what their direction would have to be. But whether one arrives at this early or late means less than that one arrives, for we can only truly arrive when we allow the energy of the universe to act through us. George Harrison put it beautifully in a PBS TV interview when he said that the Beatles hadn't changed anything: "It was the time. We just happened to be there." It's a wonderfully humble comment from someone who had been one of the world's most famous guitarists, and he implied not just that the Beatles were there by chance, but that they were tuned into something the world wanted and needed, and they expressed it better than most others could. You could call it Zeitgeist, or the Collective Unconscious, or historical determinism, or God, or anything you wish. You could put it in the form of the popular saying that tells us, 'Comes the hour, comes the man' – the idea that when the world needs a certain type of leader, then that person has a habit of turning up. What we call it matters less than the fact of the existence of this energy. The Magician is in touch with it.

We are routinely prepared to accept the existence of this power, but alas, it seems we can only do so when we see it on the movie screen. The vast numbers of Star-Wars fans who know about 'the Force' believe, if only in an oblique way, that this power exists. Unfortunately the power of belief is for many of them something that can only occur with the realm of fiction. And that is a great pity, since there most certainly is something there to believe in. We all know that heart, devotion, and determination really can move mountains, yet we routinely see this as what others can manage, not us. The Magician believes directly. Everywhere in this world determined, resourceful, selfless people are changing the things that once seemed unchangeable, working with limited resources and boundless faith in their work.

Now, this theory of the stages may seem all rather convenient. Yet it is not as clean and tidy as we might wish. For anyone is capable of rising, and anyone is capable of slipping back on the scale, at any time. When we look at examples taken from literature, we'll see figures who seem to slip back to a lesser level when confronted with threats. And this is, after all, what people everywhere tend to do. We come across something we haven't dealt with before, and fear or uncertainty pushes us to play safe. Sometimes this is called a cognitive downshift – which is a way of saying that we may tend to forget all those practical helpful lessons we've read about when faced with a real crisis.

The trouble is life has a way of sending us fairly regular crises so we can expect to see that progress is not linear; it may be one step up, one step back, two to the side … and so on. I suspect that if we are to make any sort of comparison, it might be that human progress is closer to a spiral, or a helix. At times it may look as if we are circling back to deal with the same old problems again, but in fact the challenge is to see whether or not we are dealing with them from the same mindset as before. Are we just revisiting the situation? Or are we now seeing it from a slightly different point of view? Just as a helix drawn on a page seems to go past the same places, yet only a fraction of an inch further away each time, so it can be with people. But that shift in position can make all the difference.

In addition, a spiral line is a line that is the entire length of itself. It's not just the point it ends up. So, we all have all the stages within us, all the time. Our challenge is to be able to live, for the most part, from the most developed part of ourselves, and yet still be able to mobilize the best aspects of the earliest stages when that serves the best interests of all concerned. So when the Warrior aspect of the Warrior-Lover emerges she certainly is not always going to be helpful or even right; and the Warrior may need to drop back into Pilgrim thinking in order to clarify what he or she will need to do as a Warrior-Lover. Perhaps, in its most comprehensive sense, that is what the Monarch does. Just as a Monarch is the whole kingdom of citizens (good, bad, indifferent, clueless, and so on), so the Monarch must be able to access all the parts of the psyche in order to understand fully how to respond. Only then can he or she act with fully conscious meaningfulness. This means being able to operate intelligently at all levels. So the wise parent can see and feel a child's disappointment and yet not be as helpless before that emotion as the child is. The Warrior-Lover does not forget what it is like to be an Orphan, and the Magician likewise does not expect others to be anything other than their own, perhaps confused, selves.

We see glimpses of this in unexpected places. Winston Churchill comes to mind because he seemed to have an intuitive grasp of what the British people needed and wanted. Yet he was born the second son of a duke, and received a most privileged education. One could have excused him for being entirely out of touch with the ordinary man. That his eloquence could be so persuasive was one thing – but he will also be remembered for his down-to-earth prose. When commenting on Hitler's request that Britian should surrender his reply left no room for doubt: "What kind of people do they think we are?" It struck exactly the right note of ordinary colloquial astonishment – spanning all social classes. It also made the moral point. Fascism was evil, and could not be dealt with in a normal civilized way. Perhaps the example is somewhat remote, but it reminds one of President Truman's famous statement: "The buck stops here." He spanned all classes in that statement, too. The Monarch doesn't need spin-doctors, or spokesmen, or press agents in order to say what needs to be said, and what needs to be heard. A Monarch who cannot be trusted to speak out is no Monarch at all. The true Monarch speaks out by utilizing language that will appeal to all, which expresses what others in their best and strongest selves truly feel. To do that, he must have some awareness of what others think and feel, and he can do that because he's lived in that space, too.

So the Monarch must be able to remember her roots. In doing this she is able to rise to be a Magician, articulating what many people may have felt, but which they had been unable to put into expression. Alexander Pope, the great English poet, called this type of action by its true name. He called it poetry, and defined it as "What oft was thought, but ne'er so well express'd." Truly great poetry does that – it expresses what many of us have felt but have been unable to put into words as yet. And when the words appear we're likely to say – 'that's exactly what I mean'. Poetry, like all great art, comes from those who can access the Magician in themselves, even if only temporarily.

What does it feel like to be a Magician?

Lonely, in a word. The Magician is somewhat remote from the rough and tumble world of the ordinary, and as such is not able to be part of the fray or make friendships based on unity of purpose that others may find. The Magician sees more than most; she has to foresee dangers, plan ahead so that threats don't get out of hand, and ensure that there is someone available to serve as a Warrior-Lover and face those threats. Sometimes seen as an ivory tower recluse this is in fact the Passive incarnation of the Magician; alone, self-involved and remote. The true Magician chooses to be part of the world as a director or a nurturer, rather than as a participant.

If the Magician can find another Magician then there is indeed an end to loneliness, and so the task the Magician faces is to be out in the world and find other like-minded souls.

A Magician will find that people will keep coming to her hoping she'll solve their problems without any effort on their behalf. Part of what any sage has to do is to refuse the temptation to show off what she knows, which is only a sort of ego-gratifying sleight of hand. This is the incarnation that typifies the Active Magician, and it must be rejected. Instead the Magician must return the question to the person who has it, so that the individual most directly concerned can solve it and take possession of the personal power that comes from solving one's own dilemmas. In this way that person can learn how to deal with the situation, therefore ensuring psychic growth. That's how future generations of Magicians can be trained up. And so the Magician may find he has substantial friendships with his or her equals, and extensive but less powerful friendships with those who are, as it were, in training.

One can think of this in terms of the various magic-wielding figures who appear in folk tales. Merlin is a remote wizard who intervenes only slightly in human affairs, but always decisively. He doesn't tell Arthur what he should do so much as allow him to be educated. Morgan le Fay is the distant witch who chooses to test the understandings in Arthur's court, but rarely appears in person to do so; Dumbledore is the distant but kindly chief wizard who steps well back from the fray almost all the time; Don Juan is the mysterious shaman living in the desert. The wizard (for the name is derived from the word *wise*, and means a person who is wise in unusual ways, beyond the practical realm of knowledge, closer attuned to spiritual paths) attracts students, must attract them, in order that they may grow and eventually surpass the master.

This figure has one major attribute that, perhaps, includes all the aspects so far named. The Magician is able to be fully present in this world; not reactive, not defensive, and always keeping an open mind. As we've seen keeping open is something that the Pilgrim has to learn to do, and that the Warrior-Lover has to keep on doing, even when she has chosen a particular path. The Monarch has the task of keeping the open-ness as a way of life, constantly conferring with others while still holding true to a sense of purpose for the whole kingdom. The Magician takes this ability one step further.

The way to think of this is in terms of the person who does not lose his head, who does not panic. This person will look at a troublesome situation and see past the surface confusions to what is really at issue. It's hard to do this. Even the very finest of us can only do it for short periods. When someone tries to harm us it can be very difficult to see past this to the hurt, lost individual who is stuck in a destructive way of thinking and being. In fact most of us want to avoid being hurt and we care very little what our assailant is thinking. We just want to be safe and make sure the aggressor is punished. This is all very natural. The Magician will have to step forward as a Warrior-Lover first to contain the threat, and afterwards will have to try to work with this person in some form, if possible. That involves another way of relating to this person.

As an example, think of a therapist. A gifted therapist will be able to keep sufficiently detached from the client so that she can give guidance that is not based in seeing only the surface issues but is rooted in a full awareness of the whole of the person's situation. Since clients don't always tell the truth about themselves (often because they can't see it, sometimes because they wish to conceal it) the therapist has to rely on those flashes of intuition that provide information that has been suppressed. A therapist can do this because she sees the client for only an hour or so at a time, and this enables her to keep the distance that permits her to understand more clearly what may be going on, and to access compassion. A parent of a distressed child may know the child better in some ways, but will inevitably be caught up in a whole history of hopes, fears, resentments, disappointments, and so on. The enlightened therapist will see all this, understand it, and use it as data, but will not slip into the same confused mindspace that helped to create the problem. If she does all this she can achieve the Magician's poise, and that will enable her to see the good and promising aspects of her client. To take the old Hindu greeting, we could say this is a form of *Namaste* – that which is holy in me salutes that which is holy in you. For when we greet what is holy and eternal in others, and when we turn aside from what is diseased and distressed because we recognize it as that part of the person that needs to be healed, we approach the realm of the Magician. Healing comes from nurturing what is good, not from focusing on what is diseased.

The Magician will be in tune with the magic of creation. Life has mystery, beauty, and passion for this figure. Every day is a miracle. Notice that we need mystery, beauty and passion all together. Mystery, ugliness and passion will lead us only to a place of ugliness, for the ugly and evil aspects of the world can be just as mysterious and inspire passions every bit as strong as what is beautiful and good. Beauty is more than what one sees as pleasing. Beautiful and loving actions happen in grubby and impoverished settings. It's up to us to make sure we see the beauty and look past the rest. Then every day will be extraordinary.

When the Magician dies, when this figure is able to use her death as a tool to teach others about life, courage, and meaning, the loss can be felt as a huge spiritual gift, and death itself becomes beautiful. In part we enshrine this everyday when we see obituaries in the newspaper, or on those occasions when we hear funeral addresses. The purpose of these speeches is to let everyone know what the deceased did for loved ones and the world, so that we can be grateful for his or her life, and learn about what matters even after death. The death is a loss, and it can also be a gift.

Put another way, a woman said to me about her dead friend, "It wasn't until she died that I realized how much she had given to everyone around her, just by being herself. I shan't forget that."

Notes

1. Goethe, Johann Wolfgang Von. Widely reported, although the precise provenance is uncertain.
2. Dyer, Wayne. *The Power of Intention.* Hay House, 2005.
3. Fox, Emmet. *Find and Use Your Inner Power.* New York and London: Harper, 1941.
4. PBS TV series *The Sixties.* 2006.
5. Winston Churchill, addressing the US Congress, December 26, 1941. See the original documents including this quotation at: www.loc.gov/exhibits/churchill/interactive/_html/wc0147.html
6. Truman had a sign on his desk with this engraved on it. It was made at the Federal reformatory at El Reno, Oklahoma.
7. Pope, Alexander. *An Essay in Criticism,* Part II. l. 288.

Chapter Ten

The Sub-Stages

If these six stages seem somewhat glib, they are also very flexible – almost confusingly so. The fact that an individual wanders around does not guarantee that he or she is a Pilgrim. An Orphan can wander; so can someone at any stage. What's important is the quality of the wandering. The Innocent may wander like a lost child, but will be doing so as a way to find attachment – and almost anything will do. The Orphan may wander, but the Orphan will be unhappy doing so, and be desperate to find a likely adoptive parent or clique. It is only when the individual is conscious of the wandering as an important part of the process that she can be a true Pilgrim. The Pilgrim actively decides not to be attached, knowing full well that a time will come when attachment becomes necessary and desirable. When the Pilgrim does choose to take that step, the attachment is entirely different. A child seeking shelter does not have the same attitude as a newly emerged Warrior-Lover deciding to take the actions that will create shelter. They both seek shelter; they do so in completely different ways.

What makes the difference?

Simply stated, it lies in the consciousness one can bring to the situation. The Innocent starts with not very much consciousness of what she is doing. Like a baby, it is mostly a case of instinct, at least at first. The Orphan is not that dis-similar, for even though the Orphan is conscious that she may be making what amounts to a provisional deal, the need to find a parental figure is so strong that the individual consciousness is willingly sacrificed to the more immediate need to fit in. Consciousness seems to begin to grow when Pilgrim stage is reached – and in that case it is a conscious decision to take to the road.

And this is where things become more intricate. Each phase has to be lived through, and each archetypal phase *contains the other five phases*. We have to work through them all in order to reach the next level. So, the Innocent has to move through all six miniature stages before becoming an Orphan, and as an Orphan has to go through all six again ... and so on.

Think of this in terms of the Innocent. A baby is born and at first is truly helpless. It has no real control or ability to make choices. It is the Innocent in its Innocent phase. After a while, the child begins to become more aware and can make some decisions about whom she is attached to. Mom may be OK, but Aunt Joan is greeted with wailing. The Innocent is "deciding" who to be attached to: the Innocent as Orphan. Then the child learns how to walk and crawl, and is most definitely a Pilgrim and experimenter, gathering knowledge, experience, impressions. Soon enough, the child becomes demanding, often obstreperous, and has a mind of her own: Innocent as Warrior. Cookies are good, at this stage, and are demanded with energy. Green beans are right out. Tantrums, and the child's ability to control these, are part of learning Warrior-Lover stage. Once the awareness is present, and the child chooses what to do based on concerns that are not merely selfish, we have the start of the Innocent Monarch. Another way of describing it might be to call it socialization. Children learning how to play harmoniously together might be an example of this. Mastery of this stage brings the child to Magician level. Any parent will be able to supply examples of young children who seemed, instinctively, to be much wiser than anyone could ever have expected them to be, offering love and even advice to others in a way that is astounding.

A woman in one of my workshops gave a beautiful example of this. She worked in a day care facility and at the time was having problems with an abusive boyfriend. She came into work one day with a group of children she did not know very well. One little boy came and snuggled up to her, and asked why she was sad. Surprised that her distress showed (we all think we can fool small kids) she said in the simplest terms she could muster that her friend hadn't been very nice to her, and had made her cry. The little boy listened and then said, "Someone who makes you cry isn't your friend." Those words, she said later, opened her eyes to what was truly going on in her life, and prompted her to begin the necessary steps to make sure she changed her situation. Now we may say that the little boy was just repeating something his parents had said to him, but the point here is not whether we can be critical and discount the source of the information. The point is that this was exactly what the young woman needed to hear in order to wake up, and the hint came from a completely unexpected source. Perhaps that's why she was able to hear it, when she couldn't hear similar comments coming from her friends and she would not act on her own intuitions – until the little boy spoke. In fact the Innocent Magician is often much more aware than we can readily comprehend, and is more than ready to become the Orphan, at the Innocent stage.

This is about the point where school is a really good idea, because the Innocent is ready to leave the family and attach easily to another type of experience. Most children are excited by the prospect of school; they are ready for something new, despite what they may have observed with older children who may complain about teachers and homework. The younger children don't seem to register too much of that. They just know that they're eager for the next stage so they can find out what everyone's talking about. So the child, when taking on any new task, such as a new school year, will begin as an Innocent again, and move through all the sub-stages, with luck, in that year, and repeat the same process again at a slightly higher level the following year. In the greater sense of her life trajectory she will remain at Orphan level for perhaps some years to come, gaining the confidence as a learner that will enable her to move towards Pilgrim level later. Yet each year, and in response to each year's new tasks, she will recapitulate at a micro level as many of the six stages as she is capable of achieving.

And the cycle continues.

I think you can see what's being proposed. We have six stages to go through in life, and we go through the six sub-stages of whatever main, archetypal stage we have arrived at whenever we take on a new task. We can go through some of these sub-stages very rapidly, since the earlier stages will be familiar to us from experience. Even so, the sub-stages are important.

In this particular sequence, as in all the major archetypal stages, it is vital that we notice that the sub-stages have to be completed successfully. If the child doesn't learn how to love and to trust as an Innocent Innocent then it will be very hard for her to feel the confidence necessary to go to school, for example. Children can get stuck at the fearful Innocent Orphan level and remain overly cautious or fearfully rejecting. That takes us right back to the Passive and Active incarnations we've looked at earlier. In some ways the sub-stage that is most vital here is the Pilgrim, since this is when questioning and self-definition occur. As we've already seen, the move to Pilgrim level on the larger scale of the archetype is what propels the individual forward. Just the same thing seems to be the case in these sub-stages: the Pilgrim level is the point at which growth can occur, rather than regression.

If this is true, then we may want to consider what it is that makes a Pilgrim out of a child. I think the answer to this is that the child's experience of love and support leads to a sense of confidence that the world is a good and relatively safe place to explore – and this love allows the child to have the courage to move forwards. Early trauma in children can lead to fear, and it's very hard to get a fearful child to learn from new experiences.

If we apply this to the Orphan, what we'll see is that the Orphan who is fearful will be very likely to conform and not question (the Passive stance) or be afraid and rebel in a way that is rejecting and terrified (the Active stance). This is the Orphan Orphan, who must work out a balanced stance that allows for inquiry. It is only by going forward into Pilgrim sub-stage that the child can begin to work out the true nature of who and where she is. As an Orphan Pilgrim she will begin to ask questions that will allow her to form her own views, and as an Orphan Warrior she will decide to stick up for those views – and just like the full Warrior-Lover archetype she will have to learn when to argue and when it's not worth the effort. For the Orphan's task is always to leave the adopted home, but the challenge, as any parent will know, is for the Orphan to leave home successfully. Anyone can get thrown out and anyone can run away; but the best way to leave is in full appreciation of what has been home until now, recognizing its benefits and limitations, and knowing that, for all its advantages, home has to be left behind for learning to occur. This is the sense of the balanced archetype we have been considering. The young adult who can leave the home she has outgrown and do so in appreciation and love is the Orphan Monarch, and if she can do it in such a way that everyone can feel this to be a growth point, then she has achieved Orphan Magician level. This is when the child can move forward, and when the parents may feel they can move into a new phase of life, too. Whether we see this in terms of the child leaving home to go to college, or the person leaving a job to begin a new phase of life, or even the person getting divorced, leaving is something that is not done in a haphazard fashion without paying a heavy price.

For instance, every so often one comes across a divorced couple who are actually extremely supportive and loving of each other, who raise their children competently although living apart, and who recognize that as a couple together they were not good for each other any more. This situation is comparatively rare, but it is not impossible and I have seen it in operation more than once. This is what I mean by this concept of leaving a situation productively, with love, and it is the mark of the Monarch who has become, in this action, a Magician. Everyone benefits, especially any children the couple may have. In support of this I can say I have witnessed the dissolution of marriages in which, despite the obvious initial upset, all parties concerned have been better off. The parents both became more cheerful, and the children stopped acting out at school and getting into trouble. Unfortunately I'm sure we can all think of many more instances of the opposite scenario.

We all know people who have been angry at work and who therefore arrange to leave at the most inconvenient time, thumbing their noses at the chaos they leave behind. Some people fantasize about doing just this. Others choose their sick days in this spirit. The person who leaves in this angry fashion sows disorder and, most probably, is not likely to be going anywhere much better. With an attitude of disrespect like that he is going to poison the next place he works in the first few days. Unconsciously such people have projected all their discontents onto the place they are leaving – which is another form of blaming, and thus of avoiding full responsibility for one's own role while there. This is the realm of the Orphan who is stuck and regressing. The illusion is that the new job, place, or spouse will provide a clean slate, and that the new start will be effortless. However, as we all know, when we leave a place we always take all our baggage with us.

In divorces the tendency for one person to want to take the other to the cleaners, and to pursue an unforgiving financial settlement stems from a desire to punish – from the sense that one is owed something. It seeks to avoid looking at the problems in the marriage itself, which are always the business of both partners. When one looks only at how much money one can squeeze out of the other it's hard to come to any intelligent assessment, and so no learning can take place.

These sub-stages may seem somewhat over-analytic. They are not intended to replace the ideas we've already been dealing with. The sub-stages definitely exist, and can be utilized to diagnose where someone may be stuck, as well as where we ourselves may have difficulties. The concept of Active, Passive and Balanced incarnations works well in a different way because it allows us to say not just what level and sub-stage we may be operating from but, more importantly, what direction our energy is taking us. So the passive version of any archetype will always tend to bring the individual down to an earlier level, and the active incarnation will tend to leave us isolated, in a dead end mindset, one that is very often dominated by anger. Fear causes us to regress, and anger causes us to adopt rigid postures in which we can accept very little in the way of help or new ideas.

Part Two

Chapter Eleven

Where Did These Stages Come From? A Brief History

In the summer of 2004 I had an opportunity to work with a very gifted student, Jane Deering, a graduating English major. She was puzzled because she'd read so many self-help books based on journal writing, and she felt they told her how to write more, but not what the changes she was going through might be nor how to assess them. As a result, she felt these books, however well written and successful, didn't deliver anything very much. She pointed to the seven volumes of her journals stuffed into her shoulder bag and said that she knew she'd changed since those earliest days, but she still didn't know what the changes were. "I'm still confused," she said, "and in some ways my writing isn't that much better. But I seem to be confused in a different way."

That set us both thinking. After all, self-awareness and the practice of writing were supposed to lead to clarity. But the clarity wasn't there, although we had every right to expect it, and there was even less clarity about what the process had been. Intuitively I knew that Jane had put her finger on a topic that had been troubling me for some time – how exactly did writers mature? And how would they know they had?

After some false starts we decided to look at Jane's work in the terms proposed by Paul Radin, in Jung's book, *Man and His Symbols*. Radin's chapter on the life stages of the Winnebago Indians suggested that their tribal myths identified several distinct stages in the growth towards maturity. They are:
- The baby
- The trickster
- The transformer
- The hero, and
- The twins.

These are similar in general terms to the six stages we have been discussing, but they are also significantly different, and it's worth taking the time to see how this works. The Baby is essentially innocent and trusting and vulnerable, since it has no real power. Once the child grows, she gets a sense of her own effectiveness, and this is shown in being able to "trick" adults. Those all-powerful big adults can't be right all the time, and so the child learns to outsmart them, much to her delight. For a child in this stage, one can expect to find tasks not really completed. Tidying one's bedroom tends to mean hiding everything under the bed instead of putting it away, and April Fool's day becomes a major festival, from fake dog poop on the carpet to plastic fingers dripping "real" blood. The youngster discovers she has some power in being able to deceive others.

The Transformer stage occurs when the child begins to develop a creative side, and use it. Fantasy, construction toys of various kinds, collecting objects, assembling 'camps' or building tree houses: these are some of the many ways the Transformer stage works. The ordinary is transformed, through imagination and skill, into something that shows the child's competence. I used to make plastic model airplanes by the dozen. My nephew did the same thing, and to a much higher standard, too. The pleasure we took in creating objects that were after all, just toys, had far more to do with the poetry of the toy itself: a small plane that represented power and freedom, a miniature armored vehicle that suggested the personal invulnerability we longed for, even though we had years to wait before we would be allowed behind the wheel of a car. This is what the Transformer stage can look like. It is characterized by the tendency to assemble new objects using various parts, just as the Pilgrim will assemble different notions as she works towards a creed by which to live.

As this stage begins to close, it can spark another stage (although one never completely loses the earlier stages) and that is called the Hero. In Hero stage, the child identifies with heroic figures (those superhero plastic toys have an enduring appeal) and may need to test his own courage. The haunted house at Halloween becomes a test of unflappability – just as it will transmute into a tough attitude for the late teenage years. Around this time young people love to go out into the world. Wilderness camping may test their courage and allow them to practice skills learned in the Transformer stage. In the city, the emphasis may be on not showing fear while going into bad neighborhoods, and using trickster techniques to get hold of illegal substances, perhaps. Shoot 'em up movies can be a favorite with this age group. The real task of those at the Hero stage seems to be to take their sense of personal power and test it in the real world.

If the young person emerges from the Hero phase with an intact sense of who he or she is, and knows when to use courage (and when to run away), the development will be quite noticeable in the young confident person we see. This is when the person is ready to become "The Twins."

The Twins of the legends are both kings and their challenges are very much like those we have seen facing the Monarch. One twin is hard and cruel. The other is understanding and soft, according to Winnebago lore. The challenge is to balance the two, since an overly strict ruler will incite reaction and rebellion, and an overly lax ruler will spread contempt that will also cost him his rule. At this stage in life, the young person has to balance executive ability with careful thought in order to be master of himself and of any situation that he may reach. This is an ongoing struggle that each person has to be fully aware of throughout life. And since some people never really grow up, they may decide to remain stuck as Tricksters, say, always trying to get away with something they don't quite deserve. Or they may always be fighters, in Hero stage. And so on.

When we applied this mythic outline to Jane's journals it seemed to work exceptionally well as a way of assessing her words. She embraced it enthusiastically. It seemed to explain her writings and her experience with some exactitude, and gave her a place outside her own experience from which to look back upon what she had recorded and how she had recorded it. We could see her on those journal pages moving through the stages, occasionally slipping back into an earlier stage in times of stress. And in her writing at the time she seemed to be aware of this uneven progress. The vocabulary and the imagery fitted the Winnebago template. We were more than a little surprised at how closely it did fit.

It seemed as if we had stumbled across an important way of looking at writing that had eluded so many of the self-help gurus. And the irony was that this way of seeing had been around, unregarded, for many many years. We had simply connected the dots.

Around this time Dr. Mary Hall, one of my colleagues and a social worker who teaches at Smith College, alerted me to the stages of assessment she had been using when assessing young minority mothers with addictions. Her organization used a five part series of stages to describe the progress a client was making. These are:

1) Precognition
2) Cognition
3) Asking for help
4) Action
5) Maintenance.

This is a rather cold and clinical arrangement, or so it seems at first glance, so perhaps we'd better take a closer look to see how this works in practice. At the Precognitive stage, the client may not want to know he or she has a problem, or may simply be unaware. "That's just the way it is for me" is an attitude that denies the possibility of change. At the stage of Cognition, the individual has accepted that addictions may be problematic, for example, but there is as yet no real desire or knowledge about how to change. At this point, the client may well seem like a *Trickster*, seeking to lie, or obscure, or avoid what obviously is the case. In stage 3, the client begins to see the problem for what it really is and asks for help, fully intending to do something about the situation. Just as Paul Radin's *Transformer* uses readily available resources, so the stage 3 client seeks for what supports there may be out there, and begins to think about how she can use them – just like a Pilgrim. The all-important stage, however, is stage 4, where the individual decides to take action – to take charge of her own life. This is directly comparable to Radin's *Hero* stage and the Warrior-Lover. The last remaining challenge is stage 5, in which the person has to maintain the progress she has made – by staying substance free. It is at that stage that clients return to the clinic, it seems, to re-mind themselves of how far they've come, to be reassured, and to reassure those still fighting their addictions. As role models, they have their feet in two worlds; they know the addict's plight, feel it, and yet try to stay above it. This seems to be a good description of the awareness and balance the *Twins* need to maintain, just as the Monarch does.

What is worth noting is that these two models – although coming from entirely different backgrounds and contexts – seem to have excellent functional validity. They reinforce each other almost perfectly. The Winnebago Indians had lived by their model for generations. The five stages model works for the social workers who use it to assess clients, and it makes sense for the clients themselves. People see themselves more clearly as a result. And both models are concerned with the human journey of growth to fuller awareness. The Win-nebago version is more colorful, since we can identify more easily with an im-age-name such as *Transformer* or *Hero*. It speaks more to the imagination than "stage 3", for example.

I began to wonder if these stages could be used as a way to relay to students how they can expect to see change in their lives. Change is, after all, not just a function of growth. One can grow old, die, and never have learned anything much worthy of the name, let alone anything that will cause change.

So I tried these ideas with students, asking them if they felt there was any value to them. They responded with enthusiasm. Many applied them to their lives, and were even able to identify friends who had remained stuck at certain levels. For many of these students the idea of stages helped to explain what seemed like heartbreak – why had some of their friends become almost strangers to them? Why did some of their peers seem so childish and undeveloped? Were they the "weird ones" for being interested in ideas, or were the others? Sometimes the anti-academic bias of their peers was so strong that these students felt the stages concept as an immensely helpful support to help them stay focused despite the opposition.

All this brought forward the basic idea that a schematic representation can be truly helpful as a way of knowing what really might be going on and why. Such a structure could act like a road map. It lets us know roughly where we are, how far we've come, and what the road to the destination looks like, even if it can't tell us about every pothole or holdup on the way. In fact, many of my students felt empowered by the stages idea, and they were able to monitor when they moved forward from one stage to the next, and when they slipped back.

As a general rule people do not change unless they see that change may be necessary or beneficial. We all prefer to keep on doing whatever it is we feel comfortable doing. The notion of there being stages alerted my students to the possibility that there was more to discover, more to know about themselves. If one doesn't know that a possibility exists it, to all intents and purposes, is invisible. My students began to see there might be a way ahead for them that was not defined in terms of having more material wealth only.

In addition this idea of stages of development works at two levels. The first was that on a micro level, as I could see, it referred to a specific task of mastery – whether that was the task of going through four years of college, or shaking an addiction. And it also worked at the macro level: one could trace one's complete life development in this way, as the Winnebago had clearly intended. I concluded that the larger pattern of life development was replicated, in miniature, every time we took on a new task and moved towards mastery of it. The more I observed my students – moving from innocent fresh first-years, to questioning sophomores, to juniors who had identified a major they felt good about, to graduating seniors ready to face the world of work – the more I could see these archetypes as templates that reflected some vital aspects in the processes learning and growth. So the idea of these various developmental stages had proved itself as a theory that had some practical application, as far as we could tell.

And then another idea emerged which seemed to work even better, even if it came from an unusual source.

The pioneering analyst and friend of Carl Jung, John Weir Perry, had suggested in many of his writings that the schizophrenic goes through certain recognizable stages as he or she struggles to come to the understandings that will allow for psychic healing. He identified twelve image centers that his patients seemed to share when they described themselves to him; some reported all, others only eight or nine, but they were sufficiently distinctive and coherent to provide a recognizable pattern. What was remarkable was not just that patients who did not know each other shared a common language of imagery, but *that the sequence in which the images appeared was almost always the same.* Startled by this, Perry went one stage further. He linked these images to ancient rituals of kingship, reflected in eastern mythology, of which he had made an extensive series of studies. In Jungian terms it seemed as if Perry's schizophrenics were able to reach into the wisdom of the collective Unconscious, which communicated itself to them in archetypal images, and that these archetypes, when responded to and welcomed, were capable of leading the clients back to mental health.

This idea seemed worth exploring. Certainly it was a topic that Joseph Campbell had written about extensively, although not in quite the same way as Perry. In fact, in his 1972 book, *Myths to Live By*, Campbell devotes much of chapter ten to Perry's work, noting his "considerable amazement" that Perry's observations matched so well with his own 1949 study *The Hero with a Thousand Faces*.

Perry has his own technical terms for each stage based on the images his patients used, and describes six specific stages involved in psychic rebirth.

The Mother-baby:	Madonna and Child
The Mother-boy/girl:	Great Mother and Son Lover
The Father-son/daughter:	Sky Father and Hero
The Group-youth:	Secret Society and Initiate
The Lovers:	Royal Brother and Sister Pair
The Adult Couple King + Queen:	Sky God and Earth Goddess.

The first column is Perry's formulation of the type of life situation each person has to resolve, while the second column reflects the imagery the patients used to describe that struggle.

He postulated that each stage was about an essential "love bond" relationship that needed to be successfully completed so the individual could grow to the next stage. "The archetype of the self is found taking a new, specific form for each of the major stages of life" (867). He suggests that we instinctually know what our "path" is towards healing.

What is so remarkable about Perry's observation is that his clients seemed to go through almost identically similar stages, all of which were expressed in image-generated terms that are astonishingly similar. Furthermore, the clients came to these images entirely on their own, and in this process were able to heal themselves. In his writing Perry emphasizes that he listened to his clients without offering anything except empathic receptivity, so they could validate their own feelings. Since this allowed the images to emerge into a non-judgmental environment it also helped to keep each patient's images uncontaminated by suggestion. He concluded that not only do we have within us an innate ability to heal our souls in the case of schizophrenia, but those particular image-expressions that helped his clients were direct echoes of some of the oldest literature known, even when the clients had no knowledge of literature at all.

This should not surprise us. We do already have observable abilities to heal ourselves. When we are hurt – a cut hand, say – the body knows what to do. The blood flows, then clots. The white corpuscles do their work, the red also. The scab forms. Under it, the flesh knits. When it is ready, the scab falls and new, delicate flesh is ready to face the world. The body knows what it has to do.

As we grow up, the body continues to demonstrate its knowledge of what we need. Our bodies change, fill out, develop hair in expected places, voices and chest dimensions may change. It all happens. And as any adolescent knows, it can happen in such a way that our brains can hardly comprehend what's going on. We fall in love, we mourn a loss, and no one has to show us how to do it. We already seem to know.

The extensive changes of adolescence – physical, psychological, and sociological – happen without much conscious input from us.

I would like to suggest that the same thing happens in our souls; we just may not be aware of what is going on. The literature of our modern era, spanning the last three thousand years or so, seems to spell it all out, since literature is almost always about someone – usually the main character but often the readers themselves – learning something that will help him or her become more fully human.

Very often literature records the adventures of a soul as it grows. This is one reason literature can fascinate us several hundred years after its composition, even when translated from another language.

It was then that I discovered Carol Pearson's work, which she describes in *The Hero Within* (1989). Her stages of development are The Innocent, The Orphan, The Wanderer, The Warrior, The Altruist, and The Magician. It is immediately obvious that the stages are very close to Perry's. The Madonna and Child is close to the Innocent; The Mother-boy is a prefiguring of the Oedipal stage that may lead to the child feeling Orphaned, and so on. Yet these outlines are not the same. Surprisingly Pearson makes no reference to either Perry or Radin or their extensive researches. She seems to have come to her ideas without this background information, which is, in effect, so vitally important.

Since Pearson's archetypes were those observed in the world outside, I felt uneasy about their overall usefulness. She supports her choice of significant archetypes by referring to contemporary literature and film, some of it not very impressive, and some of which seemed to know about Jungian archetypes already and was specifically set up to exploit Jung's ideas, determined to prove them in action. This seemed to be putting the cart before the horse.

In contrast, Perry's set of twelve images was uncovered as a result of his work with schizophrenic patients over more than a decade. He does not link the imagery directly to the six stages he mentions; he hangs back from that. What he does say is that the imagery almost always appears in the exact order he describes, and it appears in patients as they move from psychic collapse to recovery. This cycle of dismantling and rebuilding, he claims with persuasive examples and extensive scholarship, exists already in the myths and rituals of kingship, from Europe to China. Perry has the observed quantitative data that validates his six stages, and that is what Pearson lacks.

Perry implies that these are universal stages, marked by specific imagery, which signal the realignments of awareness that come with growth and wisdom. That's a big claim. I'm not surprised he held back from making it directly.

Perry knew schizophrenics; he knew psychology; and he knew myth. What he knew less about is literature. If those stages he talks about really exist within us, then it would seem inevitable that literature would reflect them in some way. Since literature – if it is any good – speaks to us at a profound level, and since good literature tends to survive because it is remembered as being satisfying, then there ought to be plentiful evidence in the great literature of our culture that we as developing humans go through these stages.

And there is. There is plenty of supporting evidence. My training in literature allowed me to see that right away.

This is the way the outline of the six stages described in this book came to my notice. I have since tested these ideas in the outside world, and I am more than satisfied that there is validity in them that goes beyond the ordinary.

The thing to recall here is that in this chapter I have attempted to show that these six stages are not just random terms dreamed up out of nothing. They come from the deepest structures of the human psyche, and as such they may even be genetically encoded in each of us. Whether one believes in Jung's theories and Perry's findings or not, there is enough evidence in the literature to suggest that these six archetypes may be the most important ones we have. And that's worth recalling because there are many books presently circulating that suggest there are any number of other archetypes – the numbers range from four, to six, to twelve, to a thousand. Very few of those writers offer any solid grounding that explains why their archetypal systems are the way they are, or why they have chosen the ones they have. And so, well-intentioned as they no doubt are, they have succeeded in muddying the waters.

Jung himself is infuriatingly vague as to what archetypes might be, and how many there are. Yet he is powerfully aware of their effectiveness in directing the human pysche. What we may want to consider is that there are six main archetypes – those presented here – and that there are also many other lesser archetypes which are variants of these. So, as we have seen, the 'Caretaker' figure could be either a version of the Orphan, trying to be useful and fit in, or it could equally be a version of the Warrior-Lover, extending love. The result of such thinking is confusion, and the term 'Caretaker' is likely to be misleading.

My task has been to suggest that there is a specific order to be found in all this, and that it may be readily identifiable. I seek to bring logic and order to an area of discussion that has been fragmented until now. Order is not achieved by imposing a random template upon what can be observed, but by showing that what can be observed demonstrates its own coherence.

In the pages that follow I will be tracing the six stages we've already outlined and pointing out how frequently they recur in different texts, how similar they are to each other when they do, and that they exist always in this specific order leading on, one after another, as vital components in the greatest literature the Western world has seen. That they've done so over three millennia is convincing evidence for their worth and enduring applicability. We could say that the proof of the archetypes' existence in this specific order is spelled out in our stories, legends and literature, over and over again. It may be, in fact, one of the ways we shape reality.

Notes

1. Jung, C.G. *Man and His Symbols*. New York: Dell, 1971. Paul Radin's work first appeared as *Winnebago Hero Cycles: a Study in Aboriginal Literature*. Indiana University Publications in Anthropology and Linguistics: Waverly Press, 1948.
2. Campbell, Joseph. *Myths to Live By*. New York: Viking, 1972.
3. Campbell, Joseph. *The Hero with a Thousand Faces*. Princeton University Press: New Jersey, 1972.
4. Perry, John Weir. "The Reconstitutive Process in the Psychopathology of the Self" *Annals of the New York Academy of Sciences*, Vol. 96, 3, 1962. pp. 853-876.
5. Pearson, Carol. *The Hero Within*. New York: HarperCollins, 1986, 1989.

Part Three

Chapter Twelve

Literature: the Dynamic Expression of the Six Stages

Now that we've discussed the six stages it should be clear how knowing about them can help us see how we live and how we might grow. What should astonish us is that this information has been in our culture's literature for as long as humanity has been writing – perhaps for as long as we've been telling stories. It just hasn't been spelled out quite as clearly as one might have wished because stories of any sort have to be seen as a whole, and are not nearly so compelling nor so memorable if the information is presented analytically. We can see this easily if we think of children. Tell a four-year-old to 'be brave' and the child is probably going to be a bit confused as to what that means. But tell that same child to be as brave as her favorite story book character was when she met with some challenge the child has been told about and then we have a child who has an image of how to behave – and often this is far more powerful than any appeal to abstract concepts. This is the power of the image – since all such images are based on felt emotions.

In the following section we'll see how the archetypal structure of the six stages underpins some of the greatest works of literature our western civilization has produced. I will confine the discussion to the Western Tradition because I suspect most of my readers will be more familiar with the western canon, and I see no reason to make life difficult by dealing with esoteric references. I also choose to confine the discussion in this way because our Judaeo-Christian and Greco-Latin tradition is not at all the same as many far Eastern traditions. Eastern cultures see some things differently, and they also express similar ideas in a very different way. Bridging this gap would require more scholarship than I possess, and it would also require this book to be far longer than it is. What we are concerned with here is attempting to understand elements of what is obviously present in the literature that has made up our culture and, to some extent, us. To establish this we will move through the literature chronologically, from the ancient Greeks to contemporary times. What we'll see is that not only does the literature raise issues that seem to use the six stages, but it also seeks to explore facets of them we have not yet examined. We can learn a huge amount from this.

This is a detailed discussion, and some readers may find it challenging since it will deal with literature you may not have read for some years, or perhaps that you skipped over – as we all do. The reason we look at literature at all is because great literature reflects humanity's struggle back to itself, and as it does so it confirms what people may feel, since it explores those feelings further than the individual may be able to do on his own. It would, perhaps, have been even better if I could have given examples of casework with thousands of clients, spread over a period of several decades showing how the stages have worked in many different lives; but obviously this is not possible within the scope of one lifetime. Instead we have literary examples that many hundreds of thousands of people have identified as to some extent articulating their own concerns and struggles. Both Freud and Jung found the method to have its uses, as did Bruno Bettelheim, Joseph Campbell, Robert Bly and others.

More important than this – for our purposes here – is that literature shows the stages in a *dynamic* fashion. We are able to observe characters moving through the stages in a way that would be almost impossible to record in real life. In the real world we can know only a few people intimately, and some of them may take a whole lifetime to move through the stages before we can begin to assess their progress. Literature does not confine us in this way – which is another reason it is so useful. It can show several characters developing, contrasting each other and revealing similarities that help us to understand the author's vision. This is, in part, why literature was so important to ancient civilizations such as the Greeks, because it presented a synthesis from which they (and we) could learn more about what it means to be human.

The choice of literature that is part of the western canon is not accidental either. Literature survives only if it feels true. Literature that doesn't express something that the readers can identify as accurate and wise about human nature tends to be forgotten quickly. Literary works can get lost in other ways too, of course, but it's worth considering that the stories that survive, that get told again and again with real pleasure, are preserved and valued because they express something that each successive generation recognizes as valuable and worthy of preservation. Wisdom is a good word for it.

In order to understand the dynamic nature of this way of looking at life we have to plunge into a select few of the accepted masterpieces of Western literature · in some detail. If you do not care for this you may wish to by-pass this section all together, in which case you should proceed to Chapter Eighteen: What the Literature Has Shown.

The idea of life's formative stages being reflected in literature is not new. Joseph Campbell discussed them throughout his very prolific life as a scholar and researcher. In *The Power of Myth* talks, recorded and rebroadcast widely on PBS, he quotes Nietzsche as stating that man goes through three stages: the first is the Camel, when we take in information and knowledge. The second is when the Camel goes into the desert and tries to throw off the burden that's been laid on him, and in doing so he becomes the Lion; the heavier the burden, the stronger the emerging Lion. The Lion has a task, however, and that is to kill a dragon called "Thou shalt." When this happens, the Lion becomes a child, living authentically from its own center.

Campbell used this example as an instance that seemed to sum up the myths of many cultures. I'd observe here that the Camel could well be an image of the Innocent and Orphan, and that the departure for the desert and Lion-hood is analogous to the Pilgrim and Warrior-Lover stages. The rebirth, or emergence as a child, reminds us of Monarch status, not because the Monarch is helpless, but because the Monarch has to act from direct motives, unclouded by distractions. Like a child, a Monarch does best when he or she does not have a prior agenda or prejudice, and the Monarch has to let meaning come of its own accord rather than straining to squeeze a meaningful life out of circumstances. "Thou shalt" is the weight of orthodoxy that threatens us all. Conform and be an Orphan – and you risk throwing away your own real genius in the process.

Campbell uses Nietzsche as a way of saying that the world's mythologies shared certain attributes. In this he is fully in tune with Jung's concept of the Collective Unconscious. Meanwhile, as we've seen, Jung's associate John Weir Perry demonstrated that rituals of kingship across the world were remarkably similar, and they seemed to be an acting out of psychic processes that are inherent, inborn in human beings.

Other approaches have also proved fruitful. Twenty years ago Jean Shinoda Bolen suggested most persuasively that the Greek and Roman gods and goddesses provided entertaining stories that were also instructive character studies. From them the ancients learned about how people tend to act in relation to each other. It seems unlikely that the ancient gods were seen as role models to be emulated, which is what we tend to see in Christianity, Judaism, and Islam, if only because the Olympian gods and goddesses behaved in such outrageous and extreme fashions that it would be absurd to see them as guides to how mortals should behave. Zeus' compulsive sexual exploits while disguised as all sorts of unusual animals tell us a great deal more about the nature of the sex drive than about morality, for example. The gods and goddesses provided a language that the ancients could use in order to discuss very human situations, and that dysfunctional family on mount Olympus, riddled with incest and intrigues, served perhaps in a way that daytime talk shows do for us presently. We can turn on our TVs and see extreme and bizarre behaviors, witness shocking confessions, and perhaps as a result comprehend the strangeness of the psyche more fully. We may find ourselves discussing the latest Oprah show on child abuse, and as a result we are all able to consider a topic that had been hitherto taboo. Suddenly we have a safe way of addressing puzzling or troubling situations without having to share the personal details of our lives. It gives us a place from which to begin the conversations we need to have. And thus the silence is broken and our awareness grows. The exploits of those amoral and devious immortals of Greek legend functioned in roughly the same way.

And yet the Greeks knew a great deal more than this about the psyche and about the healing power of stories. The plays that were staged at the great theater of Epidaurus and elsewhere were not just entertainments, but part of religious festivities that citizens were obliged to attend. They were very often regarded as educational, concerning the nature of human drives and behaviors.

To see how this works, let us start with two of the most famous of the ancient Greek tales. One we've already mentioned, *The Odyssey*, which dates to about the ninth century before Christ; and we'll also look at its partner-piece *The Iliad*.

These tales have had a huge readership, and as a result have been influential in ways that run so deep we can hardly assess them. *The Iliad* tells the tale of the siege of Troy and in it we see many examples of so-called heroes who are anything but good role models. In fact they're not really Warriors at all in the sense we have been considering. Achilles behaves like the worst kind of over-paid sports star, prima donna, and diva rolled into one. He sulks and will not fight. He does not care about any of the principles that have been used as reasons for the war's continuance. He cares only that his battle loot has been taken from him, particularly a slave-girl, although later he does show courage in facing his death rather than living a long life without glory. The Greeks generally squabble and plot and behave poorly. These are examples of supposed heroes who do not always embody the highest ideals of the warrior, and who find themselves engaged in a struggle they're all thoroughly fed up with pursuing. Even Menelaus, who is supposed to be besieging Troy in order to get his wife Helen back, doesn't seem to care about her very much. He's hardly a Warrior or a Lover. Worse still, the victorious strategy of the wooden horse is, after all, a fairly disgraceful trick that allows sleeping Trojans to be butchered. This is not exactly heroism.

Of course the poem is not quite as bleak as I am making out. Homer constructs this background deliberately so that he can show how his characters change. Achilles does finally come out of his wounded-ego sulks when his friend Patroclus is killed. Enraged, he then tracks down and kills Hector even though he knows from a prophecy that in doing so his own life will be cut short. Is this righteous rage, or true loyalty, or just revenge? Hector, for his part, is possibly the most gracious of all the Trojan fighters – the scene with his wife and son is extraordinarily moving – and he makes it quite clear that he is fighting for them, for Troy, and out of loyalty to his king, and that he thoroughly expects to die. He is cheerful, even though he does not really support the grounds upon which the war is being fought or expect that much good can come of it. It's ironic that the finest figure in the conflict – one who really seems to be a true Warrior-Lover – is the one who is both doomed and on the losing side.

When Hector's father Priam comes, in disguise, through the Greek lines to Achilles' tent to beg for the return of his son's body, and he meets Achilles who is still mourning his dead friend Patroclus, we have one of the most poignant moments in the poem. The two mourners weep together, no longer Greek and Trojan, but fellow sufferers facing loss. By giving us these scenes Homer is asking us to consider what the conduct of a hero should be. Is it Achilles' passionate attachment to a personal friend? Is it Hector's sense of duty even to a tainted cause? Or is it, in fact, Priam's action in risking death by begging for his son's body and forgiving the man who killed him? The religious rites and moral obligations are important to Priam, and so are the personal yearnings for a proper burial for his son. Certainly Achilles' ego-based anger is melted into compassion by this meeting. Perhaps Homer is suggesting that the true hero needs to make the transition from selfish anger to humility, and we can see that this is closely tied to what we have been observing in the Warrior-Lover archetype.

It would not be going too far to say that Achilles arrives at Troy as a Pilgrim, but one who seeks personal glory rather than truth, and that places him perilously close to slipping into the role of the Orphan – one who has just come along for the gain. He is, in fact, a fairly typical example of many young fighters, even to this day. When he goes out to avenge Patroclus his actions – and his loyalty to his dead friend – cause him to display Warrior attributes, and also to question what their value is. When he recognizes that it is not Hector who is at fault for his pain, but the whole situation, then he can understand the pain of Hector's father, and grow in spiritual stature. He can leave anger, revenge, and ego-based destruction – his desire that Hector's body shall be disgraced and desecrated – and see that Hector's soul requires certain rituals, and that the gods have to be respected. It's a major shift, and brings him away from the ego and into something very close to real Warrior-Lover status. He seems to learn about compassion for the first time. Achilles has met his opposite, Hector, has killed him – and in the process recognizes that he is just like his enemy. He is, at this point, a Warrior-Lover facing the certain knowledge of his own expendability, and of the limits of war. Homer has deflated the conventional idea of the hero as ever-victorious bruiser, and has given us instead a more subtle image, one that is remarkably similar to the fullest expression of the Warrior-Lover.

The *Odyssey* continues this discussion and provides some of the answers to the problem of what a hero should be, yet it does so in a different way, since in it we see all six stages enacted, in order.

The *Odyssey* is obviously a story in which the hero wanders as a Pilgrim – or something like it. Odysseus is on his way home from Troy, and it takes him a number of years as various adventures detain him. He has been, already, a successful fighter at the siege of Troy, but perhaps now he needs to learn something different so he can return home and be a successful leader during peacetime. This would seem to define the poem as a discussion of the stages of Warrior and (possibly) Monarch. I'd argue that we have before us a careful assessment of much more than this.

The poem opens with Odysseus as Calypso's captive. He has been stuck on her island for seven years as her lover whom she will not allow to leave. Calypso offers him a deal that seems too good to be true – marry her, and become a king, and also a demi-god. He could have it all, through no real effort of his own, just because someone loves and idolizes him. Fortunately, he has the sense to reject this offer. After all, he's already married, so he'd have to break his vow, abandon his wife and son, and betray the trust of his men who rely on him to get them back to Ithaca. We can, any of us, get ahead fast if we choose to betray our allegiances and act immorally.

This is a highly dramatic place at which to start the story. Not only does Homer plunge us into the middle of the action, but he does so in order to show Odysseus at a point of moral decision. Odysseus appears before us as a man who is not going to take the easy road to kingship. His rejection of Calypso (and later he'll have to reject Circe and leave Nausicaa, who certainly loves him) allows us to see him as a man who has personal attachments that he values, and that perhaps this is the time when he discovers just how much he does value them. He's an Orphan, looking for his true home, but when he chooses to reject Calypso's offer – which would be a sort of adoption if only he complies with her wishes – he steps forward and refuses to slip back to passive Orphan status. He discovers he is a Pilgrim who has more values than those of the "Heroes" he has been campaigning with. Until now he has been, in fact, a mercenary, out for loot and fame. He is not an authentic Warrior-Lover at all because he has not yet discovered what it is he wants to fight for beyond self-gratification. Odysseus, in rejecting the temptation of Calypso, is just beginning to define his beliefs, to seek out what he does value. And it is this exploration of authentic values that is embedded in all the adventures he has before he arrives back at Ithaca.

As if to make the point even clearer, Book II opens with Odysseus' son, Telemachus. Telemachus is having a terrible time dealing with the men who are courting his mother Penelope and who try to convince her that Odysseus is dead long since. Telemachus is the helpless Innocent, supported by his mother, although she's under siege herself. Telemachus is forced to get advice, so he leaves Ithaca, effectively an Orphan already, and travels to talk to Nestor. He then voyages on to seek the advice of Menelaus. He is, in effect, an Orphan who is becoming a Pilgrim as he tries out different mentors. In a few short sections we see him rise to the same level as his father.

The action now goes back to Odysseus who has been released by Calypso and we see him as he tells his tale to Nausicaa and her parents, the tale being a flashback that lasts from Book IV to Book XII, which brings him back to his description of the Calypso episode. He tells a tale of adventures, all of which show him repeatedly rejecting what he sees as unsuitable options – and this places him at Pilgrim level. In fact the story is highly detailed about the ways a man like Odysseus can be derailed from his tasks as a Pilgrim. First of all he must reject the temptation to forget his situation. The Lotus Eaters offer oblivion in narcotic relaxation, which Odysseus refuses even though some of his crew succumb. Next he encounters the Cyclops, and he must use cunning to get the Cyclops drunk, blind him, and escape. A second narcotic (wine) has to be used, wisely in this case. Unfortunately, Odysseus' ego gets in the way, as he insists on triumphing over the Cyclops by taunting him. This flash of pride earns him the anger of Poseidon, the god of the ocean. The Cyclops may have been blinded, but Odysseus' pride has made him blind to consequences. For the Pilgrim the ego and personal pride can often be the source of trouble. Odysseus may have escaped the Cyclops, but he still lost several men in the process, and he really has nothing to be proud of.

As we can see around us every day, people who lose their way in life quite often resort to self-medication, and sometimes that addiction or dependence helps to prevent them moving forward as Pilgrims, as seekers after something of real value to live for. Instead they opt for dependence, and slip into Orphan mode. Odysseus has no problem rejecting this option; the one that is more dangerous to him is his ego-based pride. Today we can see, any time we choose to, those who have stopped growing spiritually and opted instead for the grooming of their public image. They have to prove to themselves each and every day how clever they are, and it keeps them stuck in a repeated cycle of behavior. Whether it's 'keeping up with the Joneses next door', compulsive shopping, or the over-reaching of the stock market inside traders, the effect is roughly the same. Outer success is valued over real wisdom or awareness.

Odysseus then meets Aeolus, the wind god, who helpfully agrees to confine all the bad winds to a bag, and sends the boats off with favorable breezes. Greedy crew members think the bag contains treasure and open it up, releasing the winds, and the fleet is blown back to Aeolus' island. Aeolus refuses to help again. One could see this as a splendid metaphor that shows how people will help us, but if they feel that we are misusing their help or using it merely to satisfy our own greed, they stop. This is in many ways what the Pilgrim has to learn – not to rely on unlimited handouts and not to inflate the ego.

In Book VII, the Laestrygonians seem to have a perfect harbor, and a delightful island. But it is a trap, for they are cannibals who greedily devour most of the sailors. Aeolus and the Laestrygonians are perhaps opposite images that suggest we should control our greed and suspicion, and yet be suspicious because others will try to destroy us to serve their own greed. Balance seems to be the issue. Each of us will encounter the greed of others who will try to exploit us, and we'll also have to be aware of our own greed as we may try to take advantage of those who are friendly to us. The Pilgrim may be a person who feels self-important, on a mission, but that does not permit him to misuse others, and neither should he allow himself to be misused. A man I worked with exemplified this almost perfectly. Ambitious to get ahead in his chosen career he seemed oblivious to his employer's tendency to squeeze more work out of him while all the time saying he was 'building his reputation'. In his personal life he was living with a young woman who seemed to love him, but for whom he felt only physical attraction, he said. He saw her as convenient since she accepted the long hours he worked for his 'career' and she paid her half of the mortgage. This Pilgrim's selfishness had to be brought under control and understood before any real progress could occur.

So far Odysseus the Pilgrim has rejected several short cuts to what seems like fulfillment. He has rejected narcotic amnesia, he has had to learn about greed, and he has refused the bribery of power and sex. This theme is now about to be developed more fully.

In Book VIII he meets Circe, who raises the issue of sex and subjection. Now we already know that Odysseus will later learn more about this from Calypso, which adds poignancy to the fate of Odysseus' men, who are turned into animals (therefore they are less able to be moral) as a result of Circe's seduction. Circe either dominates and degrades, or is dominated – which Odysseus achieves with the help of the white flower moly. There is no such thing as equality in such a relationship. Sex is power, and Odysseus gains the upper hand. Fortunately he has the sense to see that this is not a healthy relationship.

Leaving Circe, Odysseus now descends into the underworld, where he meets Tiresias. Tiresias has the distinction of having been a man who was then turned into a woman, and who also has the gift of prophecy. As a balance between male and female, he represents, perhaps, the balance of awareness that Odysseus has to learn. Significantly it is the spirit of his mother that Odysseus meets during this episode. Odysseus seems, as a man who has been in a predominantly male environment, to be getting an education as to what relationships with women could be like, and how he can achieve some sort of balance.

He gets a chance to explore this further when he has to steer the course between Scylla and Charybdis – on the one side the dangerous rocks which could be seen as a male phallic symbol, and on the other a whirlpool which could be interpreted as a female vaginal symbol. Steering too close to either ensures destruction. Interestingly, Scylla is actually a female monster with twelve feet and six heads, who sits on the dangerous rocks, while Charybdis is a male monster who lives under a fig tree and swallows the waters of the sea three times each day and three times vomits them up again. This male/female reversal is suggestive of the whole discussion of male and female power balances which the poem examines.

If Circe's actions are about sexual domination and humiliation – she seeks to control and winds up having to surrender – and the encounter with Calypso is about power and refusing to be sexually manipulated, then the Scylla and Charybdis episode has similar overtones of the male/female roles and how destructive each extreme can be.

As if on cue, following this, Odysseus hears the Siren's song. The rest of the crew have sealed their ears with wax, but Odysseus, with open ears, has had the sense to have himself tied to the ship's mast. Again, the temptation is obviously sexual. What distinguishes this episode is that Odysseus knows about it in advance; he knows who he is and that he's susceptible. He is not merely a thrill-Pilgrim looking for another experience to rack up; he wants to know his limits, and he wants to be prudent. He recognizes that there are some temptations that are too strong for him to resist. This is a more personal and harrowing test. It does not leave us, as readers, with a smug sense of, "I could have beaten that one." Instead, it shows us that we are not as strong as we think, and we need to take steps to guard ourselves. Odysseus is testing his personal limits, recognizing them in the same way as the Warrior-Lover archetype is called upon to face his own limitations of courage. Indeed, in visiting the land of death with Tiresias, Odysseus has already faced one aspect of personal his limits, and the inevitability of death.

But there is more testing to come: the dangers of hubris are once again at the center of the next episode, where the sailors make landfall and see some fat cattle. They kill and eat the cattle, not waiting to find out to whom they belong, and they learn too late that these are the sacred cattle of Helios and they have violated a dreadful taboo. The sailors, like so many people, seem to think they can help themselves to whatever they wish, since they've been through so much. Perhaps we could paraphrase this as the sort of hardship that causes the sufferer to feel entitled, whereas all that any suffering really does is give us the chance to become wiser. Our past sufferings do not entitle us to anything, and certainly not to be-coming greedy.

I can recall a woman in one of my classes who used to want to talk about her disastrous life, and no matter what was being discussed periodically would announce, "I've been through all that; you ought to listen to me." Eventually, I had to tell her that her experiences might well have been extraordinary, but that did not entitle her to hijack the class discussion and put herself center stage. Wis-dom we would listen to, but not just another tale of woe. Odysseus' men behave exactly like any bunch of disreputable sailors arriving in port after a difficult voy-age – they think the normal rules don't apply to them and that someone, some-where, owes them something. This false sense of entitlement acts as an excuse for greed, and does not allow them to behave decently or access their wisdom. Homer's sense of the psychology of traumatized individuals is eerily accurate, and he makes it clear that Odysseus has to move beyond, and stay beyond, this childish motivation.

Odysseus the Pilgrim has learned about himself, and what he values. The episodes he undergoes are the lessons he has to learn in order to become a true Warrior-Lover and not just the cunning fighter he was before. Each episode also offers him the chance to slip back, into a passive mode, which is why it is impor-tant that he should reject each one in full awareness.

If we need further evidence of this, we could look at the fact that Odysseus is relating the whole tale to Nausicaa and her father. Odysseus could have wooed Nausicaa, intending to deceive her. Instead he asks for her help, respects her, and she in turn gets her father to help him. Without this help, Odysseus cannot get home again. As a seasoned Pilgrim he knows when to ask for help, and as an emerging Warrior-Lover he knows now when to control his behavior. This is an important lesson which has echoed throughout the epic, made all the more obvi-ous because the original Trojan war was fought over the abduction of Helen, and it is therefore a tale that again and again refers back to how men see themselves and how they treat women. For the first time in this tale Odysseus treats a woman, Nausicaa, decently. This is vital, since he will soon return to Ithaca and to the woman he left so many years earlier in order to pursue war, the warrior's fame, and loot – which would certainly have included slave girls for his pleasure. In fact, if we think back to the opening of the *Iliad*, the action is set in motion precisely because Achilles is upset that his captured slave girl has been taken from him. Women were merely sex objects to these Greek fighters.

We can therefore see Odysseus at this point returning home with a new ap-preciation of Penelope and his son Telemachus. In treating Nausicaa well he is able to establish the balance of male/female attributes that will be put to the test in Ithaca when he reunites with Penelope. He is prepared for the challenges of the Monarch.

When he arrives in Ithaca, he is ready to be a fighter, but he has nothing to fight with and no followers. He must, therefore, curb his anger and use his mind. He is recognized by his old nurse and by his old dog. These two figures have no hesitation in seeing that this bearded and sun-blasted stranger is their old master, and this in itself conveys some important information. For both of them knew Odysseus in specific ways. The nurse knew him from birth and from well before he could talk. We could say that she knew him in his pre-verbal innocence, from the stage before life got complicated, and her recognition is proof that this nature is essentially unchanged. The Innocent in him, that fountain of energy and creativity, has not been damaged in all his time away. The old dog therefore acts upon the plot in a similar way. The dog knows the true inner, non-verbal part of Odysseus. Both the nurse and the dog are used here to signal that the hero remembers his emotional attachments in Ithaca and also that he is unaltered in spirit. They remind us that his strength comes to a great extent from his ability to remain in contact with who he most truly is. It's a powerful life lesson for anyone.

These two images of fidelity are touching but they are hardly of military worth. So Odysseus uses his cunning to set a trap for the suitors. He asks Penelope to require them to move the royal bed (which has been made from a rooted tree, around which the house was built) and she also requests that they string Odysseus' bow and shoot an arrow through the loops on the top of a row of ax-heads. These are feats of strength none of them can accomplish. They are also aspects of insider-knowledge. The suitors fail, of course, and Odysseus kills them all. Thus, the false lovers (who want Penelope's wealth) are vanquished by the real Warrior-Lover, who is fired by pride and righteous indignation. Odysseus becomes not just a Warrior, but also a judge – which elevates him to the level of Monarch. He is also, now, working with and reunited to the female part of himself, Penelope, whom he values fully perhaps for the first time. He has achieved the balance required of the Monarch pair.

There remains just one obstacle – which is that the families of the men Odysseus has killed are mightily upset. This is solved when Odysseus' father, Laertes, kills the father of the leader of the dead suitors for Penelope's hand, and the opposing army is defeated. This fits exactly with the schema we've been discussing, because Odysseus is able to work with his father to regain the old man's lost honor, and the old man is, by his efforts, able to stop the revengers and so help his son. Athena then appears and guarantees peace. Odysseus has rescued his old father, and his father in turn rescues him. We sense that a deeper healing has happened here, which is being gestured at by the events, and surely there is in this episode a sense of redemption for the older man who is now able to show Odysseus his love, his trust, and his fearlessness. It's hard to tell who is helping whom – and that, really, is exactly what the Magician stage is all about. Great things are achieved, and it is not the triumph of any one person. Athena completes the magic.

Athena, we may recall, is a goddess usually shown clad in armor. She was not born, but sprang fully formed from Zeus's head. She is therefore a fitting image of the balance of male and female attributes we've seen illustrated as a major theme in the poem. Since she protects Odysseus and advises his son Telemachus we can see her as a way in which the story is thematically unified as male and female power, Warrior and Lover, King and Queen, come into balance.

I've repeated the plot here at length because I think it shows us more than just a string of bizarre and entertaining adventures. It shows us a program of personal development that we can learn from if we choose. In the Greek world the emphasis is certainly upon male development, and yet we cannot see this is an exclusively male application. The female figures are powerful. Calypso – the woman who wants to buy loyalty – cannot manage to do so. She is contrasted with Nausicaa, who works with her parents to help Odysseus – and does not seek to imprison him. Another comparison exists when we see Circe as the female who degrades men, reducing them to beasts since she stands in contrast to Penelope the faithful wife who uses her cunning to buy time, but knows where her loyalty lies. Penelope is more than a match for the siege of the suitors, promising that she will choose a husband when her weaving is complete, and then unstitching it each night so it never progresses. It's not just coincidence that the Siege of Troy (brought about by the abduction of Helen) is mirrored by the siege of Penelope, who manages to fight her suitors off far more effectively than the passive Helen ever did. The schema for women's development is less clear than for Odysseus, but Homer seems to see it as roughly the same. Penelope has used what power she has with courage and determination, valuing her marriage vows and never giving in to despair. We see less of her, yet it is clear she has been a quiet Warrior-Lover all these years.

Only when Odysseus and Penelope are reunited as husband and wife can the Monarch status become truly complete. The Monarch is both fighter and patient lover, man and woman, a fusion of opposites that have been balanced. We know that Penelope can run a kingdom by herself – she's managed to do so for twenty years. She is close to being a balanced Monarch in herself, but she needs Odysseus' help to get rid of the suitors, just as he needs her cooperation to achieve the same task. The story of Odysseus can be seen, therefore, as a template of how we develop, and the miracle of the story is that it does not conceive of human development as either a straight line or as being inevitable upon completion of a certain number of years. The man who brought defeat to Troy still has a lot to learn before he can return home and become a successful Ruler.

If we go into detail here we do so because this important aspect of the poem can best be understood in this way, and it is a line of inquiry that has often been ignored by others. For example, Tennyson's poem 'Ulysses' focuses on the contrast between the rambunctious adventurer, who is Odysseus in old age, and his more plodding son Telemachus. While Tennyson makes some interesting observations about how demanding and even boring Kingship is, and therefore how frustrated the old campaigner has become, this is not even close to considering the same ground that Homer covers. Ulysses emerges as an irascible old pirate.

In Homer we see every stage from Innocent to Magician reflected in the drama of Telemachus, Penelope, and Odysseus, combined. The poem is many things, yet as we've seen it is a discussion of how a man can make the transition from the ways of war to the ways of peace – and to do so he has to learn about the strength in a united male and female pairing. For peace to be achieved we have to have Odysseus and Penelope working harmoniously together. That's when the gods bless the situation.

From Homer we now skip forward several centuries to Sophocles (496-406 BC), possibly the most famous playwright of his age. Almost everyone has heard about Oedipus and we'll be looking at the two plays that make up his story, *Oedipus the King* and *Oedipus at Colonus*.

The story of Oedipus deserves to be repeated in detail if we are to make sense of the real subtlety of this tale. I retell it here because many of us are not as familiar with the details of the plot line as we might wish.

Oedipus' father is a king who hears a prophecy that his son will kill him and marry his mother. Horrified, the king takes the child, puts an iron rivet through one ankle, and tells a soldier to leave the child on a hillside to die. The young Oedipus is therefore a splendid example of the unprotected Innocent. The soldier feels pity and gives the child to a shepherd in a far country. Oedipus grows up, a happily adopted Orphan who knows nothing about his real parentage. At a certain point, he hears the prophecy that he will kill his father and marry his mother. Shocked, he does the only thing he can think of to avoid this – he runs away from home and becomes an Orphan in the truest sense. He wanders the world trying to plot his next move, as a Pilgrim might. As he is walking along a road one day, he encounters his real father, unknown to him, who is driving a chariot and who attempts to whip him out of the way. Enraged, the pseudo-Warrior mode appears and he kills his father and all the attendants. He feels he's a warrior who refuses to be a slave when the whole event seems to have more to do with a slighted ego.

He journeys further and meets the Sphinx who asks him a riddle. If he cannot answer correctly, he will die. The riddle is as follows: what walks on four legs in the morning, two in the afternoon, and three legs at night? The answer is a man, who crawls when a child, walks upright in adulthood, and uses a walking stick in old age. Even the riddle has to do with the life cycle and maturation process of the individual. Oedipus' intuition and intelligence allow him to see the riddle as a metaphor, and when he answers it correctly, the Sphinx disappears. He proves he isn't just a fighter, but he is insightful and intelligent too, and he can think in metaphors – which is what the play requires the audience to do, also.

When the citizens of Thebes discover that Oedipus has got rid of the Sphinx they are so grateful they make him their king – which is a job left vacant since Oedipus unknowingly killed the previous king, his father, on the road. He marries his mother, the widowed queen. In *Oedipus Rex* the drama centers upon Oedipus' attempt to remove a plague from the city by finding out what wrongful deed the gods are punishing. He becomes, in a sense, the detective of his own crime. Unfortunately Oedipus cannot face the truth when it emerges, and he blinds himself in self-condemning rage. For it is only when we can truly admit the way we may have felt about our parents at times, those desires to get rid of them, and the desire to be sexually valued by the opposite sex parent, that we can begin to understand the experience of childhood more fully. Oedipus has run away from one set of parents and is unaware of the identity of the biological set, so he has had no chance to examine this relationship first hand. What Oedipus discovers is that he may have reached what looks like Monarch status, but he has done so as a result of a crime, which stemmed from his ego. Did he have to *kill* the old king? His ego impulse of anger caused him to do so. He has risen to his political status as a Monarch without first having learned the discipline required of the Warrior-Lover, and so he can be seen to have inadvertently taken a short cut.

When Oedipus recognizes his crime he takes immediate action and blinds himself. He must now look within only, and give up the kingship. His wife/mother Jocasta kills herself, so she cannot grow in understanding. She may be seen to represent those people who cannot face the loss of public esteem, such as those who pose as Monarchs and underneath are passive Orphans. It is as if Sophocles says to us that there can be no short cuts to self-knowledge. Oedipus has to go back and re-learn the lessons he missed. Evicted from Thebes, he becomes an Orphan. His sons disown him, although his daughter Antigone stays with him as a guide and he is, to all intents and purposes, a ghastly parody of the Orphan, led around by his daughter who is also his incestuous sister.

Modern readers who encounter the play tend to be confused as to what it is saying, since Oedipus seems to be trapped by circumstances he does not control.

If we chose to see it in terms of the six stages we can re-assess it. It reveals itself as a cautionary tale about how anyone who attempts to skip over any of the vital developmental mileposts will be forced to return and relearn the lessons he needs to know, no matter what strange fate has been destined for him.

The second play of the series, *Oedipus at Colonus*, shows Oedipus still in this Orphan phase – which is now characterized by him refusing to acknowledge any culpability for what he did in killing his father and marrying his mother. It is all the fault of the gods, he claims. Typical rejecting Orphan that he is, he's always claiming victimhood. He's also very old and tired, and he's looking for a place to die – which means he has the temptation to slip to passive Orphan status rather than becoming a true Pilgrim.

The king of Thebes, Creon, now appears, wanting Oedipus to return since Oedipus is such bad luck in everyone's view that no one would dare attack a city he is attached to. Creon is so desperate for this "defense" of his city that he attempts to kidnap Oedipus and his daughters (Ismene has now joined Antigone). Oedipus resists this forced adoption and is aided by Theseus, the king of Athens, who becomes a protector of sorts. When this happens we could say that Oedipus has now been adopted by a benign figure. He tells Theseus he wishes to stop wandering and give the gift of his body to Athens to help protect it, which is the same reason Creon had given for wanting Oedipus back in Thebes. Oedipus also rejects a request from his own son, Polynices, to return to Thebes – another sort of bogus re-adoption – because Polynices has heard the oracle's declaration that whichever side Oedipus allies with will win the struggle for the throne. We could claim that the old blind man, in his outrage at being exiled, rejected and disgraced by his sons, is also upholding a moral point. Here he is like a Pilgrim, who refuses to make a morally shabby compromise for the sake of personal comfort. In fact, if he accepts any of the offered homes he must, inevitably, hurt the prospects of those he has turned down, and so the only truly moral choice is to refuse them all.

As he rejects his sons and their ethically shifty conduct his emerging courage allows him to take on the role of a moral Warrior. He is, in addition, ready to accept the oracle at this point, seeing his place in the divine order. You will remember that it was his father's non-acceptance of the oracle (it had told him that his son would kill him) that led to the whole story being set in motion. This acceptance of the situation, of what is, allows the wandering Oedipus to find his place in the universe.

Now, as the play draws to its climax and the storm clouds roll in, Oedipus knows he must die and that the gods are waiting for him. He accepts the demands of the gods and does not reject them or blame them. He does not weep or sorrow for his wrongs. He seems to accept that the will of the gods is their will, and it is not to be fought against. He takes charge of what he has to do to die – to meet his fate appropriately. Even though blind, he knows where he must go in the sacred grove, and he sends everyone away. He makes Theseus promise not to reveal the site of his grave, and he states that this grave will now protect Athens. In many ways he is Theseus' equal at this point. Symbolically we see this when he gives orders to the king.

In the final section of the play, a messenger reports that the earth has swallowed up Oedipus. The gods have claimed him, and Athens is now blessed.

The play allows us to see the spiritual rehabilitation of Oedipus until, in death, his grave becomes a magical defense for a city and he achieves Magician status. We may not necessarily agree with the ancient Greeks' ideas about the gods, but we can see that the Oedipus of *Oedipus Rex* is a king who originally reaches power through no real action of his own, but believes it is all his own doing. His ego deceives him. Even his self-blinding is an ego-based punishment. This is the "everything's my fault" attitude, which is only a mirror image of what Oedipus expresses later, which is "nothing is my fault." Neither is realistic; both are aspects of the unbalanced incarnations of the Orphan. Yet he finds his way back, in this drama, not to actual kingship, but to an active moral sense in which he can point out the false kingship aspirations of his sons and of Creon, all of whom care only about power and not about any higher purpose. Notice how Theseus, the just King of Athens, prevents Creon from kidnapping Oedipus and his daughters. Theseus doesn't want Oedipus to stay (he is bad luck, supposedly), but he will not allow injustice, even if it might benefit himself in the short term.

Now, having seen the overall shape of the drama we need to look closer. Oedipus, in seeing his sons and Creon's offers as insincere, takes an important step forward. He castigates his sons for their failure to be humane to him because that goes against all standards of what is civilized. He rejects the offered 'adoption,' and as he does so, he shrugs off the offer of Orphan status, moves through Pilgrim status (including the recognition of moral values he must uphold) and attaches himself, militantly, to Athens as a Warrior and Lover of decency. For Theseus is decent, God-fearing and morally triumphant.

In rejecting his sons, Oedipus refuses to validate the male lust for power of potential tyrants, and at the same time revalues the nurturing and caring attributes of his daughters. In balancing the male and female aspects of his life Oedipus can be seen achieving the Monarch's balance. The drama shows us just how rapidly we can move through the stages from Orphan to Monarch when we are truly ready, and how even in death we can move to Magician stage, making our ending a gift to all.

It's a complex and fascinating story. In so many ways, it is part of our Western Civilization. It certainly discusses what a good king is, and how that figure should act. In so doing, it shows us the way we can all develop to full awareness, no matter how cataclysmic our lives may have been. And arriving at awareness is something the Greeks seem to hold in very high esteem. Oedipus could, at any point, just take the easy way out. He could give in to Creon, or one of his sons, and become a passive Orphan figure, a person who clings to victimhood. The same temptation is waiting for any of us, today. We could give up trying in our work, our relationships, with our children, with our own souls. Think of those people who seem to be holding onto a job until they can draw retirement pay, when they can, finally, do nothing at all. Or consider those men who have stronger relationships with their cars, their ball game, and their beer than they do with any person. These are the people who seem to have given up on any sense of spiritual richness, let alone of personal growth. The drama of Oedipus lets us know that even if we're old and blind and disgraced we still have important work we can do for our souls.

Perhaps even more important for us today is that the drama of Oedipus tells us that in the serious business of spiritual growth there can be no easy promotions. Oedipus is a little like someone who is born into a highly privileged situation and whose life seems to be blessed. Such people have a temptation – which is to believe that they created their luck because of their sheer merit. Indeed, we've seen enough wealthy celebrities behaving badly to know that good fortune is not the same as being a good and moral person. Sophocles' play shows us that real spiritual growth has nothing much to do with temporal power, and that our position in the world can blind us to our deficiencies.

Let us take a look now at another major figure in Greek drama and myth, Orestes. Aeschylus' trilogy *Oresteia* (458 BC) is the single most complete treatment in drama of the long complex story of the House of Atreus, which is a list of horrors by anyone's standards. It's a tale of fratricide, seduction, rape, incest, murder, and it shows us just how confused a society can become when the moral order is based simply upon revenge.

And this brings us to Orestes, who is certainly born into a morally chaotic world. He is quickly Orphaned (even before his father is dead, his sister Elektra has seen trouble brewing, and whisked him away) and is attached to Strophius and his son, Pylades, as a result. Perhaps only an Orphan can attach so strongly, since Pylades will stay with him throughout. When Orestes' father is murdered, Apollo tells him he has to kill the murderer – his mother. The Orphan is catapulted into an action he would rather not have to do. He is, one may say, forced to do the actions normally required of a Warrior, but questioning why he has to.

In Euripides' version of the story, Orestes seems to go through the six stages with some exactitude, although he starts as a somewhat incompetent murderer.

The play opens with Orestes recovering from a bout of madness induced by what he has done.

"It is a disease called knowledge. I know what I've done is a crime. ... I'm an outcast," he declares in anguish.

He's a passive Orphan and is not prepared to see events as if he were an active agent in any of them. When his grandfather Tyndareus appears, he blames *him* for the situation, then, seconds later, he blames Apollo.

"When I killed my mother, I was obeying Apollo."

He then asks Menelaus to save him, playing on the connection that his father risked his life for Menelaus at Troy, so he is therefore duty bound to save his, Orestes', life. Even as he says it, he doesn't like his arguments, admitting in an aside: "What a sad man I am to be reduced to this ploy!" True to his Orphan status, he looks for others to save him. Just at this point, his friend Pylades appears – his father has disowned him for helping Orestes in killing his mother. Orestes, Pylades, and Electra (Orestes' older sister) are all Orphans together, now, and they prepare for the verdict of the citizens. They expect death. Orestes argues his case to the citizens, but they do not seem impressed.

Returning home, they prepare for death; they are Orphans with nowhere left to go. Then Pylades comes up with a plan. If they kill Helen, Menelaus' wife who is in the house, then the angry citizens will praise them for killing the person who started the Trojan war that robbed them of their sons. Then, if the trio can hold Menelaus' daughter, Hermione, hostage, they can force Menelaus to take them all away to safety. The generation of a plan seems to mark a turning point for them all. They no longer act like victims, and their efforts to save themselves can be seen as a re-valuing of their lives and direction. Symbolically Orestes remembers who he is:

"I am the son of Agamemnon, a king who ruled Greece by consent, not force – the power he earned was something like a god's."

The image of the complete Monarch, ruling by consent, not force, inspires him to take action, working cooperatively with his co-plotters. This sense of morality and personal values is what the Pilgrim achieves, and acting upon these values is the province of the Warrior. Notice that he states, "I am..." The statement is so much stronger than his previous, ego-centered "I" statements. "I'm an outcast" is a statement about what others have done to him, whereas this is a proclamation that reaches back into the past for inspiration to act in the present. He connects to who he is in the deepest sense of where he has come from, and so he can be seen healing the fractured relationship with the parents in his chaotic life. He accepts the good aspects of his lineage, not the confused and murderous parts. This is important, because Agamemnon did sacrifice his daughter Iphigenia to the gods in order to gain a favorable wind for the voyage to Troy, and that's what led to his own murder. It's difficult to draw a modern comparison so that we can understand Orestes' problem, but one that springs to mind is the work that must be done by those children who have parents in jail, or by those people who were sexually molested by a parent. One has to make peace with one's history and take the good while not being overwhelmed by the bad. Orestes does exactly that.

Newly energized, Orestes is no longer an Orphan, but is instead a determined Warrior, one who can work with Pylades and Electra. As one who fights for what he believes and for the preservation of his friends he can be seen as moving into Warrior-Lover status. The trio captures and wounds Helen (who is spirited away by Apollo) and holds Hermione hostage. Orestes then captures and cross-examines one of Helen's slaves who is attempting to flee, and the man's craven replies serve only to emphasize Orestes' change. He is no slave; he is his own man, and that changes everything.

Euripides ends the play by having Apollo descend from the clouds, which some have described as the ultimate contrived ending. Apollo then gives Electra to Pylades to marry and Hermione to Orestes. Helen is not dead, but translated into a star, and Menelaus has to fall in with all this. Orestes will take over Mycenae, after a year of exile and a trial to exonerate him. We expect that he will remember his father's example and be an effective king, a true Monarch. In all this, Menelaus is seen as blustering and useless; he will not help his nephew, and will not speak for him to the citizens. The Menelaus who used family connections to wage the war against Troy won't do anything to help his nephew and niece. He's an example of a poor king and an ineffective man, while Helen appears as merely vain, lacking the courage to go to her sister's tomb, which is her sacred duty, because she fears the citizens may insult her. She is seen in sharp contrast to the determination of Elektra who is principled, brave, and thinks of others' welfare before her own. The sham king and queen are contrasted with the genuine qualities of the young plotters.

This play – this whole myth – is clearly about how we should act properly in a world beset with revenge and injustice. In it Orestes first moves from haunted, helpless Orphan to one who does try to state his own case – even if it is only in order to avoid responsibility in the eyes of the court. But it's not until he takes decisive action that the circumstances change. Until then he wanders from person to person, looking for help, blaming when he feels he can; switching between being an Orphan and a passive Pilgrim. He becomes a Warrior when he chooses a course of action. Helen, after all, was adulterous; and in Greek terms she deserves punishment. In a world that has an Antigone – who hangs herself rather than leave her brother unburied – or a Jocasta, who kills herself when she discovers her unintended crime – it is not too severe to assess Helen in this way. Helen is, in some ways, the passive Orphan who fails to be concerned by her own lack of a home, since she can usually fit in somewhere. She is also perhaps the passive Innocent who refuses to notice that anything is wrong. In fact Helen fails to be anything but an object, moving from one protector to the next and back again, without any moral discomfort. She is a figure who disgusts anyone who has a sense of right and wrong. By contrast, Orestes' madness exists *because* he has a moral dilemma to resolve; and he does resolve it.

Orestes' madness is in many ways a fitting image for the struggle the Pilgrim must go through in an attempt to make sense of the contradictory aspects of the world. It also suggests how exhausting such a struggle can be, and how willingly anyone would give it up if they could.

Euripides' play is elegant in another way, also. The warring brothers Thyestes and Atreus set all this chaos in motion generations earlier. Now the problem is solved by the brave, open actions of the adoptive brothers Orestes and Pylades. If the intervention of Apollo can be seen as the ultimate easy ending, yet it would also be worth considering that it is symbolic of what happens when people take bold risks for what they believe in – they align with the energy of the gods and miracles really can happen. This is in marked contrast to the machinations of the previous generations who tried shamelessly to manipulate the words and intentions of the oracle and of the gods, and succeeded only in creating mayhem.

In the play we see Orestes and Elektra, brother and sister, working together moving towards a version of the Monarch Pair. Elektra has already shown herself as a canny Orphan since it was she who made sure Orestes was taken to safety with King Strophius years before. Now we see her as critical of the shallow Helen, and brave in her support of Orestes, a Pilgrim after justice who is ready to become a Warrior. Helen's fickleness is in sharp contrast to Elektra's steadfast Warrior-Lover loyalty. Orestes works with Elektra and the balance of male and female elements seems to be honored as they do so. Since we already know that Orestes has been the resolute executioner of his mother, and yet is tormented by his conscience, we could say he already possesses the male and female attributes of decisiveness and compassion that must now be brought into balance as he becomes a true Warrior-Lover.

The final double marriage of Pylades and Elektra, Orestes and Hermione is not just sound political sense that can keep the peace, but it seems also to be based in them having achieved the qualities of the Monarch. Obviously Orestes can't marry his sister, yet the play has shown brother and sister (and Pylades) each able to work bravely and honor the other's abilities, which amounts to a convincing demonstration of their capacity to be part of a Monarch pairing, and therefore ready for the marriages Apollo proposes. This is not just a contrived ending but a resolution that requires us to see the symbolic growth of the characters towards maturity.

In other terms the ending works just as satisfactorily, too. The marriage of Orestes and Hermione may seem odd to our eyes, yet it is the ultimate political marriage. Orestes may wish to revenge himself on Menelaus – following the male principle of pride – but since he's married to that king's daughter his pride will necessarily be softened by political and family considerations. Hermione is therefore a central factor in him maintaining his balanced Monarch state. She will provide the feminine balance to him throughout their lives. There is every reason to believe they will be effective rulers together. Elektra and Pylades have, of course, already shown their qualities in the course of the play, growing through each stage, as we have seen, and so the audience would be able to identify their potential for right ruling. The stage of the Monarch has been achieved in each case. Better still is that in reaching this stage they have taken actions that Apollo approves of. In contributing his divine power he has raised the results of their actions to Magician level.

The road to moral competence, to effective and peaceful rule, again seems to be described in terms of the six stages we have been looking at.

This point is worth making in such detail because for the Greeks the story described the way in which a new moral and legal order emerged. Bolstered by Apollo, the new moral code ensured that the sort of feuding that had caused so much destruction in the past would now be held accountable to a higher sense of justice than simple revenge. Orestes, driven mad by his need to follow Apollo's instruction to kill his own mother, represents the inner crisis that the whole of his society needed to solve if it was to remain healthy itself. The old family vendetta always put family first, but, as we've seen, this code of conduct falls apart when one family member kills another. For the Greeks and for those who followed, this myth marked an important division between the old way of ruling and the new way. And what we see is that rulers have to grow into awareness and competence, and they do so by moving through the stages we've been discussing. This is the only way the chaos caused by the old law can be put right, and kept right, for the future. This is the new model. Wrongdoing must be punished, even if it is done by one's own parents. It's a code based on an abstract sense of justice rather than upon concrete family ties. This was a revolutionary moment in history. It's not surprising that the Greeks felt so strongly about this drama.

In Aeschylus' version, *The Eumenides*, the same considerations are seen in a slightly different form. In this drama it is Apollo who pleads for Orestes at his trial, when the judges' vote is tied, by saying:

I bade him avenge his father. I bade him, as a supplicant, seek my shrine. It was but just that the wife who slew the lord should die at her son's hands, that there be no dishonor to the holy tie of marriage, which Zeus and Hera instituted. Not justly do ye chase Orestes; let the goddess Pallas judge our strife.

It is Pallas Athena, the Warrior-virgin goddess, who decides the tied vote in favor of Orestes. She then has to appease the outraged Eumenides, who consider this new law-giving by the new gods as an affront to the "old" ways of the Titans. They are only able to relent when Athena gives them a sanctuary temple, acknowledging their claim in the new order of things.

I'd suggest that this discussion of what is right or not – the sense of outrage at killing a mother as opposed to the idea of justice – is at the center of the question of how to be a moral human being that both plays address. *The Eumenides* presents a view of morality in which family is sacred. Apollo states that laws need to be followed for the public good, and that it is our duty to be aware of this. This position is surely the one faced by any person aspiring to Monarch status: what do I feel like doing, and what am I moved to do by a higher sense of what is right? Sometimes even one's blood relatives commit crimes, and they need to be held accountable. The highest court anyone could stand before vindicates Orestes and peace is restored between the Olympians and the Eumenides.

As before, we notice that Orestes has been an Orphan, a Pilgrim (he goes to Delphi, for knowledge), a Warrior, and finally, in court, he is asked to account for his decisions. This allows him to make the next step: to become King, and use his new knowledge.

Why does all this matter? Because the clear hint in each of these plays is that the chaos of the old way of doing things can only be set right by those who have grown into meaningful understandings about what leadership might be. It's no longer enough for a person to be strong and ruthless to be accounted successful. And the new, higher, standard involves completing all six stages. Euripides and Aeschylus may not have divided the stages into the same categories we have been using here, yet they had a strong sense of what a leader needed to have achieved and seen on his way to the top, and the sequence in which he had to achieve them. Specifically, the point they seem to emphasize is that in order to become a true Monarch one has to confront and struggle with the accepted and 'parental' attitudes one will encounter. The struggle may be hard but it leads, ultimately, to a healing of the relationship with the troublesome parental history. If Homer seems to stress Odysseus' need during the Pilgrim stage to understand love and attachment, we could say that Euripides and Aeschylus seem to stress the need, at the Warrior-Lover stage, to re-adjust the relationship to the parent and the parental world, in order to create a harmonious future. Being right by the old standards has been shown to be inadequate. The Warrior is therefore a figure who has to be seen as growing into a far more constructive figure – the Warrior-Lover. The playwrights' visions are presented as a synthesis, of course, while the idea of the stages is an analytic one. Yet they cover the same ground.

These plays and poems survived because they spoke directly to the ancient Greeks, and to subsequent generations, about vital psychological processes we have to undergo on our path to full personal authenticity. They felt true then, and their great beauty is they still feel true today. All of us will reach a stage when we disagree with our parents' views. Sometimes this may be over trivial matters, and sometimes it may be because of profound differences. The 'Apollo' in each of us – the sense of what we see as absolutely right – will propel us into this conflict. If we choose to ignore it we could, in theory, become passive Orphan figures and accept the existing injustices. Unfortunately one cannot ignore the gods in Greek drama without paying a price, which could be a metaphor for the inner torments we face if we give up what we truly feel compelled to do. Orestes' struggle is at its most tortured when he is trying to keep everyone happy about what he's done – when he tries to explain to the citizens why he killed his mother on Apollo's orders. Perhaps from this we can see that none of us can do what we feel we have to without upsetting others, those whose judgments we fear. For example if a young woman decides to be a political performance artist then someone in the family or community is going to object. We can be sure of that! Sometimes that's good, since it will cause the individual to think about whether or not this is a good match for who she is. In the end, though, if we choose to live our version of our lives it is almost inevitable that such conflicts will occur, and in facing them we find out what our strengths may be.

Greek dramas were, in a sense, the psychology texts of their day, and they show with remarkable exactitude the notions of spiritual development we have discussed so far. They do so in terms of myths that are case-histories, showing what any of us can expect, in general forms, as we grow in spiritual awareness. Behind all the difficult names and obscure references they are identifiable as being about people remarkably similar to us, if we're prepared to look.

What is truly important for us is that each of these writers seems to be redefining what it means to be an evolved and aware human being. These heroes achieve peace, learn the skills necessary for maintaining peace, and in return the gods bless them. This, the writers seem to say, is the way forward. The old ways will just not serve anymore. Wars can bubble up at a moment's notice, but peace takes time and effort and awakened consciousness. Odysseus and Penelope, Achilles, Orestes and Elektra, and Oedipus – these are the great names of Greek drama that are still alive today. Their effect upon all subsequent literature has been huge, and they all demonstrate the six archetypal stages of development in action.

Notes

1. Bolen, Jean Shinoda. *Goddesses in Everywoman: Powerful Archetypes in Women's Lives*. New York: Harper, 2004. See also: Bolen, J. S. *Gods in Everyman*. New York: Harper, 1990. Ms. Bolen has several other titles that are to do with archetypes.

2. The *Iliad* addresses the Trojan conflict, while the *Odyssey* is about Odysseus' return from Troy, and so could be seen to be the sequel. Things are made complicated because it is possible that the poems were composed out of sequence; scholars also doubt that Homer was one poet, and suggest the poems were reworked over the ages. For our purposes we can use this information to read the poems as folk tales that examine important topics – demonstrating an integrity of thematic matter even if reworked by many hands.

3. Euripides *Orestes*, translated Andrew Wilson, available on www.users.globalnet. co.uk/~loxias/orestes.htm. This translation was used by the Foad Theatre Company, at the Square Theatre, Edinburgh, August 1993.

4. Aeschylus *The Eumenides*, from *The Drama: Its History, Literature and Influence on Civilization*, vol. ed. Alfred Bates. London: Historical Publishing Co., 1906 pp.78-104.

Chapter Thirteen

Literature from the Bible Onwards

The next major story to consider occurs about four hundred years later. It is the story of Jesus, as relayed in the Gospels. There is considerable variety in the Gospels but in the form that they have been handed down to us in the Bible we have a fairly coherent series of events describing his life. As we will see the Gospels, which have circulated for the best part of two thousand years, reflect the six stages of development and also deepen the discussion in several important ways.

The four Gospels agree that Jesus was born in a town that was not Mary and Joseph's home, and he arrives on the scene a little like Oedipus, already in danger. The story of the flight into Egypt certainly suggests the theme of Orphan, although it's not until the young Jesus stays behind at the Temple that we see him as the Orphan who is already aware of his future role. "Wist ye not that I must be about my Father's business?" (Luke 2.49) he says, when his parents return to collect him for the journey home.

It is not until Jesus goes out to meet John the Baptist that he genuinely leaves home, a Pilgrim looking for a mentor. John agrees to baptize him, but recognizes that Jesus is the one who is to come after him, "whose shoes I am not worthy to bear." (Matthew 3:11) In fact we would do well to pause here and consider Jesus' baptism by John, since it is most probably the gospel writers' way of signaling to us that Jesus is getting ready for the spiritual struggle ahead, rather than being washed clean of his past sins, or marking that he is joining a particular group. Jesus immediately goes into the desert for 40 days and nights. The baptism seems to mark the beginning of his life as a Pilgrim.

This idea of wandering in the wilderness seems to be a major component of many stories. It is a trial undertaken by the Buddha, by Moses and the Israelites, and by Mohammed; as such it represents a time of leaving one place that had been a home of sorts, and seeking a personal identity that results in a clear awareness of personal knowledge. So Buddha comes to a sense of his life mission, Moses is given the Ten Commandments, and Mohammed is told to write the Koran.

Jesus, in going into the desert, is doing the same thing. He becomes the Pilgrim tempted by the devil, and as he rejects each temptation, he gives a solid reason that counterbalances Satan's insinuations. As he rejects, he also makes clear his acceptance of an opposing view to that which Satan offers him. Asked to turn stones into bread since he is the Son of God, he replies, "It is written that man shall not live by bread alone, but by every word that proceedeth out of the mouth of God." (Matthew 4:4) The next temptation is to throw himself down from a high place, and Jesus replies, "It is written again, Thou shalt not tempt the Lord thy God" (Matthew 4:7) When Satan promises him riches and glory in return for worship, he replies, "It is written, thou shalt worship the Lord thy God, and Him only shalt thou serve." (Matthew 4:10)

In these three temptations we have, actually, a series of responses that amount to a spiritual credo every bit as strong as the Ten Commandments. To understand this we need to look closely at what he says. Jesus says first that 'bread' – the daily things of life, food – is not what is important; it is the spirit that must be looked after and fed. In a world of orthodox Jewish laws about what one could or could not eat this would be a startling thing to hear! He seems to be rejecting the strict laws of dietary restraints that are still so important within Judaism, as well as the 'bread' that symbolizes the concerns of ordinary life, suggesting instead that we re-evaluate our spiritual practices.

The second temptation concerns not tempting or testing God, and we could see this as a fairly uncomplicated statement about how to think of the Almighty. Yet if we see it as a statement about faith, it becomes a declaration that says we do not need to worry about whether or not God is working for us, because we just have to have faith that God always is. God is looking out for us all the time, Jesus says, and whether we're just about to dash our foot against a stone matters less than God's spiritual connection to each of us. This is an important statement about the relationship of man to God, and one that does not exist in the Hebrew teachings. Again, because we may be familiar with the words we may find that we look past the almost shocking quality of what Jesus says when viewed in the context of orthodox Judaism at the time. Just have faith, says Jesus, and know that God will look after you all the time – you don't need to worry or beg or agonize.

The last statement Jesus makes is also somewhat unusual. We may see it as quite reasonable – that one should worship only God. Notice, though, that Satan offers him 'glory' if he will worship him; this may be the key. Jesus says, in effect, that one should worship God even though there may be no obvious worldly glory in it – that prayer is a private and personal communion, and not a public display. 'And him only shalt thou serve,' He says. No one can serve God and serve the world. We have to choose one, Jesus tells us. The clear hint is that the spiritual world is the only world that matters. All of Satan's questions are aimed at the physical world; food, comfort, and glory; all of Jesus' replies are concerned with the spiritual world – spiritual growth, faith, and devotion. These three replies are rich and deep and complex and they spell out a framework of spiritual values with great clarity. If ever a Pilgrim figure formulated a coherent system of belief, defended it, and became a Warrior-Lover, this surely was it.

One more fact should strike us. Since Jesus and Satan are alone in the wilderness, which is symbolic of that lonely place of self-assessment we all must go to, we have a practical consideration. Who was at hand to record this information? Satan wouldn't be much of a note-taker. The only possible answer is that Jesus himself repeated these events to someone who relayed the information to the writer(s) of the St. Matthew gospel. We miss the point if we see this as just another odd episode. There are no wasted words in the New Testament. The writers seem to have been fully aware that they were recording information that is of major importance from the point of view of the spiritual teachings of Jesus, and of vital importance in Jesus' spiritual maturation. As a Pilgrim he defines himself through what he rejects and *at the same moment* by what he endorses in the contrast. It's a 'not this, but that' moment which brings him to Warrior-Lover stage. It signals to us, in fact, that Jesus' life is to be seen as something that involves him growing and maturing. He may be the Son of God, but he is also expected to grow into his personal power. The gospel writers seem to go out of their way to let us know that he is just like us. He is therefore a model for us to emulate, and that is exactly why this episode is dramatized in the gospel.

Jesus is a Warrior-Lover at this point. He is tested for physical greed (bread) but also in terms of his ego. Satan's words, "If thou be the Son of God…." have a needling quality, and the temptation is to show off his power. Similarly the dare that he should throw himself from the high place is a test that attempts to lure him into relying on his father's power, not his own wisdom. The third temptation is an effort to get him to divert his spiritual aims into worldly ones. Satan seems to be asking directly, what do you believe and why do you believe it? Jesus replies each time with "It is written…" Jesus isn't just parroting the scriptures. Elsewhere he quotes Holy text with some reverence, saying, "and the scripture cannot be broken" (John 10.35). And this is another clue that can help us see his statements more clearly. What is written, if it is true, has absolute value. Jesus' words can now be paraphrased as, 'I believe in these things because they are *right*, not just because they are convenient.'

After this Jesus goes off and finds his disciples, with his moral code clear. And he certainly does challenge the existing status quo almost immediately. The Sermon on the Mount, which is his next major public teaching, offers some startling new perceptions, such as: "Blessed are the poor in spirit..." (Matthew 5:3). This must have rocked more than a few preconceptions at the time, and is almost as stunning as the famous statement: "Love your enemies." (Matthew 5:44) Again and again, Jesus asks those who speak with him to think, not just to take instruction. As a Warrior-Lover he does not tell people what to do; he asks them to reconsider what they have been doing. The battle is now inside the conscience of each person.

When Jesus first enters Jerusalem, it is in triumph. The temptation is that everyone will believe this to be a victory, although Jesus knows where it will end. On the cross he faces the Warrior-Lover's ultimate test – the recognition of his own limits in the encounter with death. Mocked as 'king of the Jews' he may seem to be a failure, but as a person who will die for what he holds true he has the power to shake every person who knows about him. His is a kingly sacrifice of himself. It is interesting also that when Jesus dies he has Mary and Magdalene at the base of the cross. Most of the male entourage has fled. It is the women who come to the tomb, also, and find it empty. As a veiled reference to the fusion of male and female we have been discussing, and of the balance required of the Monarch, this can hardly fail to attract our attention. The balance of male and female, the Crucifixion that is simultaneously a defeat and a victory, all this indicates the equilibrium of the Monarch. And after Jesus rises from the dead he can be seen as achieving the level of the Magician because his disciples are now not just followers but leaders in their own rights. He has empowered them to teach and work miracles themselves.

This schematic account of Jesus' life is not here so we can discuss doctrine in detail. It is here because this story is surely one of the more influential stories that has shaped the western world, and it seems to conform with some precision to the six stages idea. If indeed Thomas à Kempis is correct and we should imitate Jesus, this may have all the more resonance for us since it seems that this is an archetypal journey and Jesus is one more example that fits into this very ancient pattern. We know this, broadly, to be true because it so often feels true. To take just one aspect, we could say that Jesus' experiences in the wilderness are now part of therapeutic orthodoxy. We all have to wander in the wilderness for a while so that we can work out what we value. Outward Bound courses are predicated on the idea that lost and at-risk youth (Orphans and fledgling Pilgrims) can benefit by being part of a real wilderness experience in which, with luck, they become Pilgrims and begin to discover their own inner resources. Outward Bound courses seem to work, much of the time. This may be because they allow individuals to complete a series of physical actions that articulate the unconscious materials we all need to come to terms with. If the experience works it does so because it reflects how people actually are and what they need to develop. So-called 'primitive' societies have rituals of this exact type that allow young people to be alone and decide who they may be, usually at around the time of puberty. The Australian Aborigine on his 'walkabout' is doing something very similar.

Another way to look at the Jesus stories is to ask not what it was that Jesus went through, but rather, does his trajectory coincide in any meaningful way with what Jesus asked his followers to go through? It is, after all, one thing for us to stand back and decide what framework the Gospel writers had at the backs of their minds, and quite another to ascertain what vision Jesus himself might have considered as the way humans develop. We can, however, hazard a few guesses. Jesus had a reputation for sitting down to dinner with all sorts of disreputable people, tax collectors, prostitutes, lepers, the poor, and so on. The thing that is most remarkable is that these people did not remain disreputable figures. Indeed they seem to have been inspired by Jesus to leave their miserable existences behind and follow a higher calling. What is most clear, though, is that Jesus did not turn them into passive followers, although the gospels refer to them as followers or as disciples. Instead he challenged them to think for themselves. He resolutely refused to announce himself as the Messiah, preferring instead to lob the question back to the twelve in such a way as to force them to make up their own minds: "Whom do men say that I am?" he asks, and then follows it up with a second question, "But whom say ye that I am?" (Mark 8.27, 28) And that is his answer. It is not up to him to make meaning for anyone; each has to find his or her own meaning. If Jesus had simply collected followers he would have been just another person picking up passive Orphans – those who perhaps would have wished for nothing better than to be told what to think. Instead he spends his time with Orphans who know there is something more to find out – since so many of them are on the edges of society they know exactly what it is not to fit in to the consoling mainstream of life. By asking those he meets to think for themselves Jesus sets up a situation in which his questioners have a real opportunity to become Pilgrims after truth for truth's sake, not for the sake of belonging to a movement.

From our point of view I'd suggest that Jesus was encountering the lost, the dispossessed, and the downtrodden, and he was able to show them that beyond their Orphan stage there were other possibilities for development and growth. His genius certainly seems to have been to be able to talk with the Orphans of the world and introduce them to the idea that they could become Pilgrims. And from that point on there was no turning back.

Of course, he didn't just deal with the poor. When asked by the rich man's son how he could enter the kingdom of God, Jesus instructed him to take all he had, sell it, and give the money to the poor. The man, we are told, went away sorrowing, "for he had great possessions." (Mark 10.22) Jesus seems to be saying that money is a stumbling block, and this is certainly an acceptable interpretation. Yet one could add that at another level Jesus is urging the man to open himself up to the experience of becoming an Orphan when he gives away his father's money. Without wealth and without status he will be forced to attempt to decide what is truly valuable, and that will be the first step towards becoming a Pilgrim. *Then* he can begin to grow. Unfortunately the young man does not seem to want this, and goes on his way 'sorrowing'. The Bible is quite clear about the nature of the challenge, and how hard it can be for some people to give up their comfortable situations. Not everyone can manage to take up the offer to become a Pilgrim.

The purpose in these pages has not been to go against religious doctrines of any sort – but rather to show that the Jesus story also functions as an illustration of what the journey towards truth is likely to be for all of us, no matter what our religion. When we decide to become Pilgrims, to find expression for what is true within us, we step towards a realm that has a different energy, one that seems to be based in questioning. When we have our own sense of what the answers to those questions might be, as Warrior-Lovers, Jesus' example can show us that we have to allow others to ask their own questions and not feel compelled to answer them. For if we do so we may take away their opportunity to make real understanding happen. Any teacher knows that if one tells the student the answer rather than letting her come to the solution in her own way, then very little learning takes place. If personal or spiritual growth is to happen it can only occur in a situation in which each person is supported in his or her questioning process. We know this now, and yet we cannot forget the many previous decades in which education was defined as learning-by-rote, when questions were asked only by the teacher with the intent to find out whether the students had been attentive. There is a place for learning-by-rote; and there is also a place for inquiry.

The Jesus story also introduces a new element – which is that one can lose the earthly struggle but still win the spiritual struggle. The earlier myths have a tendency to let the heroic figures achieve vindication in the eyes of the world. In the Jesus story, it is Jesus' seeming failure that is vital to the sense of the narrative.

A different example of the six stages at work is in the Arthurian legends, where the knights-errant go off on various quests and return after their adventures older and wiser. One of the most famous of these, *Sir Gawain and the Green Knight*, has come down to us in an anonymous version written down in 1375, presumably after having been in circulation in an oral tradition for some years.

The tale opens at Camelot, at Christmastime, and it is a scene of pleasure, warmth, and comfort. The food is good and there is plenty of it (which was not always the case at that time). Everyone is happy and looking forward to several days of feasting. It is an Innocent's dream: safety, loyal friends gathered together, while outside the snow piles up.

The idyll is shattered when a monstrous man on horseback gallops into the hall, and what is worse, he's completely green: skin, hair, clothes, even his horse. The giant proposes a game in which he will receive one blow of an ax and then will return the favor. This seems bizarre to everyone in the hall. But no one jumps forward to accept. King Arthur, dismayed that his loyal followers aren't responding, agrees to the contest. Gawain begs to leave the bench and take his place. Gawain, the Innocent, steps forward.

He swings the ax and cuts off the giant's head.

The Green Knight then picks up his head and says that Gawain must meet him a year from that day, at the Green Chapel, to receive his return ax-blow. The giant green figure then leaves.

Gawain, knowing he has no magical powers that can save him in the way the Green Knight was saved, has been roughly thrown into Orphan stage. When spring comes he goes on his quest, homeless, and a Pilgrim after his own fate. He is a faithful Pilgrim, however. He does not run away or leave the country. Before Gawain leaves Camelot the poet takes care to tell us that the knight has the sign of the pentacle on his shield – the five pointed star that can be drawn with one unbroken line – which symbolizes the interlinked chain of virtues he is sworn to uphold. On the inside of the shield is a picture of the Virgin Mary, to remind him of chastity and mercy. He may be off, homeless in the world, but he has beliefs that he cherishes and chooses to honor publicly, so he may feel himself to be closer to a Warrior-Lover than to a Pilgrim. What he doesn't know yet is that his moral code is about to be severely tested, forcing him to ask the questions about his beliefs that a Pilgrim usually asks. As an untested Warrior he is really only a pseudo-Warrior.

A few days before the deadline Gawain is still lost, and he seeks refuge in a castle. Here he meets the ebullient Sir Berkilac, who entertains him and proposes a game: that each evening they will exchange all they have gained that day. Since Sir Berkilac knows where the Green Chapel is – only a few miles away – he tells Sir Gawain to relax and enjoy his stay.

This is easier said than done.

The next morning, Sir Berkilac goes out hunting deer. Sir Gawain stays behind, asleep. Sir Berkilac's beautiful wife comes to see him, clad in very little. She slips into his room, gets inside the bed curtains, and perches on the side of the bed. Gawain pretends to be asleep.

For a man of honesty, to pretend – even if it is only pretending to be asleep – is not comfortable. In fact the lady tempts him, making suggestions of a vaguely sexual nature, which become more insistent on each subsequent day. He fends her off not just once, but on each of the three days, refusing her sexual invitations but agreeing, reluctantly, to accept a few kisses. These he dutifully gives to Sir Berkilac, her husband, on each of the three days he returns from the hunt.

What this means in terms of the six stages is that Gawain, the knight famous for his good manners and courtesy, is being tested in various direct ways that have nothing to do with the traditional methods of swords and shields. He, who carries a picture of the Virgin Mary on the inside of his shield, is tested for his purity, his honesty, and his truly "courtly" virtues. Can he reject his hostess without causing offence, or will he give in (the easiest way of not causing offence in the short run) his ego flattered by her regard for him? This is where Gawain, in refusing her, upholds the causes he fights for, which are purity and keeping one's word to others.

On the third day the lady realizes she can't seduce him, so she offers him jewels – appealing to his ego-based greed. He refuses again. Then she offers him a green girdle – a belt – that she claims will save the the wearer from any mortal wound. Gawain accepts. This is the one item he does not surrender to Sir Berkilac. Like any Warrior, he knows when to be afraid. He'll need that belt when he meets the Green Knight.

Notice that Gawain does not slip into the easy role of Lover (the other side of Warrior-Lover) because he recognizes that he loves his principles more than he loves sexual indulgence. In a very real sense, he knows the true nature of his role.

He then goes off to the Green Chapel and what looks like certain death. On the way, the servant sent to guide him urges him to flee. He refuses.

When he meets the Green Knight again, he bares his neck for the ax and waits. However, hearing the whistle of the blade, he flinches. The Green Knight protests, and demands another swing. Gawain agrees that he has not kept his end of the bargain, and allows another swing. This time, the Green Knight halts the ax an inch from Gawain's neck. He was just making sure Gawain was not about to flinch again, he says. Annoyed now, Gawain agrees to the third strike.

This time the ax whistles down and just nicks Gawain's neck. Immediately he jumps back, draws his sword and says that the next blow will be in full battle only. The Green Knight just laughs, and explains the situation. The three blows, he points out, were for each of the three days of temptation. The first two days Gawain kept his word and his honesty. On the last day, however, he held onto the green girdle, and this dishonesty is rewarded by the nick on the neck (which would produce a lasting scar). Fear of death can turn anyone into a dishonest person, it would seem. The Green Knight had known all along exactly what was going on, since the entire situation had been set up as a test by the witch Morgan Le Faye – King Arthur's half-sister – who had played the part of the lady.

We can observe a number of things right away. The three temptations are a direct echo of the temptations of Christ. Indeed the Gawain poet intends us to see this specifically because he has the lady say things such as 'If you be Gawain …' (l. 1481) which cannot fail to remind us of Satan's words: 'If thou be the Son of God…'

Gawain returns home to Camelot, tells his tale, and declares his defeat and disgrace. King Arthur's response is to announce that this was surely a test no one could have passed, and he orders the entire court to wear the sign of the garter, to remind them of Gawain's trial.

How does this match our stages? Gawain, as we see, learns his limits as a War-rior-Lover. What he learns is the fear of death. In order to be a true Warrior, to fight and kill, one must have some idea of what it is one is doing, and that involves facing fear and understanding death. Anyone can die, but freely offering oneself knowing one may be killed – that requires self-awareness. Similarly, anyone can love, yet what makes love magnificent is the knowledge that life is short and the deep feelings that arise will be tested, and cut short, by death at some point.

Gawain's return to Camelot, and to his king, allows Arthur to point out that this is not a personal, ego defeat and neither has Gawain, as Camelot's representa-tive, let the side down. It is, rather, a situation that has shown the limits of what even the finest of us can do. Doing the very best we can in an impossible situation is, in its own right, a victory. Arthur converts a particular incident into a general lesson for all, and shows both the male executive power of the king and the female sense of compassion typified in the queen. He acts, therefore, as the integrated Monarch. He brings out the balanced viewpoint so we can all become wiser. In so doing, Arthur is not just being the Monarch – bringing an orderly end to a situ-ation and re-validating one of his best knights – he is also close to being a Magi-cian. He knows that Gawain will be a stronger, better, more moral knight for his adventure, and that this is not a defeat but a refining process that brings the best qualities forward. Arthur trusts his knight, and he knows that Gawain will from now on trust himself more fully. Arthur's trust in his follower allows him to take a situation that could be damaging to the whole belief system the court operates by, and he transforms it into a lesson that will strengthen the court as a whole. The Magician can make something positive out of even a seeming defeat.

Again, Christ's temptation, the seeming defeat and disgrace on the cross and his rising up from the dead on the third day to a more triumphant role are mir-rored in Gawain's three days with the lady, his defeat, disgrace, rehabilitation by the Monarch, and the subsequent larger moral triumph of the court as a whole.

Since the knights of the Round Table and King Arthur's court were role mod-els for an entire era, it is not unreasonable to pluck this one tale and see in it such important material. The story of Sir Gawain is perhaps first and foremost a rattling good yarn, and it is also a series of instructions about how a man should live, and what challenges he will face. Most important of all, it suggests that even if a man has a rigid code of conduct – in this instance the code of chivalry, at which Gawain is very practiced – it will not provide complete protection against the challenges that life will inevitably send us. We may achieve 100% on the exam, but life will not be playing by those rules all the time. The poem is a reminder to keep our minds open, for at Warrior-Lover stage we will be tested again and again.

The lady's temptation in fact offers a short cut to Monarch-hood, perhaps, if Gawain becomes her lover, gets rid of Berkilac, and abandons his quest. Yet this would be Monarch-hood based in a series of lies and disloyal actions. Gawain is not fooled, and he is not an opportunist, so he is able to move up the stages in an orderly fashion, learning the lessons he has to. Notice, though, that Gawain ascends only so far – to full Warrior-Lover status. Arthur is the role model for the Monarch and Magician stages. It is the totality of the tale that matters here. Focusing on just the main figure will not tell us the whole story.

Notes

1. All bible quotations are from the King James Authorized Version.
2. Thomas à Kempis, (1380-1471). *The Imitation of Christ.*
3. *Sir Gawain and the Green Knight,* trans. Marie Boroff (1967). *The Norton Anthology of English Literature,* vol.1, 8th ed. Greenblatt, Abrams et alia, New York: Norton, 2005. See also line 1293, 'Our guest is not Gawain' and line 1779, 'I find you much at fault'. The lady insinuates that Gawain is an imposter

Chapter Fourteen

Shakespeare and the Six Stages

Moving forward in time we can apply this six-part pattern to the structure of Shakespeare's plays. The History plays are obviously concerned with questions of kingship, rule, and what an effective Monarch should be, and since the King was thought of as God's deputy these plays offer a way to consider all the stages from Innocent to Magician, and how they are linked. It is a concern Shakespeare returns to again and again, even outside the strictly historical confines. *King Lear* is not really historical; neither is *Macbeth*, yet they both ask questions about how rulers should act. This was a question of vital importance to Shakespeare and his age. As the king was, so was the realm, and all the people in it. Right behavior was not just a matter of politics ensuring peace, it was a question of whether or not one would get into Heaven or be flung into Hell. Behind that important consideration, of course, lay another, which was how one should live one's life, whether or not one actually was a ruler.

The clearest example of the six-part system at work is probably in the *Henry IV* and *Henry V* sequence of plays. *Henry IV, Part I*, contains two stories. The first concerns the king, Henry, who has pushed his predecessor Richard II off the throne, and is therefore tortured by the anxiety that he may be a usurper and not a 'true' king. His politically questionable situation and his own anxiety seem to bring about the very thing he most fears: challenges to his right to rule. He managed to seize the kingdom, but can he keep it? The second and parallel story is the saga of his elder son, Hal, who seems an unpromising youth. Companion to the dissolute and drunken Sir John Falstaff, Prince Hal looks like every father's nightmare; and he seems to be God's judgment upon the king for taking the throne, since Hal will be next in line. Hal is a shortened version of the name Henry, of course, and this use of names suggests that Prince Hal is an incomplete version of the person who will become the next King Henry.

The Elizabethan audience would have been fascinated by this play, because it asks how such an unpromising youth could have evolved into one of the most successful kings the nation had known. Hal, the roistering lout of the early scenes, would have seemed no different from any of the rough apprentices in the audience, and almost interchangeable with any of the tavern roughnecks one might have run into every day in the squalid streets of London.

The plot develops with Hal as the central character. He is surely no Innocent: he seems to be the self-Orphaned son who has mistakenly attached himself to the worst of all adoptive fathers – Falstaff. Can he really not see the error he has made? We, in the audience, have the point made for us when Falstaff jokingly pretends to be the king, and he laughs at how Hal will be greeted with tears and admonishments when he returns home. Then Hal insists that they change places in this role-play, and so he plays his own father and Falstaff pretends to be Hal. From this vantage point Hal freely criticizes Falstaff and says that any prince worth his salt would leave the old scoundrel's company. Falstaff, pretending to be outraged, remonstrates, ending his speech with: "Banish Jack Falstaff, and banish all the world." To this Hal replies, "I do. I will." (2. iv. 462-4). This is the hint we need. Hal has seen through Falstaff's bluster and deceit. The Orphan Hal is Falstaff's adoptive son no longer. He is about to reject this way of life. Until now he may have acted like the Orphan, but in this scene we watch him closely for he has just become a Pilgrim seeking after real moral values. When the time comes, he will step forward and put those moral values into action, becoming the Warrior he needs to be.

And, on cue, he has his chance. The rebellious Hotspur prepares for battle – a man so full of fire and fight that even his wife relates to him combatatively. Arguing with him, she seizes his hand and says, "In faith I'll break thy little finger" (2. iii. 84), unless she gets her own way. Hotspur loves to fight and is very good at it. Yet when he meets Hal on the field at Shrewsbury, it is Hal who wins their duel. The better man really does win. Hal, in killing Henry Hotspur, has been blooded as a Warrior and as a Lover of what is right. The good Harry kills the evil Harry for the sake of his father, also called Harry. Symbolically one could say that Prince Hal meets and defeats an aspect of his Shadow self, the unbridled angry part of himself he has to contain and understand so that he can become a balanced Warrior-Lover. He has fought for the cause he loves, where Hotspur was simply fighting for wealth and power. Significantly, the cowardly Falstaff hacks dead Hotspur's carcass and tries to claim he killed him, pushing forward his own ego-claim – and Hal does not argue. After all, it doesn't matter. Hotspur is dead, and the situation does not need any display of personal glory. Hal knows the truth. True Warrior-Lovers do not need ego rewards.

Hal's performance in battle helps in great measure to heal the rift with his father, too, although it will not be until Hal becomes king on his father's death that he will be able to appreciate the full burden of what his father has had to struggle with. In an important scene the old dying king is lying asleep and Hal picks up the crown and wanders into the next room, meditating about kingship and his father, coming to understand the man he once rejected. The king wakes unexpectedly and assumes the worst of his wayward son, and has to be reassured that the young man has not been overly eager to take charge of the kingdom. In this, the climactic moment of the play, prince Hal speaks of his loyalty to his father, and of how he put the crown on his head in order to try to comprehend the burden of kingship. The king, moved, believes him.

> Oh my son,
> God put it in thy mind to take it [the crown] hence
> That thou might'st win the more thy father's love,
> Pleading so wisely in excuse of it!
> Come hither, Harry; sit thou by my bed,
> And hear, I think, the latest counsel
> That ever I shall breathe *(Henry IV, pt 2:* 4.v.178-184).

The difficult relationship between father and son is healed. The Warrior Hal has shown himself as Lover of what is right. In fusing these two aspects he shows he is ready to become the Monarch, and the dying king is able to explain himself to his son. This touching scene is dramatically moving, and it is also something more. The king is able to tell his son he loves him, and to appreciate his son's words as 'wise'. Love and positive regard, which until recently had been withheld, are now admitted, and without these the relationship cannot be made whole. Hal's borrowing of the crown, which precipitated the whole discussion, can be seen as him appreciating for the first time the difficulties his father has faced. In this one scene they begin to understand and trust each other fully.

It is this trust that allows the king to confide in his son as an equal and to confess to Hal that his fears for his claim to the crown, which he took from Richard II, have worn him down. Hal's response is worth quoting:

> My Gracious Liege,
> You won it, wore it, kept it, gave it me;
> Then plain and right must my possession be (4.v. 221-3).

The downright pragmatism of this is surprising. It's yours, says Hal, and that's all that matters when you give it to me. There is no moral quibbling here. What we are in fact witnessing is not 'finders-keepers' thinking. This is Hal reassuring his dying father that as king his father had displaced an incompetent ruler who needed to be removed. In saying this he is becoming the parent to his parent. As he hears his father's confessions he is also a substitute for a priestly father confessor. The son becomes father to the man.

When Hal does ascend the throne, his first action is to reject Falstaff. He has seen what it takes to be king, and is now ready to step forward. He has met this second aspect of his Shadow self, Falstaff, and rejected that wonderful, anarchic figure as a ruling force in his life, but not before he has become thoroughly acquainted with Falstaff's charisma and energy. What Falstaff teaches Hal is how to talk with ordinary people – a skill we will see Hal using to formidable advantage in *Henry V* with his address to his troops. For Falstaff has many attractive qualities. He is hilarious, even though thoroughly immoral, and he contrasts with Hotspur who is similarly selfish, but no fun at all. Falstaff's way is the way of short cuts. The old knight wishes to be on good terms with Hal because he sees a chance to gain a leg up in the kingdom when Hal is crowned. But Hal, who allows himself no short cuts, will not play that game. Hotspur, too, wants a short cut to power and his co-conspirators are just as devious as Falstaff's gang, although better funded. The parallels are elegant.

If we take Jung's sense of the Shadow self and apply it to these events it will be important to spell out that Jung saw two aspects of the Shadow. The first was that the Shadow self is made up of those personal aspects of oneself that one chooses to repress, but which one has to recognize as a legitimate part of one's psyche. So we all tend to repress emotions like anger, yet we know we have to acknowledge and use them at some point. The second value Jung gives to the Shadow is that it is the impulse of pure evil, and that this chaotic urge is ready to overwhelm us if we let it. Hotspur's mad desire to fight, no matter what, is this purely destructive impulse – an impulse that turns out to be suicidal for him.

It is essential that Hal conquer both aspects of the Shadow, and he does. The repressed aspects of the self, as embodied in Falstaff's influence on Hal, can be just as destructive, and yet Hal learns to use what he observes. Having spent time with Falstaff, Hal will never again be easily led astray by a plausible and attractive rogue. Having fought Hotspur, Hal will never be tempted to the sort of suicidal ego-striving he has witnessed in his opponent. Shakespeare is extremely careful to show us a Hal who has mastered both sides of his character. This is essential for the successful completion of the balanced Warrior-Lover stage.

In *Henry V*, the newly crowned King Henry receives his first major challenge. The French, who even squabble among themselves as to who is in charge, refuse to acknowledge Hal's claim to various lands in France. The French court is seen as acting childishly and provocatively. They send a gift of tennis balls to Henry, suggesting that since he was such a dissolute youth, he'd prefer to be playing rather than fighting. True Warriors do not, of course, provoke fights by sending insults. Hal's response is righteous but controlled anger. He checks with the lawyers and the archbishops to make sure his cause is just, and he sets sail for France. Notice that he does not respond to the insult to his ego or act rashly. He is deliberate, controlled, and very much determined to fight a righteous war. The ego, which the French thought was the totality of this man, is not what dictates policy. Shakespeare is very careful to let us see this, since we need to see the king as the principled Warrior-Lover who loves justice.

The play continues with Henry as a fighting king, taking risks in battle, leading from the front. He is not, however, merely a bruiser. When some of his old drinking buddies desecrate a church by stealing the furnishings, he doesn't shrug it off; he has the offenders hanged. Moral codes matter to him. The French are shown as less honorable. When they are losing the Battle of Agincourt, they turn aside from the main fight and slaughter the unarmored baggage handlers and servants. Fluellen the Welsh captain is aghast. A professional soldier, he cannot accept this atrocity. "'Tis expressly against the law of arms. 'Tis as arrant a piece of knavery, mark you now, as can be offert" (4. vii. 3-4), he storms, in a Welsh accent. The comparison is clear. Warriors are neither angry nor vengeful, and certainly not wanton butchers. They take up arms in full knowledge of the terrible things they may have to do; but random destruction is not part of their code. Henry's response when he sees the dead boys and baggage handlers leaves us in no doubt what to think: "I was not angry since I came into France until this instant" (4. vii. 52-3).

Just before the decisive Battle of Agincourt, Henry walks amid his troops, disguised, and listens to them as they air their thoughts. This is thematically a reprise of *Henry IV, Part I*, where Prince Hal is 'in disguise' when he spends time with the disreputable Falstaff and company. Here, on the night before a battle he looks likely to lose, Henry listens to his soldiers discussing their fear that the king's cause may not be just, and whether that means his supporters will be damned to hell as a result. Henry sidesteps the issue by announcing that "Every subject's duty is the king's, but every subject's soul is his own" (4. i. 178). Shakespeare may not provide the answer, but he has at least asked the question. The implication is clear for our purposes: the Monarch has a greater moral responsibility than anyone else, and that is his particular burden. The army will be made up of all sorts of people, some Innocents, some Orphans, some Pilgrims, and quite a few Warrior-Lovers. The king's job is not to force them all to be at the same level of awareness. His task is to make sure they function as an army so that wrongs can be corrected. Where they are spiritually is their own business.

One detail is worth noticing: before the battle Henry utters the famous 'band of brothers' speech in which he emphasizes his links to his men. He also states that anyone who does not want to fight may leave without shame. This is brilliant politics, since no one will now dare to slink off from what has been acknowledged to be a dangerous situation. It has the added value of turning each man into a volunteer – and Henry's point is clear. He only wants people who want to be there, since only volunteers will have the heart for the hard fight ahead. His maneuver has, in fact, just empowered his men with a sense of their own valor. The king is not only brave, but he knows how to produce bravery in others. He makes a virtue of their small numbers and difficult situation. He has learned from his time with Falstaff how to relate to the common rank and file, and now he uses that skill to excellent effect. In this he shows the unmistakable signs of being a Monarch who can lead and manage others successfully, bringing out the best in them. The astonishing victory against overwhelming odds can be seen as the Monarch's ability to make extraordinary things happen – King Henry has contacted the realm of the Magician, and (in Shakespeare's terms) God has completed the work. As with Orestes and Odysseus, when a figure works with selflessness, courage, and determination he can align himself with the energy of the universe, or God, and miracles can occur.

The play concludes with the now victorious Henry wooing the French princess, despite the lack of a common language. This wooing makes political sense, of course. Yet Shakespeare is careful to give us a Henry who actually wants to marry the princess, who promises her a "true" soldier's heart, and a real marriage. He asks, "Can'st thou love me?" (5. ii. 194). Rather than attempting to convince her of his love, he simply announces his own intentions. The king has just won a stupendous victory, against the odds, by the exercise of courage, faith, and moral belief in his cause. He now offers love. These four attributes make him a true king, and possibly a true Magician. Certainly defeat can be turned to victory; and war can be turned into peace if one offers the losing side love and honor.

Shakespeare's interest in kingship and how a person can reach that exalted level returns in a different form in the tragedies. In *Macbeth*, Macbeth is a military hero who knows what it is to command, and to fight and kill. His error is that he confuses killing enemies (which brought him promotion and success) with murdering a friend and benefactor, Duncan, just to bring more success. Commanding soldiers is not the same as ruling a kingdom. He is the Warrior gone astray, unable to activate the Lover aspect of himself. Significantly, almost all his actions in the play are killings. He just can't stop. "I am in blood stepped in so far, that should I wade no more/ Returning were as tedious as go o'er" (3. iv. 136-138). There is no way forward for him except destruction. When his wife kills herself she destroys his dynastic aims, too, which means his reign can only be self-serving. He has no children, no future beyond himself. Worse still, he cannot unite with the softer, kinder, feminine aspect of himself. Even while alive Lady Macbeth was hardly the embodiment of those virtues. Without that aspect of himself he cannot become a true Warrior-Lover, let alone achieve the level of the Monarch.

But Macbeth cannot see this. This is because it is his ego that is involved. He wants to be king as the crudest form of ego-gratification in his lust for power. He has no thoughts of making Scotland a better, or even a halfway decent, place. As his spiritual aridity becomes more and more obvious he descends through the stages. His compulsive returning to the witches for reassurance is a ghastly inversion of the Pilgrim's struggle for personal direction. He puts himself more and more in their deceptive power until he can no longer find a sense of meaning in the universe. Life is a "tale told by an idiot, full of sound and fury, signifying nothing" (5. v. 26-27). He may nominally be a king, but he is as spiritually lost as any Orphan, clinging to the witches' words.

Macbeth is eventually killed in single combat with Macduff. Macduff is pure, moral, and has been in exile (a Pilgrim with his own beliefs about what should happen) following his family's murder, which reduced him temporarily to Orphan status. When the time comes, Macduff the Warrior, avenger of his loved family and lover of Scotland, faces and kills Macbeth in a fair fight, fulfilling the prophecy, which seems to give the divine seal of approval to Macduff's status as a true Warrior-Lover. Macduff, acting for what is morally right, is supported by God, is fully aligned with God's will. The genuine Warrior-Lover defeats the bogus Monarch, and Malcolm can now ascend his father's throne in rightful succession. Shakespeare is careful to have the very next scene present us with the veteran soldier, Old Siward, hearing about his son's death. Malcolm praises Young Siward, and when assured that his son had wounds only on the front of his body (therefore he was not killed running away), Old Siward declares;

> Why then, God's soldier he be!
> Had I as many sons as I have hairs
> I would not wish them to a fairer death (5.viii. 49-51).

This image of a young warrior, about whom we know almost nothing else, stands in stark contrast to the desperate figure of Macbeth we have seen meeting his death just moments earlier. Young Siward is the epitome of martial rectitude. He is 'God's soldier' and his youth suggests that he is the sacrifice that must be paid in order to purify the kingdom.

The play clearly is about many things – and one of them is that Warriors like Macbeth can go astray when they try to transition to Monarch status if they have no idea what that process involves. Notice that Macbeth has to suppress his humanity. It takes him considerable mental effort to steel himself to kill Duncan, which is the equivalent of killing off the Lover aspect of the Warrior-Lover archetype he so nearly achieves. Moreover Lady Macbeths' famous 'unsex me here!' speech demonstrates how her ego ambitions have led her to deny her softer, compassionate side; and so she too becomes a ghastly parody of the Warrior-Lover. In fact, this kind of self-serving ambition is, as we have seen, always the realm of the Orphan.

Just as with Oedipus we see that those who attempt to achieve Monarch level by shortcuts condemn themselves in the process. Malcolm, who actually does inherit the throne, may not have been through all the stages we have observed, because we don't see very much of him. But the implication is that he has witnessed them all and learned from them, and so he has an absolute right to claim his political and spiritual place.

The precise nature of Shakespearean kingship, and what it means, is not for us to discuss here. For one thing, Shakespeare's society was very different from our own, and the legal system was quite unlike anything we have. Shakespeare's vision, therefore, is not likely to correspond exactly to our own idea of healthy government, especially as that very topic is under continuous debate each morning in our newspapers. The aim here is to show that behind the superficial differences there can be discovered this same six-part system. Where Homer's Warrior-based society emphasized the Warrior stage, the New Testament's religious context emphasized spiritual issues, and Shakespeare tended to focus on issues of power and government, and their moral foundations. To each according to his needs.

Shakespeare stayed with this issue, and this way of looking at it, for most of his career. In *King Lear* we see how he extended an idea that is already present in *Macbeth*. Again, he does not attempt to show one figure growing through all the stages so much as he lets a range of figures act out different aspects of this progression. By the end of *King Lear* we have witnessed all six stages, and yet only we, the audience, can see them all in their completeness.

We'll need to go through the play to explain this.

The aging King Lear attempts the unthinkable at the start of the play: he's going to divide the kingdom up and live off the good will of his daughters. This is about as realistic as a Mafia boss announcing he's going to retire. Everyone thinks he's gone mad, and the "licens'd fool", the court jester, tells him so. Certainly he seems mad, since he exiles the one daughter who really does love him, Cordelia, because she will not play the game of declaring before the court how much she loves him. She refuses to engage in his ego-fuelled charade. So Lear rejects the figure who can be seen as his loving, compassionate aspect, his Anima (his queen is presumed to be long dead), and commences his downward path through the stages.

In these early scenes of the play Lear claims he's a king; and yet, as he rides about the country with his hundred knights, he is acting more like a pseudo-Warrior, and we should be sensitive to this since he seems implicitly to accept this demotion he has engineered for himself. Even as a pseudo-Warrior he does not behave appropriately. His daughter Goneril complains about the riotous actions of his knights, suggesting that he is unable to keep them under control. Enraged, Lear storms out, vowing to go and stay with his other daughter, and we have a glimpse of him as a man who has hoped for love and acceptance. He's not a true Warrior, and he's not a true Lover, since he doesn't know who he loves or who really loves him. Shocked by this he becomes a Pilgrim after truth. He wants to know who truly does love him. The whole kingdom will say it does because he's nominally the king, but who, actually, does so? He seems very much like a Pilgrim as he shuttles between his daughters' homes, hoping for acceptance. Little does he realize that he is about to be manipulated into a fit of rage in which he will evict himself from even these uncertain lodgings. He's about to become an Orphan because of his absurdly naïve, ego-based behavior. After all, the role of the Monarch is not to be loved but to be effective at running the kingdom justly. Lear seems to have forgotten this first principle.

Alone on the heath, in the storm, Lear is a true homeless Orphan. He stops talking to the jester (the Fool) because he finds another more basic fool, Poor Tom. Poor Tom is literally almost naked and seems out of his mind. He is "bare unaccommodated man" in the most basic sense. He is as clueless as a newborn Innocent, and about as well dressed as a newborn, too.

We, the audience, know that Poor Tom is in fact Edgar in disguise, fleeing for his life. Edgar, the noble and legitimate son of the Duke of Gloucester, has been forced to flee because his illegitimate half brother, Edmund, has spread slanderous rumors about him. Now in a realistic world, Edgar would hardly be so naïve as to buy into anything his thoroughly evil half brother might say, yet Shakespeare does not want us to think Edgar is half-witted in his credulity. Edgar is unsuspecting because he is noble and pure. He becomes an Orphan and as "Poor Tom", descends to the level of an Innocent.

Lear, naked on the heath, devoid of his wits, really is an Innocent too, and he sees the injustices of the world with the shocked clarity of the Innocent who cannot understand why things are that way. His madness is, in fact, an inability to accept that the world is not as he wants it to be, which is the basic reaction of the Innocent who suddenly is faced with Orphanhood. It takes Cordelia's return from exile with the French Army before he finds a "home".

Just as it seems as if everyone of note is busy descending through the six stages we notice that another development is moving the action in a contrary direction. Edgar, in disguise, is guiding his old blinded father, Gloucester, around the countryside. The echo of Oedipus is hard to miss. Gloucester begins to realize how misled he has been about the true nature of his sons. Both Edgar and Gloucester are Orphans (each has 'adopted' the other, one may say) and it is up to Edgar to lead his father to some truths he needs to know. This impulse is what connects him to the Pilgrim stage: he has specific moral ideas he needs to examine and he knows that his father must do this as well. This is made clear when we see that Gloucester wants to kill himself – a sure sign of orphanhood and depression – which Edgar sees he has to coax his father to reject. Edgar pretends to lead him to a cliff, and Gloucester tumbles forward, and faints. Edgar now approaches again, acting another part, and claims that Gloucester was led to the non-existent cliff by the devil and has been saved by angels – thus teaching the old man that despair is unacceptable. Gloucester ceases his self-pity (for the Orphan can be endlessly self-pitying), and begins to face the disasters of the world with more courage as a Pilgrim. Edgar may be literally without a home, but his rescuing of his father, and his desire that this broken, blinded man should see the truth about them both has turned him into a Warrior-Lover. At great personal risk he has sought and found his father, gone with him with a disguised voice as his father has started to recognize the truth of his own sins, and in so doing he has quietly upheld important moral values – not the least of which is filial loyalty.

Courage is the next test, of course. Oswald, the courtier, tries to kill Glouces-ter, who is a walking advertisement for the cruelty of Goneril and Regan, Lear's wicked daughters who now rule the land. Armed with only a walking stick, Edgar kills Oswald, proving himself the "better" man in the fight to defend the person he loves. Next he hears of the challenge his half brother is issuing to fight any contestant to his claim. The Warrior-Lover in him begins to emerge more fully. Edgar leaves his father, fights the duel, and wins. Shakespeare makes it abundantly clear that while the evil Edmund is fighting to try and consolidate his grasp on the throne, Edgar is fighting because he wishes to oppose evil and has nothing directly to gain. The righteous Warrior-Lover who defended his father now rises to be the Monarch who has successfully championed the entire kingdom.

When Edgar recounts the story of where he has been all this time, he speaks about the services he has done for his father in protecting him. During this time it is clear he has been healing the relationship with his parent at the same time as he guides him towards knowledge and a peaceful death. Edgar tells us that just before he went to fight his half-brother – his Shadow self in its most self-serving embodiment – he revealed his identity to his father. Here is how he describes it:

> [I] never – O fault! – reveal'd myself unto him
> Until some half-hour past, when I was armed;
> Not sure, though hoping, of this good success,
> I ask'd his blessing, and from that first to last

> Told him my pilgrimage. But his flaw'd heart –
> Alack, too weak the conflict to support! –
> 'Twixt two extremes of passion, joy and grief,
> Burst smilingly'. (5. iii. 191-8)

Edgar has been able to heal their relationship, during what he describes fittingly enough as a 'my pilgrimage'. Despite all that has happened both are able to see the love they have for each other. Edgar has also shown his father the truth about Edmund, and in the process has become the parent to his own father. Edgar shows all the signs of being the Warrior-Lover who is ready to be a Monarch.

Lear has a similar reconciliation with his daughter Cordelia. She rescues him when he is mad and running naked on the heath, but all too soon her army is defeated by those of her sisters. Lear, the naked Innocent, given a home and 'adopted' by his daughter, recognizes anew the love of the daughter who truly does cherish him – the same daughter he had banished for not speaking publicly of her love for him. Finally he knows who he is and what is important, preferring to be in jail with Cordelia rather than free in a world run by her cruel sisters. His idyll is not long lasting, however, and they are led out to be hanged. Lear dies in a last burst of Warrior-like energy. "I killed the slave that was a-hanging [her]," (5. iii. 274) he announces, almost as an aside, after he carries Cordelia's corpse on stage. He dies believing, hoping, his daughter is still alive when she is obviously dead.

So, is this the promised image of kingship, a deluded old man? Perhaps what Shakespeare offers us is rather the totality of the play's experience, which leaves us with a sense of God's hand having brought about a united realm, newly freed of evil, under an Edgar who has seen so much and learned from it all. Lear and Cordelia have mended their fractured relationship and, as they both lie dead in front of Edgar and the others, they serve as a graphic visual reminder of the necessity of the Monarch to balance the female and male principles, and to respect each aspect. Cordelia was too loving and too verbally unexpressive, while Lear was too aggressive and impulsive. Edgar sees this, and can be expected to get the message about moderation, and how each aspect of the psyche can temper the other.

The Magician figure does not appear as a single person in this play, and this is because the magic happens when loyal, honest, and decent men and women courageously do the right thing. Edgar has guided his credulous and too-loving father back from the brink of despair. He has seen the ruin of Lear; and he has had to kill his own half brother. Our relatives are our blood, and reflect aspects of who we could possibly choose to be. Edgar decides to refuse the less helpful aspects of his family tree and as he does so he grows spiritually. The forces of good work as best they can in this play, and God completes the "magic".

Shakespeare is first and foremost interested in showing believable characters as they develop in an authentic way, and he is not concerned with demonstrating how a schematic overview works. Real human development is never tidy. Therefore Shakespeare's depiction of the stages can at times overlap in a way that tells us more about life than about anything else. For example, as Edgar recovers from his Orphan role he realizes that he must become the parent to his own shattered parent. He is an outcast, wandering the world, and yet it is by offering support to Gloucester that he learns to show his love, to exercise his judgment, and to uphold certain basic moral values. If it is the Pilgrim's task to find out what he believes, then Edgar certainly accomplishes that. He is, in fact, assimilating the values that will make him a Warrior-Lover when the occasion arises – and it does first with Oswald and secondly with his own brother. With Oswald he fights for personal interest – to defend the father he loves. When he faces Edmund it is because he is choosing to fight for a principal of right and justice. Notice how Shakespeare shows Edgar fighting to defend his father, and then almost immediately afterwards we see him fighting against another blood relation. Right actions exert a stronger call than mere family loyalty. Again, the idea of the Shadow self seems to be called into the discussion; the manipulative, egomaniacal Edmund can be seen as the pure evil of the Shadow, and Oswald is perhaps the sort of corrupt opportunist against whom Edgar has an instinctual reaction. Edmund is the opposite of the Warrior-Lover in that he is a Warrior-hater, in love with destruction, an aggressive active Orphan. Oswald's role is different in that he plays the passive Orphan, trying to hitch a free ride with whatever power is in ascendancy. Both of them represent ways of being that Edgar rejects. Here one could certainly argue that Edgar begins to show the qualities of a true Monarch.

As a result of Edgar's courage the sisters, Goneril and Regan, destroy themselves – one poisons the other and then stabs herself when Edmund is killed. Edgar's presence has precipitated the collapse of evil, and in that sense he could be seen to be the Magician. We have already noted that Edgar can be determined and gentle, so there are no doubts as to him being able to balance these two aspects, male vigor and female compassion. We don't need a female figure against which to balance him. His rejection of the evil sisters and his endorsement of Cordelia's cause are symbolic of his growth. It would be hard to pinpoint at what time Edgar moves from one level to the other, but this is less important than the fact that he does.

The play is named for Lear, but the most extensive spiritual growth is to be seen in Edgar. This is a demanding play since so many of the major figures are in a state of change. Lear, dying of heartbreak with his dead daughter in his arms, is the saddest expression of the Orphan one can imagine. And perhaps that's exactly Shakespeare's point. In life we have the opportunity, the duty, to become as spiritually aware as we can manage, but when we approach death we all feel the temptation to return to the condition of Orphans, wanting to be loved.

Shakespeare does in fact make use of a Magician figure, to considerable effect, in *The Tempest*. As Duke of Milan, Prospero becomes so engrossed in his studies of magic that he is usurped and exiled. He is then left adrift in a boat with his daughter, Miranda. He has already failed the test of being an effective Monarch, because he was neglectful of his duty. Now, an exile and an Orphan on the island, he is able to learn about hope and love from the Innocent Miranda while the negative Orphan Caliban must be tamed and confined. Caliban can be said to represent simple appetite, and he's always looking to be adopted by someone if it serves his ends: Prospero at first, later Trinculo and Stephano, the drunken servants. He even makes a song about it when he is drunk: "Ban, Ban, Caliban, has a new master, has a new man." A new form of servitude is always welcome to the Orphan who does not wish to take charge of his own life. For Prospero, marooned on his island, could choose to wallow in his wounds and sense of being unjustly treated by others. That's what Caliban does. He nurses grudges. Prospero must reject that temptation, controlling it as he controls Caliban.

When the shipwrecked court arrives wet and confused, Prospero is put to the test: will he use his magic wisely? "The rarer action is in virtue than in vengeance," (5. i. 27-28) he decides, although the fact that he has to say this to himself is proof that he is tempted. He must tame himself, not just Caliban or his opposite, Ariel, and his Warrior-Lover status is revealed in him refusing an unnecessary fight with his helpless enemies. He has the Warrior's spirit and force of will; he also has the Lover's desire to help his former enemies back to a life that is honest and virtuous.

In order to bring his plan to fruition, he has to acknowledge that there are some things he cannot do. He cannot compel Miranda to listen to him; he cannot compel others to be good; and he cannot make the circumstances. The situation has come about because of circumstances beyond his control, which he must now recognize and use properly. In fact, the magic that Prospero works is based on giving up power rather than using it. Although he can temporarily 'Orphan' the young Ferdinand by making him think his father is dead, he cannot compel him to love Miranda or Miranda to love Ferdinand. That has to happen voluntarily. Prospero's fight could be said to be one in which he must fight himself and love others, including his perfidious brother. He must give Miranda, the child he loves, to Ferdinand and trust that all will be well. He has indeed been the Warrior-Lover working all those years to support the child he loves. In doing so, and being balanced by her influence upon him, he has become a Monarch, tempering executive decision-making with mercy. Now he is tested as a Monarch. Can he do what is right and good or will he give into the desire for revenge? In not allowing his ego needs to prevail he works the true magic – bringing all to a harmonious ending.

.As if to reinforce the point Alonso, who had helped displace Prospero, could be compelled to give up the power he loves, but instead he volunteers to do so after the ordeal he has been through. The plotters Antonio and Sebastian, of course, have to agree to behave because Prospero lets them know that he, Prospero, knows all about the plot to kill Alonso. This is a threat, truly, but it's up to them to choose to mend their ways, or at least to restrain their impulses. Prospero does not seek to control others but to get them to control themselves. And that, as we have seen, is the mark of the Magician.

As a result of trust and love (Ferdinand and Miranda are promised in marriage and therefore Antonio's plotting no longer make sense), the whole cast can now return to their proper lives. The relationships that were fractured are now mended. Miranda has taught her father about love and therefore about mercy. Prospero gives up his magic and declares: "I'll break my staff.... And deeper than did ever plummet sound/ I'll drown my book." (v. 1. 54 -57) He turns to human decency, to love, to promises being kept and laws being respected. The real magic is the miraculous, everyday decency that people can achieve, if given the chance.

It doesn't take a huge amount of effort to apply the six-part idea to Shakespeare's other plays. If this was intended as a work of literary criticism, we could do just that in great detail. We'll need to take a more schematic approach here, one that will serve to remind us that the stages exist, plentifully, in all Shakespeare's plays, and since he is arguably one of the most powerful influences on the English speaking world that ever existed, we can look to him as an articulator of our lives as well as a shaper of our sensibilities. His works could not have survived unless they, in some ways, helped to explain us to ourselves.

Hamlet, for example, is a depressive Orphan after he learns the truth about his father's death and, as an Orphan, rejects everyone and everything until he is forced to go to England. Up to this point he has succeeded in hurting those he is closest to (his mother, Ophelia) as well as those who really are pawns in the court intrigues (Rosencrantz and Guildenstern, Polonius), but he has no coherent plan of action. He returns from his pilgrim-like voyage to England a fighter, but not as the raging maniac he had been earlier when he killed Polonius. He is a changed man. When he comes upon Ophelia's funeral, he declares himself to the world – for the first time: "This is I, Hamlet the Dane" (5. i. 251), he shouts. In a play that is constantly concerning itself with pretence, with acting, and with who is really doing what and to whom, Hamlet's declaration of identity is a blast of cold, refreshing new air. At this point he is both Warrior and Lover, since he goes on to say: "I loved Ophelia, Forty thousand brothers with all their quantity of love could not make up my sum!" (5. i. 263). To hear this from the man who had tortured Ophelia at their last private interview – the event that helps to unsettle her mind – is magnificently straightforward. Compared to his earlier actions, he seems a different man altogether. For comparison, let's look at how he talks to Ophelia in the first part of the play. Notice how hard it is to pin down what he may mean and what he feels.

Hamlet:	I did love you once.
Ophelia:	Indeed my Lord, you did make me believe so.
Hamlet:	You should not have believed me, for virtue cannot so inoculate our old stock but we shall relish of it. I loved thee not.
Ophelia:	I was the more deceived.
Hamlet:	Get thee to a nunnery. Why wouldst thou be a breeder of sinners? (3.1.115-123)

No wonder Ophelia thinks he's gone mad. Even the king, spying on the pair, declares, "Love? His affections do not that way tend." And yet that is exactly what is going on. Hamlet loves Ophelia but he's not sure he can trust her.

Symbolically we can see this as Hamlet rejecting the feminine part of himself in order to take on the more masculine persona of the revenger. But it is a dangerous psychic course, one which demands the throwing away of one's finer and gentler (and more vulnerable) traits. In fact this rejection, like his rejection of his mother and Ophelia's subsequent death, means he is refusing to re-establish contact with the feminine aspect, the anima, which he will need if he wishes to achieve balanced Warrior-Lover and Monarch status.

It is only after his return from his sea-trip, after he has declared his love for the now dead Ophelia, and after we see a gentler, more philosophical Hamlet, that we have a sense of him having tempered his wild masculine energies with something more compassionate. His apology to Laertes before their duel is a masterpiece of heartfelt diplomacy, but it's delivered too late for Laertes to be able to believe it. Anyway, poor Laertes is on his own course as a revenger, and so he too has had to crush out any gentler aspects of himself. He's so enraged that he wouldn't be able to hear any apology, let alone accept it. Perhaps it is in the constant devotion of Horatio to his old student friend that we see the hint we need that the kinder, more compassionate part of Hamlet is still to be found, beneath the conflicting views the rest of the court has of him.

Notice that a revenger is always working from a sense of hurt ego. It is a role and as such, the realm of the Orphan. Hamlet's refusal to accept that role outright, and his questioning of what he should do, mark him as a Pilgrim. In the graveyard scene he declares his love for Ophelia, announcing openly his sense of what his personal truths are, and shows that he is prepared to fight for them – all signs of the Warrior-Lover. But it is only when Hamlet begins to accept fate, and to see there is a 'special providence in the fall of a sparrow' (5. ii, 211-12), that he moves closer to the realm of the Monarch who is able to see the forces of time at work and to view them dispassionately.

As a Warrior, he defeats Laertes, and as a man of morality – a Lover of what is right – he executes Claudius when his murderous plots are laid bare before the assembled court. He is, briefly, the king. Even as he dies, he has enough aware-ness of his duty to nominate Fortinbras as his successor – a wise move if peace is to be ensured in Denmark. He saves Horatio from suicide, therefore making him the official historian of all that has happened: again, an important task to ensure a trouble-free and peaceful succession for Fortinbras. Even when dying Hamlet thinks of what his duty is, and wastes no time on self-pity. This is very different from the tortured self-doubting prince of the start of the play. We see that, finally, he would have made a good king if he'd had the chance. The kingdom has been purged of evil, and Hamlet (himself tainted with Polonius' death) has been the agent of the purgation and paid the price. If magic has occurred, it has been God's guiding hand that worked it by using Hamlet.

This has been a detailed discussion and it has established several important things that need to be re-stated here. First, Shakespeare's worldview seems to be very close to the idea of the six stages. Second, he examines the trajectory of his main characters from a variety of angles and situations, and in so doing he alerts his readers to the different sorts of struggles we are all likely to encounter in our lives. No one could hope to cover every eventuality, every permutation of the six stages, and make them universally applicable. The aim here has been to show that Shakespeare extended the archetypes we have already seen, asking us to consider how exactly they function under varying conditions. The advantage for us, as I stated at the start of this section, is that literature is able to present us with char-acters who are recognizably human who are in a state of development. They are dynamic, and they are distilled. The audience witnesses whole lifetimes in the course of a couple of hours and can draw lessons about human nature. Where history tends to be about political events that shape a nation, literature focuses on the personal experiences that happen to individuals. It is a supremely compressed way of viewing human experience.

The six stages seem to be everywhere. One more example may be needed, however.

Note
1. All quotations are from the Peter Alexander edition, above.

Chapter Fifteen

Literature: Continued.

If we accept the analysis of *Macbeth* I have just offered, and if we see the same ideas occurring in *King Lear*, then we can make a distinction between Shakespeare's plays. Macbeth is tragic because he fails to grow to real maturity, and actually slips backwards down the levels. His total dependence upon the witches marks him as someone who has descended to the level of a desperate Orphan. As such he remains egocentric and destructive, even when he knows he's beaten. Yet the play is about more than his failure to grow into a satisfactory king, and it is about more than how he becomes a perversion of the successful Warrior he once was. Malcolm emerges as the good and pure future king, just as Edgar does in *King Lear*. The plays are not, therefore, about the individuals but about the triumph of kingship, in its highest form. It would not be hard to argue the same for *Hamlet*. Fortinbras is an able Warrior, no doubt. And perhaps that is virtue enough in the Denmark of the period. Only the audience has witnessed the lessons Hamlet learned, and once Hamlet is dead, Denmark is not much wiser. Horatio will tell the story – Hamlet has ordered him to do so – but only those of us who have heard Hamlet fumbling his way towards understanding in his soliloquies will ever know what actually was at issue. This becomes even more poignant if we look at *Julius Caesar* in the same light. For, at the end of that play, we have a conclusion that is above all else ambivalent. When Octavius views Brutus' corpse and claims, "This was a man," he is making a bare statement of fact, which looks like praise. Yes, Brutus was a man. And like all men, he made many mistakes. Notice Octavius doesn't say, "He was a leader" or "He was a genius" or anything of that sort. This final scene, in which such transparently pious platitudes are mouthed, should leave us feeling considerable doubt as to the true qualities of the victorious Mark Antony and Octavius. We, in the audience, know that Rome is due to be swept by further civil wars, further bloodshed and sacrifice. In fact, the tragedy of *Julius Caesar* is that the disasters do not end, and the pain continues. There is no consoling sense that evil has run its course and a good person will now take charge. Antony and Octavius can be effective fighters – but we have no assurance that they can be just and decent rulers. They just aren't Monarchs. They have attached themselves only to power, and function as Orphans who buy into only one idea of what is important.

These renditions of tragedy, then, fall into two categories: the tragedies of powerful figures who fail to grow or develop, and tragedy in which, despite the failure of the main character to grow completely, the situation is advanced towards peace and harmony.

Characters who will not change, or who are in positions of power and cannot change for fear of losing that power, are the figures who are left behind. In *Hamlet*, Claudius cannot pray, and he cannot give up Gertrude or the kingdom of Denmark – his instincts as a plotter stay with him until his own plot to kill Hamlet ensures his own death. He does not change. In the comedies, those who cannot change are bypassed or contained. *Much Ado*'s Don John has the opportunity to leave his plotting, and he doesn't. It earns him prison. In *As You Like It*, Jacques' famous melancholy gives everyone a sour taste in the mouth. His seven ages of man is as gloomy a vision as we could ever hope to have of mankind. And it is inaccurate, since he considers man in isolation and having children is never mentioned as part of man's destiny and duty – a considerable oversight in Shakespeare's world. In Protestant England practically everyone got married and went forth to multiply. Significantly Jacques is the only one who decides not to leave the Forest of Arden. Everyone else has had enough exile, discomfort, and wandering, thank you very much. Jacques, unattached, sees the four weddings and will not join in the fun. Similarly, Malvolio in *Twelfth Night* refuses to change. He is "sick of self love" (1. v. 85) as Olivia points out, and even when fooled, disgraced, and mocked, he will not change his view of himself. His final words, "I'll be reveng'd on the whole pack of you," (5. i. 364) indicate his desire to stay in that injured, egocentric, victimhood. It is simply the reverse of his earlier bullying rectitude.

If Malvolio is stuck at a stage, it is surely the Orphan stage, since he has found a place (in Olivia's house) that suits him. Self-absorbed, he assumes Olivia must love him, for he is the key person in the household. He doesn't desire to change so much as he desires an elevation in his status so that he can be even more who he is. He fantasizes about being able to tell off Sir Toby, once he is married to Olivia. His idea of attending to business involves telling others how to live. As we have seen, the Active Orphan is good at doing that.

The characters who will not change, who refuse to grow, all cling to an outmoded sense of themselves. They are all Orphans.

The characters who do change, who grow and help others to grow, all start at Orphan stage.

It is in Shakespeare's comedies that we see this most clearly. In *Twelfth Night* Viola is a shipwrecked Orphan forced to dress as a boy and find a place to live (like all good Orphans). She then sets about educating her new master, Orsino. Orsino's emotional education is one of the main themes of the play: because when we first see him he is stuck in self-indulgent lover mode. Whenever we find ourselves acting a role, as Orsino does when he sees himself as 'the Lover', we are very likely to be in passive Orphan mode, adopting the conventional way of being in an attempt to avoid finding out what it is we truly feel. Orsino believes himself in love. His ego is fully engaged and he simply will not accept that Olivia isn't interested, so this 'love' is merely a mirage supported by his vanity. Worse still, he will not examine his feelings until the disguised Viola comes along to challenge him and make him question himself, which is what a Pilgrim has to undertake. Viola's task is to bring him out of the imaginary world and into the world of action, which is where emotions are tested. She makes a Pilgrim of him.

As a result of taking in the lessons about love that Viola has coached him in, he can see the real qualities she has behind her disguise, and he can recognize that rapport, understanding, and loyalty are important parts of mature love. Orsino is able to use what he has learned in his discussions with Viola – and we'll recall that Pilgrims are those who discuss and question – and once in Pilgrim mode he can redirect his love. He is able to let go of the loving-beauty-from–a-distance role, and understand true attachment. This is the realm of the Warrior-Lover. He can now marry Viola, accept Olivia's love for Sebastian, and the loving bond of loyalty all have for each other. Near disaster is turned into happiness. Linked to his 'female' other half, Orsino can now become a true Monarch, and we know already that Viola can contact the masculine side of herself since she's been in male disguise for three months, using it to teach Orsino about balance in his life. They are balanced as man and woman, and also within themselves. Harmony is achieved, and in almost no time at all. Love is what makes it happen. Perhaps Shakespeare is suggesting that love is what brings the Magician stage forward.

We'll notice that Viola starts the play shipwrecked, devoid of everything – a true Orphan – yet she never gives in to passivity. She quickly finds someone to adopt her, first the Sea Captain, then Orsino. She rapidly becomes a Pilgrim, going between Olivia and Orsino, wrestling with her own feelings. As she talks with both Orsino and Olivia about love, she expresses her own feelings about the seemingly impossible love she is experiencing. As in the old adage that the best way to understand something is to teach it, Viola is able to access her own wisdom as she attempts to explain what love is to each of them. Yet she does attempt – faithfully – to do what is right. She does tell Olivia how Orsino loves her – which can't be easy, given her own feelings. This is, one could say, her stage of growing into Warrior-hood. She does the right thing: she does not try to build up her own position. If we laugh at her near duel with Sir Andrew, it does not mean she is devoid of Warrior-Lover courage. She simply is not a brawler, and she sees no point in risking anyone's life over a stupid misunderstanding. If we want more proof of this she is, in Act V, prepared to go with Orsino, who imagines she has fooled him, even when he says:

> My thoughts are ripe in mischief;
> I'll sacrifice the lamb that I do love
> To spite a raven's heart within a dove.

In his misplaced rage he's ready to kill her. Her reply is worth noting.

> And I, most jocund, apt, and willingly
> To do you rest, a thousand deaths would die. (v.1. 123-7)

She doesn't hesitate. Her courage is in no doubt at all. Throughout the play she shows moral bravery. For example she never has much trouble correcting Orsino or interrupting him:

> Viola: "Yea but I know…"
> Orsino: "What dost thou know?"
> Viola: Too well what love to man women may owe."

She can argue, fight verbally, express her heart, and yet be patient and caring. This is where the Warrior-Lover grows towards the level of Monarch. As she grows, Orsino is enabled to grow as well, learning the lessons he needs from a woman. He learns because she gets to express what she knows – thus allowing her truly to own her knowledge – and so together they are moved to Monarch level.

Perhaps the thing that most impresses any audience in *Twelfth Night* is that Viola speaks her mind. She is unashamedly herself, and even though she cannot speak directly about her own love for Orsino (since she's in disguise and Orsino is fixated on Olivia), she does talk about what she knows about love. She does not hesitate to tell Olivia what she thinks of her, either. Viola speaks straight. She does not use her disguise as a man to conceal her essential nature. In fact, it is the very thing that allows her to help her speak her truths. What Shakespeare gives us is a detailed presentation of how a woman moves through the stages of development, and how she can raise the awareness of the men and women around her as she does so. And she's not a unique case.

Shakespeare's disguised heroines grow because they speak their own, highly intelligent, truth. Rosalind in *As You Like It* is in many ways similar to Viola. Both are nominally Orphans on the run from male parental authority, but when they take up their male disguises they refuse to be victims, and instead become Pilgrims. Beatrice in *Much Ado* is an Orphan, living with her uncle, but she refuses to be the passive female everyone expects a woman to be, and her determination marks her as a Pilgrim. Portia in *The Merchant of Venice* has been left wealthy by her father's death, and every gold-digger in the area wants to marry her and take charge of her and the money. She's an Orphan, of course, but also one who refuses to be passively adopted and so she goes into disguise to save Antonio, and, by extension, her marriage to the man who got Antonio into such trouble to begin with by borrowing money. Helena in *All's Well* is also an Orphan living in Bertram's mother's household, and her courage, skill in medicine, and resourcefulness mark her as a something more than just an acquiescent female. She cures the king and goes searching for Bertram when he deserts her, traveling across Europe in order to corner her husband. She is closer to being a Warrior-Lover even though she may seem at first glance to be in Pilgrim mode. The difference is she knows exactly who she loves and who she has to seek out.

So one might say that for Shakespeare's characters the ability to grow, to move up the ladder from Pilgrim to Warrior-Lover, requires love that is acted upon courageously, since love is one of the few emotions that can move us beyond egoism. It is only when these women take decisive action to educate the men and bring them to a place of awareness that they can become Warrior-Lovers, since in speaking out about what they feel, they explore the nature of that feeling, and grow.

The important point is that the love has to be returned, faithfully. The attachment must be mutual in Shakespeare's formulation. *All's Well* is a play with a bittersweet ending because, despite Helena's efforts, Bertram still doesn't seem to love her. It's been dubbed as a 'problem comedy' for this very reason. Whether the character experiences sexual love or familial love (one thinks of Edgar and Prospero) matters less than that the ability to attach to others is developed and tested, and then proved. Courage moves characters out of passive Orphan status, but it is love that places them on their spiritual paths.

Notice, though, that none of Shakespeare's women (nor any of his male characters in other plays) can solve the situation they are in. Time and chance has to do that for them. Viola states it openly:

> O Time, thou must untangle this, not I
> It is too hard a knot for me t'untie! (2. ii. 38-39)

The transition from Warrior-Lover to Monarch seems to depend upon the main character recognizing that time, circumstance, Fate, and God are the larger forces at work and that these must be worked with without hesitation. Again and again it is the workings of Fate that seem to bring the Warrior-Lover the chance to ascend further, whether it's shown in Hamlet's succinct 'The readiness is all' (5. ii. 216) or in Edgar's 'The ripeness is all' (5. ii. 11). The same profound awareness of being a servant of a larger power, and being faithful to that power, fuels each statement. And when Viola, Beatrice, Rosalind, Helena, Portia, and Olivia do truly take charge, it is in response to their knowing the time is right, that love cannot be put off. This is when harmony can be restored, as symbolized in the marriages, and the women are to be seen as Magicians – that is to say as facilitators of this miracle of human voluntary attachment. This is beautifully illustrated when Rosalind hears all too clearly Orlando's weariness at their playacting and discussions when he grumbles: 'I can live no longer by thinking' (5. i. 47). The time has come to replace thinking with doing, and she masterminds the rest of the play with its four simultaneous weddings. Marriage is, after all, not just about love, but also about intelligent trust between two people as they face the future together – faith, in a word.

This is given another twist when we contrast the work of Shakespeare's great contemporary, Christopher Marlowe. *Dr. Faustus* was an Elizabethan smash hit (it played to packed houses for two weeks on its first run), and it has most of the elements we have been discussing. Faustus, we are told in the prologue, is of humble origins, and he becomes famous at Wittenberg University for his studies, his lectures, and his abilities, particularly in medicine. He is an Orphan who has found his attachment in learning, and although he may seem like a Monarch in all he does, the play opens with him unable to decide how to use his skills. He literally wanders from book to book, rejecting medicine, law, philosophy, and religion before he settles on witchcraft, in the form of necromancy. He is the Pilgrim who chooses the wrong attachment to explore because he is motivated by egoism, the desire for wealth and recognition. He shows courage – or something like it – because everyone else seems to shrink away from what he does, and he does not seem to be afraid of giving up his soul, at least at first. He thinks he's a Warrior. Yet this supposed courage feels as if it's closer to the wild bravado of the gambler who places a bold stake without any true sense of what he risks. Actually, in selling his soul to the devil he is merely accepting another home – so he falls from Pilgrim stage and becomes a corrupted Orphan figure, one who merely opts for a short cut. As we've seen in all the major works we've so far looked at, there can be no shortcuts in psychic development.

And when he gets his four and twenty years of power in return for his soul, what does Faustus do? All his ideas for making Wittenberg stronger and better seem to evaporate. He cheats a horse dealer (a bit like getting one over on your local shifty used-car dealer); he gets grapes out of season for a pregnant duchess; he plays practical jokes on the Pope; he conjures up illusions of dead and famous people – but doesn't ask anything insightful when they appear. They are simply tricks done for others. How sad to be able to conjure up Alexander the Great and not remember to ask him any questions! He also summons up demons in the form of women, so that he can have a red-hot sex life. And yet his very first wish is for a wife – perhaps the most commonplace of wishes given that every man and woman in Elizabethan England was expected to marry. Ironically it turns out this is just another thing Satan cannot provide, since marriage is a holy sacrament. Faustus has no vital loving human relationship with anyone. Even Wagner, his servant, is afraid rather than loyal. In unconscious self-parody, one of Faustus' final demands is to have Helen of Troy appear before him. She appears and his response is ecstatic:

> Was this the face that launched a thousand ships
> And burned the topless towers of Illium?
> Sweet Helen, make me immortal with a kiss   (scene 12, l. 81-83).

Well, actually, this isn't the face. This Helen is an illusion. And who knows if it is even an accurate facsimile? Also, in speaking of Helen's face he makes it quite obvious he refers only to her outer attributes. She is a sex object to him. But it's also worth remembering that she didn't launch any ships. In fact, she didn't do anything much. It was a jealous husband who whipped up the fleet to pursue her abductor. Simply put, Faustus deceives himself into thinking that since he is the one who will actually get to possess her body it will make him superior to all other men, even the Greek heroes, and that kissing this woman will make him "immortal". It's an odd statement from someone who doesn't even believe he has a soul, or so he claims. Faustus wants to see himself as some sort of all-powerful male Lothario, but the scene is one he has chosen in order to delude himself. Faustus wants love and he merely gets the pick of the brothel. His only real attachment seems to be to the cynical Mephastophilis, whom he calls, "Sweet Mephastophilis" (scene 12, l. 60) – an unusual choice of adjective for the creature he knows will rip him limb from limb later. It is perhaps the same thing we see in the love-hate relationship some people have with their drug-dealers.

Faustus has made a huge error in that he fails to love – and his soul is wasted. His expertise in witchcraft is not his, at all. He has been adopted by Mephastophilis. That's all he seems capable of, and his wonderful abilities remain unused. Faustus, in failing to achieve a meaningful attachment to anyone or anything except ego-gratification, is a tragic figure to be wary of. What we can learn from this figure is just how easy it is for even the supposedly enlightened and intelligent to fool themselves. If Marlowe can offer us anything in terms of the life stages, it might be that he asks us to consider how easily we can remain in Orphan stage and yet construct for ourselves a framework of ideas that can make us feel as if we have become better than those around us. Faustus is a man who wants shortcuts, who wants to believe his own publicity about himself, and in order to do so he agrees not to look too closely into things.

If Marlowe's figures fail to make the transition to full Pilgrim stage and beyond, it may be because talented Kit Marlowe, the toast of London, was homosexual in an age when homosexuality was considered immoral and illegal, as well as a recipe for eternal damnation. His heroes do not have successful loving relationships. Tamburlaine comes closest. The Warrior–shepherd almost succeeds in ruling the world, until his beloved wife dies, whereupon he begins to lose interest in conquest. He slips back to Orphan mode. Even in *Edward II*, Gaveston, the homosexual love interest, is seen as shallow and self-centered. Marlowe made a career out of showing men who fail to love successfully, and therefore who fail to grow. Magnificent as their rhetoric may be there is always a strain of desperation in it. His characters remain alone and their downfall is sealed when they trust others based on their desperate ego demands. Faustus trusts Mephastophilis; Tamburlaine trusts his wife; Edward trusts Gaveston; and the Jew of Malta trusts the Governor; and all are betrayed by those they felt to be closest to them. Without real, reciprocated love there can be no progression.

Note

1. Marlowe quotations are from the *Norton Anthology of English Literature*, vol. 1 8th ed. Greenblatt, Abrams et alia. New York: Norton, 2005.

Chapter Sixteen

Nineteenth and Twentieth Century Literature: Failing Belief in the Stages

If we jump ahead here in our survey of the literature we may find some indicators that can tell us why more recent writing has, at times, not shown us the way forward. If we focus on Dickens, for example, we have an instance of a wildly popular writer who certainly seems to be invested in looking at how people interact. Dickens' novels are stuffed full of Orphans: Oliver Twist, David Copperfield, Pip of *Great Expectations*, and so on. *Bleak House* has several sets of Orphans or 'wards of the court', *Nicholas Nickleby* is about a whole school full of abandoned children, and *Little Dorrit* has a family confined to debtors' prison which makes Little Dorrit herself a form of orphan. What is remarkable about the orphans Dickens gives us is how often they are adopted and how, in many ways, they do not seem to progress very far through the stages we are discussing here. In *Great Expectations* Pip is an orphan brought up by his sister. Pip thinks the wealthy Miss Havisham (who has adopted Estella) has adopted him and he thinks he is destined to fulfill Miss Havisham's wishes and marry her. In fact the money that mysteriously flows to him comes from the criminal Magwitch, who has 'adopted' him after the terrified Pip has been forced to bring him food, and whose money Pip eventually refuses – he rejects the adoption. He then manages to get a job and support himself, and only later does he recognize that his friend Herbert Pocket engineered the job for him – thus adopting him in a different way. What Dickens seems to do is to show that his orphans will eventually all be adopted and (more or less) happily re-integrated into a family circle from whom they will derive their sense of personal meaning.

This is quite obviously unrealistic in the case of Oliver Twist, the child of a disgraced wealthy woman who dies. He is born into the workhouse, apprenticed to a sadistic chimney sweep, and then adopted by Fagin's merry thieves. At the end of the story he is happily reunited with his mother's family – and yet he shows absolutely no signs of any sort of maladjustment when he becomes an upper class Victorian boy after a life of extreme want and privation. It seems that Dickens did not believe that there was anything more important than a family circle, and that whatever life lessons his characters learned were less important than their ability to find some sort of a family home.

In this Dickens was a creature of his age. Economic survival in the years of the industrial revolution in Britain meant that the search for truth was less important for him and for his readers than learning how to get along reasonably with others and squeeze a little joy out of life along the way. In *Bleak House*, Esther Summerson doesn't really want to know who her mother is, and effectively refuses the inheritance she is entitled to, while Sir Leicester cares less about what his wife has done in the past than that he needs her and loves her now. The harmony of the family circle is valued above truth. And it's not hard to have sympathy with this view. Dickens had been born into poverty, and he knew many of his readers were amongst the poorest classes, so one might say he knew his readership, and he knew their plight.

The world of Dickens does not seem to require the fully-fledged Warrior. Characters go searching for meaning, and do occasionally fight for it, but they seem to settle for domesticity. This is not a criticism, since domestic peace is not so plentifully abundant that we can scorn it. It is merely an observation.

Even Dickens' most pithy statement about the Industrial Revolution, *Hard Times*, produces only the performers of Sleary's Circus show as heroic figures – characters who are otherwise comic and child-like but who share a heartfelt devotion to each other. Dickens' characters seem to move from a state of miserable orphanhood to a condition of happy and loving Orphan attachment. This is not a trivial change. Love does triumph. Yet it seems as if Dickens is suggesting that the opportunities for large-scale Warrior-Lover actions are limited within the more enclosed world of the city lives he depicts. Dickens returns again and again to scenes of family parties, or gatherings of friends (usually including a bowl of steaming punch to help things along), as his way of honoring this very human bond. The constantly broke Mr. Micawber, in *David Copperfield*, is perhaps the most memorable example of this – a jovial figure who seems almost incapable of taking any responsibility for his life and his family, but who brings a community of friends together with his good humor.

By contrast, in *Great Expectations* Jaggers, who is the finest criminal defense lawyer London, holds a gloomy luncheon party. The serving woman, we learn later, is a murderer he managed to free on a technicality. She knows she can never leave his service and he seems to delight in keeping her in his household as a sort of trophy. The sense of repression and sadistic control is chilling. The Monarch archetype of male and female in balance is, in this case, a ghastly parody of what it could be. This event stands in immediate contrast to the madcap hilarity of his legal clerk's marriage ceremony. Wemmick, who lives in a kind of scrap-wood castle with his old deaf father, decides to take Pip along to his marriage, all the time pretending that the event has not been planned in any way, and at the last moment seizing a fishing rod out of pure, spontaneous fun. Wemmick's is just one example of marriage for real affection – and the hint that Dickens gives us is that people who marry for love (as opposed to the heartless financial arrangements that Dickens records so often with his wealthy characters) are those who are the real Warrior-Lovers of the age, who become Monarchs in their marriages when real, full Monarch status is not possible. It is a domestic version of the patterns we have seen. If there is a Magician stage it is contained in the vision of a supportive, loving circle of family and friends.

This is a much more modest view of human potential than anything we have seen until now. The effects of the Industrial Revolution and the advent of mass society in the cities – both of them startling new events in human history – coincides with a diminution of spiritual expectations.

This pattern is not just present in Dickens; Henry James exhibits it also. In *The Ambassadors* (1903) we see Strether as the 'adopted' diplomatic emissary of Mrs. Newsome, with whom he has an understanding and an attachment, as he attempts to get her son Chad to return from Paris, where he has adopted the ways of Old Europe. Both Chad and Strether are changed and refined by their experience of Europe, and yet, when the novel ends, it is Strether who returns to Mrs. Newsome, knowing that she will no longer accept him because he has failed in his mission. He has learned something about himself, it is true, yet he also turns his back on Maria Gostrey, who certainly understands him and his situation with admirable delicacy. Strether does what is conventionally correct, as a good obedient Orphan, but it looks a great deal like the avoidance of a real, loving attachment with Ms. Gostrey. Strether appears as a fine and delicate endangered creature, wonderful – but his feelings and longings are bound for ultimate extinction in a crass world. Is his action in returning to the United States, an unsuccessful emissary, heroic or cowardly? James leaves it to us to decide.

This could certainly be seen as one of Henry James' themes, and one on which he works some interesting variations. In *Daisy Miller* (1879) the Europeanized American Winterbourne comes very close to taking a risk and declaring his attachment to Miss Miller, who is through and through 'an American girl' as her brother announces. Winterbourne has only his aunt as an attachment – he is an ex-patriot, and therefore a sort of Orphan, whose 'studies' make him almost a Pilgrim. But he doesn't declare himself to Daisy; she flirts with another man, catches malaria and dies. The last we see of him he is back to his same familiar routine in Geneva, 'studying' hard and 'much interested in a foreign lady'. He fails to move out of his accustomed rut, the comfortable Orphan role he knows so well. Daisy offered him the chance to become a Pilgrim, perhaps, to question his world's values and even to take his personal growth further since he would have to confront society if he decides to remain with her – and ultimately he refuses the offer. In many ways it is the offer to become a Warrior-Lover that he turns down. It is not a failure of James' imagination that he doesn't explore it – it is instead one of the important things he has to tell us. Ours is not a society in which being a Warrior-Lover can easily pay off, he seems to say. It's much safer to be an adopted Orphan. This theme echoes through James' work. When people marry for money, as James shows them doing most poignantly in *The Golden Bowl* (1904) he shows us that we must not expect them to display the heroic qualities that spring from the development of deep, vital love. The best we can expect is to see the heroism of long-suffering emotional self-denial patiently borne so that material well-being can be preserved.

Edith Wharton makes the point even more strongly. In *The House of Mirth* (1905) Lily Bart will not conform and marry for money; and society's response is to crush her. When she kills herself she does so in a gesture that is an acknowledgement of society's power – she leaves all her debts paid so as to be above obvious reproach – but her action is also an escape from that power.

If Henry James shows us the silvered bars of our cages, Joseph Conrad, the creator of modernism, presents a slightly different picture. His masterpiece *Heart of Darkness* (1899) is a depiction of the six stages as they go horribly wrong. Kurtz, a European trader, has gone into the Belgian Congo and, free from the restraints of civilization, has had himself made into a tribal god. Armed with modern advantages such as rifles and a callous cruelty to the native populace, he is a prophetic hint of the atrocities that would later be enacted against 'lesser' races by the Nazis and others. Kurtz believes himself to be a hero and a god. Conrad makes it quite clear that Kurtz and his type are not gods, but merely people without any sort of belief except in making money – the most hopeless version of the Orphan one can imagine. The whole novella, and its companion novel, *Lord Jim* (1900), is concerned with how people will often take the easy short cuts to convince themselves they have achieved Monarch or Magician status when they have, in actuality, done nothing of the sort. Instead it is Marlow, as the relayer of both stories, who emerges as the one who has gone down the path of spiritual growth. He has seen his Shadow self in Kurtz, fought with it, and won. He has found out what he believes (as a Warrior-Lover) in this confrontation, and he now knows what he values, yet he seems unable to make the transition to Monarch status. Yes, he is a captain of a ship – so he knows how to manage this microcosm of the Monarch's realm. Yet he is presented to us as someone who is still haunted by what he has seen, and who is having some trouble in making sense of it. It is almost as if Conrad is suggesting that Marlow's territory of psychological trauma is what we'll have to observe and learn from, but what we make of it is up to us to decide. In this Marlow is an example of the Warrior meeting his own limitations. Again, we can compare him to Gawain returning to Camelot, but without the consoling King Arthur to validate what he has seen. It is we, the readers, who must use Marlow's experiences to help propel us, if we are capable, to Monarch status.

In Conrad's later novels the heroes often fail to make meaningful connection to the women in their lives and as a result they remain as Orphans. In *Victory* (1914) the quintessential loner Heyst cannot tell Lena he loves her, and when she is killed defending his life he burns her body, their house, and himself; Razumov in *Under Western Eyes* (1911) reveals his duplicity to Natalie Haldin when he begins to feel attracted to her, and although he is eventually cared for by Tekla, he is at that point deaf, half crippled, and an outcast. He is an orphan by birth, a loner, and yet does not seem to be able to love anyone. In *The Secret Agent* (1907) Verloc, shocked by the explosion that has killed his brother-in-law, hopes Winnie will understand him and love him, but when he asks for an embrace he receives a knife in the chest. Although he has warm sexual feelings for his wife, she has married him chiefly as a way to ensure some financial stability for herself and her brother. Theoretically all these figures could move towards reaching balanced Monarch status, and yet none of them seems able to make the transition because the Warrior-Lover stage cannot develop completely without love. And perhaps that is the point: Conrad invites us, the readers, to make the leap for ourselves. If we can understand the situations he describes, in all their complexity and richness, then we can glimpse the realm that one has to come to terms with in order to become fully a Monarch. It's the breaking free from those limitations that seems to be so impossible.

Without surveying all modern literature in detail we would have to say that it seems to be true that the six stages are not as fully in evidence in our literature as in earlier centuries. They still exist, of course, yet it is almost as if the more modern writers do not seem, on the whole, to be able to believe in them, or believe in human progress, beyond Warrior stage.

This vacuum was quickly filled. Hitler used archetypal images, grafted onto Wagner's music, and the bastardized notion of the *Übermensch* (clearly a Warrior of sorts) was created to replace what had been a potentially useful series of ideas about human development contained in the form of legends. Given this type of manipulation, which was used in different ways by the Communist regimes of many countries also, it's easy to understand why writers might shy away from this sort of discussion. Instead, today's archetypes seem to have been redefined in ways that emphasize their glamor and not their interior values. So, we have

'Superheroes' who are ridiculous excuses for making money off children and their ill-informed parents. Thus can commercialism and propaganda hurt our lives.

We can, however, take something valuable from the examples of Dickens, James, and Conrad. In each writer's work there is a sense that after a character has been through something extreme then there is, perforce, the need to settle back into the ordinary, working-day world. When we do so, as we must, we find ourselves accepting what looks like a return to Orphan level. This seems to be the level at which most people operate most of the time. When the excitement is over we still have to make sure the electricity bills are paid, the car is repaired, and so on. We may seem, in our lives, to be surrounded by Orphans who insist on the regulations and the rules, yet we do well if we understand that some of these people are already further advanced. When the occasion demands it there will be Warrior-Lovers and Monarchs. Ordinary citizens, when faced with extraordinary struggles, will show their true qualities. Until that point, though, we all have to live by the rules in what seems like an Orphan's world.

And that's what makes our own personal growth so challenging. So many people around us look as if they're Orphans, buying into the status quo. There is a tendency to assume that nothing else and no other possible way of being exists, when this is not the case.

Note

1. All the novels referred to have been reprinted many times. I recommend the Penguin Editions.

Chapter Seventeen

Recent Literature: Harry Potter

J.K. Rowling's novels show unmistakable signs of reflecting our six archetypes. They are so wildly popular and so obviously filled with archetypal imagery that they are hard to ignore in a discussion such as this. In addition, they originally hit the reading public as something rather new, daring, and exciting, and partly this has to do with the way the characters are developed.

The archetypes are pushed upon us early. Harry the Innocent is orphaned practically at birth and left with the non-wizard Dursleys, who do all they can to make him feel like an outcast. Therefore we can see Harry as an Orphan (and he begins each new story back at Privet Drive, newly an Orphan) who becomes a Pilgrim. This happens first in the Hogwarts' sport of quidditch. The 'seeker' in the game has the task of tracking down a particular kind of flying ball, a flitch, which has more value than the other balls, and when captured causes the game to end. Clearly this is a metaphor about the different levels at which people can seek for meaning. This is re-enforced in volume seven when the very first flitch that Harry ever caught in a game turns out to contain one of the objects that Harry has been seeking for a long time. So Harry becomes a 'seeker' in the first volume, and it is plain we are to see him as a seeker after truth, a Pilgrim, from this point onwards, especially as he immediately sets about trying to solve the various mysteries that descend on Hogwarts.

Notice that in each volume the truth he has to seek is a little more sinister, and Harry has to develop and use his skills a little more fully. In each volume he has to show his courage, and he has to demonstrate love and loyalty during the climactic confrontation each tale provides – which allows him to be seen as responding each year to ever more demanding tasks. Starting each year as an Orphan, he moves from Pilgrim to Warrior-Lover archetype, and then becomes a Monarch in his mastery of the challenge he faces. The aftermath of each adventure is that there is an effect on the entire school that is in some way empowering – and the Magician in him emerges.

Another way to look at this is in terms of the endings of the seven volumes. The resolutions to the plots become steadily less cut and dried as we progress through the series. In volume one Harry and his friends save the Sorcerer's stone from Voldemort's grasp, and their achievements are acknowledged with joy by their housemates at the end of term feast. This is an overt, public triumph, and one that would appeal to any eleven-year-old. In volume two Harry rescues Ginnie Weasley, who has been possessed by the spirit of Voldemort. This is every twelve-year-old boy's dream, to rescue a younger person (and of the opposite sex, too) and yet the triumph is more muted. The Weasleys are happy, as is Dumbledore, but the celebration is less public. Volume three continues this trend with Harry and Hermione rescuing Sirius (the child rescues the god-parent, in a plot that must surely echo every adolescent's desire to show his worth to a respected adult) and Sirius escapes on the rescued hippogriff, Buckbeak, who had been wrongly condemned to death. Yet because the rescues were made possible only by use of a device called a time-turner, which is not exactly legal in Hogwarts, this is a triumph that only Harry and Hermione know about. Moreover, in doing what is morally right Harry has put himself outside the law. His success is a private one. Dumbledore feigns ignorance of the whole thing.

In volume four the gloom and secrecy seem to deepen. Harry may win the triwizarding contest, but he knows now that Voldemort is back and possessed of a body, and even his wizarding win is eclipsed by the death of Cedric at the moment of triumph. Moreover, Harry's awareness of Voldemort's true status is greeted with disbelief. This disbelief mounts in volume five as Harry finds himself more and more alone, more and more a Pilgrim rejected by his peers for his beliefs, so he in turn rejects their conventional thinking. By the end of the book Dumbledore is, to everyone's relief, back in charge of Hogwarts, and the prophecy Voldemort sought to capture has been saved, at least for now. Yet Voldemort's followers are growing in power, and the Order of the Phoenix seems divided and less than competent to contain the threat. Volume six concludes with a full-scale battle at Hogwarts and the death of Dumbledore. The victories seem to have become progressively less convincing, and steadily less reassuring. We are moved in each successive volume from a relatively simple moral world towards one that is more and more problematic. If everyone agrees at the end of volume one that Harry has done the right thing, by the end of volume six not even Harry knows if he's done the right thing.

Volume seven takes this uncertainty to its limit, since Snape, whom we had last seen killing Dumbledore, is revealed to have been a double agent that the already dying Dumbledore requested should kill him. For large portions of the book even Dumbledore's own past seems questionable. However, subtler than this is that Harry is brought to recognize that part of Voldemort is in him, and some of his blood is in Voldemort. The only way forward is for Harry to volunteer himself as a victim, knowing Voldemort will kill him and in so doing will destroy a portion of his, Voldemort's, own soul – rendering him that much easier to kill. That, Harry knows, will allow someone else to finish the task. Harry must choose to die willingly, even though he sees his life as a marvel he would rather enjoy. He recognizes this as the only way to stop evil. It is the ultimate act of love for others, the final word in ego-suppression and altruism. It is an expression of the long defeat Paul Farmer spoke of, and Harry ceases to consider personal victory. He simply desires truth and clarity rather than lies and deceptions.

As we discover, Harry 'dies', meets Dumbledore's spirit, and learns the remaining truths behind the events of the past seven years. This is convenient for the plot, of course, but it establishes two major points. For the first time Dumbledore tells Harry the whole truth, treating him as an equal. This marks Harry's transition to the highest level. Harry is aware of this and when he talks to Dumbledore we notice he does so as an equal, in the same way he'd address Ron or Hermione. There are few traces of the old master-pupil relationship. Truth leads to equality. Harry then has the choice to 'move on' – remain dead and explore the next world – or return and finish the task. Like Buddha turning back from the brink of nirvana, like Jesus returning to the disciples, Harry takes the loving route that will help others. He returns, fights Voldemort, and in blocking Voldemort's killing curse (notice that the good wizards don't usually use killing enchantments; only the evil ones do) it rebounds and kills Voldemort himself. We could say that the climax of these tales is about the selflessness of the true Magician, and since Harry doesn't do anything in the final encounter except allow evil to destroy itself, his way is less action than inaction. Evil has a way of imploding upon itself when confronted.

Behind this lies a major point, which is that in the final section of the saga the most important emotion is love. Molly Weasley's fury at the Death Eaters' attempt to kill her children is a magnificent and successful version of the love that Harry's own parents showed in attempting to defend him many years earlier. Anger that is based in love becomes justifiable. Loyalty, love and courage confront selfishness and greed, and love wins. In case we miss the point, Harry twice saves the repellent Draco Malfoy's life. He'll save even his enemies if he can.

In each tale Harry has to show his bravery and stand up for what he believes in, and what he values. His loyalty to Dumbledore is tested in all the tales, each time a little more deeply. In the sixth volume he is faced with an extreme test for his loyalty – he has to continue to obey Dumbledore's instructions even though he fears that doing so will kill the old wizard. In the seventh volume he has to be loyal to his cause even though he is convinced it will kill him.

Several things are important, here. One is that in a realm of magic and spells that can make people act against their free will, Harry's loyalty is not compelled but it comes from his heart. Yet he also has to learn to control his heart-felt yearnings, especially to strike back at others. He'd dearly love to punish the Dursleys of course, but he must learn to control his power despite provocation in each volume. He has to discover the balanced use of his abilities, which means acting compassionately. And just as Harry is left to solve many of his difficulties on his own without Ron and Hermione to help him in the final crises, so we see him moving further and further from any parent substitute, too. In the third volume he rescues his godfather, Sirius Black, as well as his teacher Professor Lupin, who functions as a father figure and friend of the family. Eventually he loses Sirius at the end of volume five, Hagrid and Lupin are left marginalized, and even the grandfatherly Dumbledore dies. As he loses each in turn he must become more self-sufficient until, eventually, he must parent himself. It is as if Rowling is deliberately stripping Harry of adult and parental figures, forcing him to grow.

The fight for what is right therefore becomes increasingly lonely with each volume. In *The Half-Blood Prince* Harry eventually rejects even the sexual attachments that the young wizards blunder through. Harry tells Ginnie Weasley he can no longer be her boyfriend as it is simply too dangerous for her to be associated with him. This can therefore be seen as an attachment that is not simply ego-based, and it is a good fit for the archetype of the Warrior-Lover, especially as Harry and Ginnie seem to be evenly matched in many ways. It's not that he doesn't care for her — it's that he cares about her survival and he recognizes that since his own may be in question hers definitely will be. This is a marked contrast to the rather silly, self-involved adolescent crushes that seem to go on around him during the greater part of the story. Perhaps the piece of evidence we need is only made clear in book seven — Ginnie understands why he's had to leave her, and accepts it while maintaining her love for him. Harry's birthday kiss leaves no doubt about that. And he never ceases to love her.

Harry's devotion to Hermione and Ginnie are a way for us to see him integrating the 'female' part of himself into his awareness prior to him reaching Monarch status. The point is made for us strongly in volume seven when Harry is merciful at important moments, accepting 'female' compassion in his life. Right at the start of the book when he's under direct attack by Death Eaters he uses blocking spells, not killing ones, and is criticized for it. In the final battle he has to restrain Ron from wanting revenge. Harry knows that Ron's desire to kill is based in love for his dead brother, but he also knows that revenge is not going to help them defeat evil. Harry's course has to be more merciful. Yet he cannot allow himself to be in any way soft. He deliberately avoids Ginnie so that he won't let his personal feelings overwhelm his greater duty, which is surely evidence of the strength of his attachment and his awareness of the need to make balanced choices. This refusal of ego-based actions marks Harry as more aware than Ron and Hermione (who are not above a passionate embrace with each other when they feel frightened). It signals him as moving towards the highest level of Magician.

In whatever way one looks at her achievement, J. K. Rowling has provided us with a series of novels that seem to reaffirm the sense that one grows through certain stages, and that we grow through the stages not just once, but we keep coming back to the same sorts of struggles except each time at a deeper and more complex level. In doing so Harry grows towards the level of Magician in a process that is cyclical. Rowling gives us a readily accessible framework since Harry progresses through each academic 'year' learning life skills and gaining personal power. In this series of stories Rowling has done something that simply was not possible in literature before, if only because cycles of novels were and are extremely rare. She has let us see that progress through the life stages is not just a one-time experience. Harry goes through all the stages, from Innocent to Magician and he does so each year: so he completes each stage in all its sub-stages, on an annual basis. We could spend a vast amount of time attempting to show this statement to be true in a detailed examination of the texts. Perhaps it is enough to say that Harry arrives each year at Hogwarts surprised by the new, heavier workload, and at the end of each novel he has just achieved a not-inconsiderable act of wizardry that seems to mark his trajectory from Innocent to Magician in each instance. I suspect, however, that since Rowling is a novelist who deals with representations of human beings first and abstract ideas such as 'stages of life' second, we might find ourselves getting bogged down early on if we attempt to show this as an even or orderly progression. Children are complex. They develop new skills and then temporarily slip back to a less aware level. And that is as it should be. It is Rowling's gift to us that she sees them as people who are growing, above all else.

We can take this insight into the adult world, as well. When any of us feels threatened or insecure we are likely to slip, for a while, a few levels in our aware-ness – no matter how evolved we may be in the rest of our lives. The highly paid executive who is laid off in a corporate re-shuffle may well move, in shock, from Monarch to Orphan level. The overwhelmed mother may find herself reduced to helpless depression and self-pity by a difficult family situation, and the Warrior-Lover becomes, for a while, a passive Orphan. This is how life seems to test us. The point seems to be that we have to bounce back.

Rowling has one other great advantage. Since she is not writing within a realist framework she is free to spend more energy examining the very areas that modern writing is often unable to approach – the realms of the Monarch and the Magician.

Let's take a look at this. If Dumbledore is an example of the fully developed Magician to which Harry is aspiring, it's worth noting that he is rarely at the forefront of the action. He is, rather, someone who allows the actions to unfold, and we see that he is specifically *allowing* Harry to use his own power whenever possible rather than seeking to control or direct him. This, after all, is the mark of the true Magician; good impulses in others are encouraged, but not forced. And, as we are plentifully informed, Harry's power stems directly from love. It was his mother's love that made the infant Harry able to resist Voldemort's killing spell, causing it to bounce back at him. Harry's place at the Dursley's, no matter how it is begrudged him, is safe because there is sisterly love behind it – Mrs. Dursley was Harry's mother's sister. Harry's loyalty to Dumbledore is based in love. This is a point we will have to return to, since it seems as if love of one sort and another is one of the greatest forces at work in moving people through the stages.

Further evidence of this is in the sense that each volume of the series concludes with an act that has to do with love. In volume one it is Harry's purity of heart that allows him to be the one person who can hold the sorcerer's stone, since he's the one person who has no desire to use it for harm. In volume two the phoenix comes to save Harry as Dumbledore points out later, only because it recognizes the extent of Harry's loyalty and love for Dumbledore himself. In volume three Harry and his friends rescue two wrongly condemned creatures – Sirius and Buckbeak, and their love causes them to contribute to the resolution of the story. In volume four Harry's task is slightly different because he has to be loyal and loving to his friends *and* his rivals – and, in the case of Cedric Diggory, this saves his life. Moreover, when he fights Voldemort he proves in fact to be the more powerful magician. Seeing the images of his dead father and mother reminds him of what love is and Voldemort can do nothing against that. Volume five is in some ways about Harry's loyalty not just to Dumbledore but to the whole sense of what Hogwarts is there to do. The school is not just a place to teach skills, but a place in which the human spirit can be nurtured, and Harry knows that. He forms 'Dumbledore's Army' as a Warrior, but also as an act of loyalty to a principle of what is right, therefore achieving his objectives as a Warrior-Lover. Notice how his concept of love and loyalty has grown! Volume six shows him remaining true to what Dumbledore asks, even in the face of tremendous temptation, and even when he sees Dumbledore offering forgiveness to the despicable Malfoy. Malfoy's name is a clue here, since his name means, significantly, 'bad faith', which is the exact opposite of love. As we've seen in volume seven, Harry's love is tested to its ultimate limit, death, and he does not hesitate to fulfill his duty to what is right, what is loving, and what is true.

So, love and loyalty seem to be redefined as we go through these remarkable books, and it is these two qualities that cause the real magic to occur. Volume six ends with Dumbledore's funeral, and yet we can be sure from the emotional reaction of the crowd that his death was in no wise a defeat for the forces of love and good. In fact, it seems to have mobilized those very qualities in the mourners. The same thing happens in volume seven when Harry is thought dead – the Hogwarts defenders become even more determined, rather than less. When Voldemort dies the Death Eaters scramble to run away in a display that is the exact opposite of loyalty to a cause. Even the Malfoys are terrified that their son might have been hurt, and they stop fighting in order to find him – placing love before ambition.

Rowling is probably not the final word in how the six stages function. I'd like to suggest, though, that she seems to have access to the same sort of template we've been discussing so far, and that this adds to the attraction of her books. Moreover, she is addressing herself to the parts of life where we can become Magicians, and she asks us to consider how we can get to that point. We could express this differently: the stories differentiate between muggles and wizards. Muggles are those who can't or won't accept that magic exists. They are, one might say, grimly utilitarian. They are the Orphans who, like Harry at the start, feel that life holds nothing more for them. Then there are those who know there is more to life, and who become Pilgrims in seeking that 'more'.

The Dursleys, interestingly, know that there is more to life than their muggle world view admits and they keep getting reminded of this; but they are deeply afraid of what they see and so they choose not to admit to what they know. Orphans of the first order, they represent the condition many people live in, as Orphans who are determined to believe in an Orphan world no matter what.

The final scene of volume seven is somewhat domestic. Harry is married to Ginnie and they are seeing their children off on the Hogwarts express, and there they meet Ron and Hermione who are also married and doing the same thing. They all look like well-adjusted Orphans, doing the socially accepted activities of parenthood. Yet we know that they are sending their children off on the first part of their own journeys of self-discovery. The parents may look like ordinary wizards, but they have a profound awareness of the nature of love. The Magic continues in their children, and it's the magic of allowing others their freedom.

Harry has made a life based in love, not power, and it has been signaled to us that he is not interested in power when we see him give up the Elder Wand, the most powerful wand in existence, in order to have his own magic wand back again. His own wand is nominally inferior, yet it has one huge advantage: Harry has felt it on several occasions showing him what to do and he is utterly comfortable in his rapport with it. This is the realm of the ultimate magician, when the magic seems to do itself because it comes from the core of oneself. Giving up the supremely powerful Elder Wand is a symbol of how Harry chooses to relinquish power for its own sake in order to accept something that is more authentic to who he is. It's a moving moment and it's utterly in tune with the six stages, and with the sense of what a Magician needs to be.

In fact, throughout volume seven we see characters acting and speaking from the heart in this way. They speak out and act directly on what they believe, even if it seems to be against their obvious best interests. Professor McGonagle's cry when she thinks Harry's dead, Molly Weasley's fury when she sees her children under threat, Ron's rescue of Hermione, Dobby's rescue of Harry which costs him his life, Harry's rescue of Malfoy, even Harry's own pronouncing of Voldemort's name – which results in his capture but ensures that Harry gets the wand he needs – all are examples of characters showing their real feelings rather than reacting with fear. The point is re-enforced when Harry argues with Lupin, forcing him to go back to look after Tonks and their child. At first sight Harry seems to be working against his own best interests. He needs as much help as he can get. Yet he's also speaking from his heart about the love bond that Lupin should be honoring but cannot because of his fear. That's why he has to reject Lupin's help. Anything offered in the spirit of fear is to be refused, because only courage can breed love and attachment. And that's part of the Magic that changes ordinary people into extraordinary people.

Rowling has given us one further important gift in this last novel and it is an insight into the nature of the highest level of Magician. We see it when Harry, in nearly dying, is blasted free of the part of Voldemort's soul that had attached itself to his soul when he survived the first attempt, as a baby. In Chapter Thirty Five we're told this information explicitly, and we also note that Harry wakes up naked, not needing his glasses, and 'unblemished'. This is surely a symbolic scene in which he is perfected, as one might be when going to heaven. He has in fact returned to being a pure Innocent, as well as being a Magician. The point seems to be this: the Magician archetype is not complete until it has welcomed back this first, most important stage – which is, as we have noted, the stage at which we all learn unconditional love. And Harry does offer Voldemort love in the final confrontation. He tells Voldemort the truth he needs to know, he offers him a chance for remorse (using that exact word), an opportunity to back down and save himself, and when Voldemort strikes he deflects the charm back at him. It is a remarkable scene, filled with symbolic undertones, and Harry the Magician is complete.

The hint is clear: we become full Magicians when we act out of a sense of truth, compassion, and love, all of which demand courage and absolute faith. The pure emotions of the Innocent combine with the acquired skills of the Magician at this highest of levels, since everything we do is in service of love. And without this highest form of love it is impossible to achieve real peace.

With this in mind, if we look at Harry's conversation with Dumbledore's spirit, it's worth noticing that he does not reproach the old wizard with how things have turned out — although he well might, given how he has been denied a fair amount of information. Dumbledore even asks, "Can you forgive me? Can you forgive me for not trusting you?" (713). It's an important moment and Harry's reply is an incredulous, "What are you talking about?" This tells us several things. The first is that even Dumbledore suffers from fear and lack of trust. Even he cannot be fully open. Perhaps this is one of the flaws that kept him from being the very highest level of Magician and which he must now put right. The second point is that we witness in Harry a forgiveness that is freely given before it has even been requested. Real forgiveness is already present in the heart of the Magician who has arrived at full integration of the Innocent's love in all its elemental power. Just as a child will always forgive and love a parent, so does Harry in this scene. Dumbledore goes so far as to admit that Harry is "the better man" for his purity and trust, and Dumbledore doesn't flatter. Harry is no pushover however, which is what we might associate with the idea of the Innocent. The flayed baby he sees in this chapter is startling to him, and when Dumbledore says the child can't be helped he accepts it. What we don't learn until later, and it is something that Harry doesn't spell out directly, is that this suffering creature is actually Voldemort's tortured soul. This is hinted at when Harry tells Voldemort during their duel that he's seen what Voldemort will become. No one has to tell Harry this. He just knows it because he recognizes what happens to those who do not love, and he knows he can't help that suffering figure even if he wishes to. It has to help itself. And from this we learn that love and compassion has its limits. We cannot help those who won't be helped, which is one of the saddest facts of our world. Ask anyone who has tried to use love to help someone they care for who has a serious addiction.

Harry and Voldemort's souls meet in an otherworldly version of King's Cross station, symbolically a point from which one can choose many directions. The one soul is whole, loving, ready to learn the full truth. The other is in the form of a squalling baby, unable to listen, wrapped in its own misery. Harry returns to the world for love, his ego almost non-existent. Voldemort returns only for gain and ego aggrandizement.

Egoism is the absence of caring for others. Carried to an extreme it becomes evil, and so evil is shown to us as the opposite of real love. We need to know this since we all have to deal with the problem of evil in our world, not just when we are school children. All the same, children have a remarkable grasp of the nature of this struggle — their playground dramas of good guys versus bad guys are evidence of that. They seem to be rehearsing for their life struggles to come. Harry's struggle is larger and more complicated than this; he has not only to fight against evil, but he also has to fight his own temptation to slip into a place of hurt and despair and anger, which is simply a form of self-hatred. Self-hatred is a lack of self-acceptance that can lead to an over-compensation in the form of the lust for power and vindication – and that can very easily create evil. That's the lesson he gets from the Dursleys. They hate him because they fear the fact that he's different, and by extension that makes them peculiar. And they want so much to be accepted by other muggles, and to fit in and gain approval. They can't just love who they all authentically are. In fact, they hate who they are when Harry is around. Harry's response to this is, frequently, to wish to revenge himself on them. Revenge, as we know, never improves anything, certainly not the existing relationships between human beings, and so each time he feels this urge Harry is tempted to act in a self-hating fashion. His education, therefore, involves loving what is right and loving others, but it also involves learning to love himself so that he can love others – even if they don't seem to deserve it.

This message about love is a major part of what Rowling conveys to us, and I have to say it sounds like wisdom and it feels entirely accurate. It may not look much like the way our present governmental and legal systems function, but that may be the whole point. It's closer to the teachings of Jesus than of Machiavelli. Rowling's achievement is that she has taken us into spiritual realms most writers never attempt. Hermann Hesse perhaps comes closest, although he keeps us in a realist world. Rowling's magical kingdom is not just a backdrop. Instead it is an important device that clearly enables her to say what she needs to say about the nature of the Innocent's power of love, and how it has to re-emerge for the Magician to become complete, and this could not be said in any other way.

This long section has shown us several things. The first is that the six stages echo throughout our literature. At times it may not be immediately obvious, but the stages are there. There is simply too much evidence to overlook.

The second thing is that since the stages are there in our most influential literature it is a fair bet that they articulate, to some extent, actual points of change that people go through that are linked to profound unconscious processes. Literature survives because it feels true in some fundamental way to those who read it, or hear it, or see it on stage.

Third is the obvious point that literature shows us in a highly compressed form the important events in lifetimes, real and imagined, and as such it shows us dynamic examples of individuals as they grow. Literature can be, therefore, a rich repository of human wisdom. As we've seen with Harry Potter, it can even take us beyond death when it needs to.

Fourth, and perhaps somewhat contentiously, is that some of what is today marketed as 'literature' or 'memoir' may be beautifully written and packaged but reach no further than the Orphan's sense of self-pity, focusing only on the dreadful childhood of the main character. While this may be sensational and sell millions of copies we have a right to ask whether or not there is any real wisdom in such a book, whether it asks us to wallow in misery or seeks to show us the way forward. The six stages may just give us a sense of what may be missing and therefore allow us to avoid what is second rate.

The fifth point is that literature comes in many shapes; good, bad, accurate, inaccurate, and mediocre. The smash hit today is sometimes deemed worthless tomorrow. To some extent I've tried to offset this by focusing on literature that has been popular and enduring and which has been accepted as a competent vision of human characteristics. Yet I am sure there will be a few people who will object by saying, "But it's just words on a page. It's not life!" And they'd be right. All I can say in reply is that literature, to date, has been the best way of rendering the inner life we have discovered. It might be a cracked and tarnished mirror, but it may be the best we've got.

Note

1. Rowling, J. K.. *Harry Potter and the Deathly Hallows*. Scholastic, 2007.

Chapter Eighteen

What the Literature has Shown: Stages and Sub-Stages

We can now return to our original outline, armed with our findings from the literature, and attempt to spell out what the challenges seem to be that face each archetype. We will need to repeat some information we've already covered, but this is only in service of building on it. If we can see where we are in terms of our whole life trajectory we have achieved part of the objective. Yet it can be hard to identify where we are within that archetype's growth, which is why the sub-stages can be so useful. And since life has a way of shaking us up from time to time, causing us to operate from a level that is less than we'd thought we were capable of, it can be helpful to see how this is mirrored in the sub-stages. Anyone confronted by a new experience can slip for a while to the Orphan sub-stage, for example. If we know this it will be much easier to get the help or advice we need so we can move back again to the fuller expression of who we are. The better the road map, the less disastrous a wrong turning will be. With this in mind, let's look at some possible ways the sub-stages can play out for us.

For the Innocent, the challenge is to develop enough sense of trust and curiosity in the outside world to be able to venture away from the home and explore successfully. The child who is ready to leave the home environment could be seen to be an Innocent who is in the sub-stage of the Pilgrim. The five-year-old who can't wait for the first day of school would be an example of this. Leaving a safe situation is not an action that produces undue fear or panic – that would be the mark of the Innocent at Orphan sub-stage, the Innocent Orphan. In school the child may well decide on topics she loves and put a large amount of energy into them, as an Innocent Warrior-Lover, gradually gaining mastery of her small world to become an Innocent Monarch. As she grows her abilities may well surprise others. She may turn out to be extraordinarily good with animals, or an inspired story teller, or a math whiz. Children do this surprisingly often. Ask any parent and the chances are good that you'll hear anecdotes about the child's unusual way of seeing things, or saying things, that take the parent by surprise. This is the Innocent Magician who enriches the world of the parent, too.

The difficulty is that many of us are propelled, against our will, out of a comfortable situation as Innocents and into uncertainty before we are quite ready. In the Bible, Adam and Eve's curiosity gets them banished from Eden, and so mankind spends the rest of eternity longing for heaven, for Paradise Lost. The Innocent Innocent has set behaviors and everything has, so far, magically appeared to fulfill the needs she may have. Like a well-raised infant, or a baby at the breast, the Innocent thinks somehow she has created the situation that is so comfortable. When life goes well, we have a tendency to believe we have made it all happen. Investors in dot com stocks in the nineties believed they were very savvy money-managers. And then the bubble burst. Some are still trying to get back to the "good old days" when life was easy.

The comparison is not lightly made. Many investors in those stocks that evaporated were almost completely inexperienced in the real workings of business or the stock market. They seemed only to see one aspect of the situation – they could hand over the money and watch it double itself, as if by magic. The situation was made worse because so many were able to invest on-line, in that strangely detached world of computer screen images that are so remote from the rough and tumble of the actual stock exchange trading floor. They really were Innocents who felt that they deserved something for nothing, and they were seduced.

Literature rarely approaches the idea of the Innocent directly. It prefers to head straight to the point when Innocence has been threatened or overthrown so that its qualities can be seen in contrast to the imperfections of the rest of the world, when the figure is already at Orphan stage.

For the Orphan the world is now tainted. She has been banished from the perfection of Eden. Whether it is a case of looking back at "summertime, when the living is easy" or the good old days the situation is the same.

The Orphan Orphan will sometimes suffer from a hankering after what has been lost; whether it be good or bad makes no difference. The Orphan Innocent will seek some sort of shelter as fast as possible and will attach readily to it, perhaps too trustingly, while the Orphan Orphan will do the same, but with a gloomy conviction that nothing can ever quite replace what has been lost. Nostalgia is a symptom of this – and certainly the desire to collect antiques or live out some version of the past is very prevalent for many people today. The past is, after all, safe. There can be few surprises in it. These are the consolations the Orphan Orphan will tend to construct as a protection against the pain of knowing that the past is gone. Nostalgia of this sort seeks to soothe the pain and at the same time memorialize it. For one can idealize the past or one can do the opposite, which is to demonize it. Those who declare that their upbringing has blighted the rest of their lives, who prefer victimhood, are those who are finding a home of sorts in the past, albeit it a painful past. We all know people who will not let go of their grievances. Any bar, in any town, after about 10pm on a Saturday will have a least one of those. The challenge is to recognize the situation and try to take charge.

This recognition marks the point at which the Orphan Orphan sets out to question the situation as she understands it, and therefore she moves into Orphan Pilgrim stage. At this level she must learn to stop blaming others, stop punishing herself, and not accept victim status. Failure to do so leads back to the passive Orphan Orphan state that can be so self-indulgent. Sometimes people can spend years hovering between these two levels. It seems to be at this point that quite a few of them seek therapy, and a successful treatment might depend upon the person developing enough courage to move out of the comfort zone of accepted misery and stay in that new space of questioning. And if the individual finds that to be too challenging, a successful treatment might also be to encourage the person to accept her Orphan Orphan role as the one in which she feels safest for now. Who knows what opportunities life may bring her in the future?

The Orphan Pilgrim typically has noticed that the world is imperfect and that she needs to take positive steps in order to get what she needs. This is a formidable challenge and when faced with it the temptation is to scurry to the safety of a home, any home, and slavishly conform to it. Conformists everywhere are likely to be, at heart, frightened Orphan Orphans who refuse to grow. Some may have come to that conformity after careful exploration. Most have not. Do as society says; inherit father's business or his business interests; toe the line; these are the pressures on the Orphan at all the sub-stages.

What we need to recall here is that when a person reaches the main Pilgrim stage, as we've seen, she begins to take responsibility for her own destiny. Just similarly, when a person reaches Orphan Pilgrim sub-stage she is moving away from the passive aspect of the Orphan and towards her own sense of self-definition. This puts the questioning Orphan Pilgrim on a potential collision course with authority figures, her parents, and her friends; and she must be willing to risk the fracture of those relationships and define herself in different terms as part of the task of self-discovery. This is the Orphan Warrior. The parent who has remained a passive 'adopted' orphan herself will be frightened by this show of independence in her child, and seek to bring the child back into the fold – using all means available, fair and foul.

A man who lived down the street from me some years ago is an example of this. He lived with his mother and was a devoted son, plump, gray-haired, who never went anywhere. He had a steady job that more than paid for his needs, and he was, as far as anyone could see, the perfect Catholic son. When his mother died he was in his mid-fifties. Within weeks the son had changed his entire wardrobe, had his hair cut, bought a red sports car, and embarked on a series of gay love affairs that were, I am told, filled with very noisy late night confrontations that spilled out onto the front lawn. I cannot say what sort of a person his aged mother was, but it seems as if she had sufficient power to prevent him from being himself, openly, for her whole life. That dear old soul had managed to keep him a passive Orphan Orphan all those years and I suspect it had done him no favors. When he became an Orphan Pilgrim he was perhaps more uncontrolled than he might have been if he'd been allowed to make his experiments over a longer period of time and move more gently through the sub-stages.

Seen another way, the entire Orphan stage is about ego development. We can do as everyone else does, in which case our ego is likely to be underdeveloped and our superego (our awareness of what society expects) is going to be somewhat overdeveloped. As a woman in one of my groups once phrased it, "I'd spent so many years being told what to think and do that when it came to making up my own mind I couldn't decide what I wanted. I kept asking: what do *you* want me to do? I had no idea what I wanted. None. I was trained to do what my mother wanted me to do. I can't even choose a flavor of ice cream when my mother's around. I'll ask her which flavor *she* wants me to have! I can't go on like this." Her ability to recognize that this had been the way she had lived for so many years, and her courage in saying it out loud to the group, represented a major step forward for her. She was announcing her intent to find out what she actually did want, as an Orphan Pilgrim. Her situation may sound extreme, yet the group members did not think so. As one of them said in response, "The more beautiful you are, the more pressure there is to do things the way they expect."

This sort of fragile ego state of the Orphan Orphan is therefore at the mercy of every fad that is endorsed by others. In contrast to this the Orphan Pilgrim feels driven to try and find out what she wants, building up a sense of ego-strength in the process, and then has to gather the courage to explore it. When she chooses to act on this courage she becomes an Orphan Warrior-Lover. At this sub-stage she will tend to look at a situation with clearer eyes, and see that a certain course of action is necessary. She sees she must leave her familiar surroundings if she is to grow, and that this is a necessary rebellion – not just a way of punishing her parents.

Unfortunately there is, as we've noted, a destructive aspect of this progress. This is the angry Orphan Pilgrim who rejects others and wishes to smash the things outside her world which she sees as threatening. This person is likely to be frightened of real exploration, and so can slip back to Orphan Orphan level. If left unchecked, this can become the realm of the terrorist, the fanatic, and the suicide bomber who has merely swapped one orphan option for another. It is a mindset that is simultaneously slavish to a dogma and yet without discipline. The Orphan Warrior-Lover has to learn to assert her own selfhood, in a loving way, within the structures in which she operates, whether that's the family, work, or the greater world. This is the child – of any age – who can disagree with the parents without making a scene, without slipping into anger. This is the young man who can say to his father that he knows what he's doing is not what the father wants, but he'd still like his father's blessing to go ahead and do it. The time honored ritual of the father's blessing has been diluted considerably over the centuries, which is a great pity, since it would seem to be an extraordinarily useful landmark, an acknowledgment of personal development that deserves to be respected. It is, in fact, a moment of re-negotiation of the parent-child bond.

If the Orphan's growth is not derailed, the Orphan Monarch will emerge as the person who is able to leave home (either physically or metaphorically) with a full appreciation of what it is that is being left and how valuable it has been. At this level the leaving will take place with love and with hope, and if the Orphan Monarch is able to allow the parents she leaves to feel satisfaction in the change, there will be spiritual growth on both sides. Then she can be seen as the Orphan Magician. This is when the Orphan is 'balanced' – the term we used at the start of this book.

The sub-stages are perhaps most clearly observed at the Orphan level, which is why I have taken the time to go through them in detail. One reason is that the Orphan archetype is in some ways the most problematic developmental point for all of us in our culture. Certainly the Orphan archetype is a real sticking place, requiring minute attention so that we can get ourselves out of the mud. Once we're moving again we don't need to be quite so attentive to the type of mud that caused the problem.

The Pilgrim is therefore the person who does choose to go exploring and truly leave the adopted home under reasonable circumstances. The challenge here is to explore life fully and with honesty, finally settling upon a direction that feels authentic for the individual's selfhood. In order to do that, one has to have a grounded sense of that selfhood, and that takes time, energy, experience, and courage. It also takes honesty. This is the single most important quality to emerge at this point, and one could say that it cannot fully emerge until this point. Anyone can search for a while and then give up. This is what can happen to the Pilgrim Orphan – who is too timid to look very thoroughly and soon heads home and back to Orphan-hood. The Pilgrim's task is to try to stay focused so that she can know what the search is really all about, and then stick to that goal. The Pilgrim Pilgrim knows that the task is to find a place in which the ego can merge with an appropriate field of action. So, for example, if she is truly fascinated with history it is appropriate that she does the work that will allow her to spend large portions of her time engaging in historical researches of some sort. But this is only a good idea if she really is fascinated by the chosen topic, and not just fooling herself. When the Pilgrim chooses, it will be a conscious choice based on real insight, not a selling out to the highest bidder, and at this point the Pilgrim becomes a Pilgrim Warrior-Lover.

We all face the possibility of selling out because we all have to live. No one can be totally independent and we all wind up making a few compromises. The struggle here is to decide what one needs to do to preserve one's Pilgrim impulse, while making sure the bills get paid. This is the balance the Pilgrim Warrior-Lover needs, and achieving it is what the Pilgrim Monarch is able to do. The Monarch is, as we recall, all about balance. This situation is most visible when a person takes on graduate work or some sort of higher training that demands sacrificing the usual pleasures everyone else is enjoying, while paying her own way. Balancing one's life at this point can be massively demanding, and the temptation to give up the exploration of the self is ever present. Over the span of a two year course of study we can expect to see the Pilgrim Orphan attach to the task; explore it as a Pilgrim Pilgrim; struggle to understand it; and move towards the Pilgrim Magician status of personal and professional competence.

The Pilgrim Pilgrim's task is to locate a sense of truth and personal honesty, and then at Pilgrim Warrior-Lover level another quality is called into play in full force, and that is courage. Honesty and a sense of one's personal values mean nothing if the individual has no determination to honor them, and that demands a more forceful courage than before. And this is where the Pilgrim Monarch comes into existence, because the moment we have a clear and balanced idea of what it is we want to put our skills toward, we find it much easier to concentrate and to succeed. What used to be so hard becomes very simple. As one artist I worked with put it, "Once I became clear in my own self about what I had to do, everything became suddenly straightforward. And I found I had almost boundless energy and no regrets at all about what I had left behind." Her sense of personal clarity came to her as a huge relief. She didn't have to agonize any more; she simply had to take action. This is the magic of connecting to our true sense of purpose, and it powers us through to the next stage.

The Warrior-Lover's challenge is to know when to fight and when not to fight. The people, the causes, the principles one decides to fight for are not things that can be handed to us by someone else. There are, after all, so many to choose from. If it is the Pilgrim's job to choose wisely, authentically, then it is the War-rior-Lover's job to put this choice into motion. The Warrior-Lover who is In-nocent will be full of energy and idealism, and that idealism really needs to be deflated. This brings the Warrior-Lover into the Orphan sub-stage. And so the gung-ho new employee discovers that the company isn't quite as marvelous as it had at first seemed to be; the young doctor discovers that patients do not always cooperate, and some aren't even reasonable. Author and physician Danielle Ofri records her encounter with one patient whom she had struggled to bring back from almost certain death. She lavished time and care on this very sick older man, only to discover that his main interest in her was in groping at her breasts. Disillusion waits for all of us, often in the least likely places, and the Warrior-Lover who is at Orphan level has to move through that experience without allowing it to upset her life.

As the Warrior-Lover deals with all this the Pilgrim sub-stage begins to emerge, and the individual is able to question carefully and realistically what he or she has committed to working for. It would be nice if we could do this before we take on a major life-task but the fact is that no one can be sure what will loom up on the road ahead. So, the Warrior-Lover may marry with a pretty good idea of what the demands of that situation will entail, but no one ever knows just what sorts of tests life may have in store for us, which is why the Warrior-Lover may have to return to this sub-stage a few times in order to work out the best way to move through each challenge. If this is done successfully the Warrior-Lover who is negotiating Pilgrim status will find herself re-committing to the main challenge of her life, choosing to declare her values and rising afresh to Warrior-Lover Warrior-Lover level.

In making this deliberate choice, the Warrior-Lover has to embrace the opposite viewpoint, which means she has to take the opposition (or the enemy) seriously, and attempt to understand that the purpose of every struggle is not to win or destroy but to make healthy growth possible. A practical example of this might be the arguments of a loving couple. The arguments can be impassioned, fierce, and may seem catastrophic to the casual observer. Yet each arguer will be fighting fair – attempting to get to the heart of things rather than just trying to win. And usually the end result is more love and a greater peace.

In the sense that Love and War are obvious opposites, the Warrior-Lover has to grow to understand each realm. Since the Warrior has to be ready to die for the cause, just as the loving mother is ready to die for her children if necessary, this stage values the moral issues more highly than the ego. The true Warrior-Lover can be outraged, but never simply because ego-based personal pride has been affronted. The pseudo-Warrior by contrast is all about ego-based pride, and will be the one who brags about his exploits. This is as unacceptable as the Lover who brags about his conquests (notice how the language of conquering is interchangeable in each case.) As before, we can see this pseudo-warrior as being basically one who is looking for outer validation, and this figure is more correctly just another version of the passive Orphan.

Interestingly enough, at this point it's not really possible to think in terms of Warrior-Lover Orphan, because a Warrior-Lover who is lost in the same way an Orphan may be lost simply cannot continue a prolonged existence at Warrior level at all, and is more properly seen as sliding towards being simply an Orphan. The true Warrior's inner fight is to put the task first, and the ego second.

The Warrior-Lover Warrior-Lover will have to fight at some point, and in doing so will also have to come to terms with the Shadow. As we've seen with Prince Hal, the Shadow has to be contained, learned from, and even defeated. Like Gawain, the Warrior-Lover Warrior-Lover meets his fear and finds himself incapacitated by it, temporarily. Then he has to forgive himself for being afraid. In the non-literature world, this is the person who has to accept that he must modify his ambitions; that his strongest love cannot save another who is bent on self-destruction; and that we all make mistakes that feel disastrous, yet we must carry on. We all must face our limits, be disappointed in ourselves, and still function. This is the personal Shadow – the parts of ourselves we have had to repress.

And yet the Shadow is more than this. In meeting our own Shadow self we meet a figure of great power, and this power needs to be understood and constrained. A Warrior-Lover can be a domestic person, and can also be brave in a fight. The Shadow, however, is that part of the fighter that is essentially amoral, uncontrolled. It is the force that makes soldiers do acts of seemingly foolhardy courage; it is the energy that seeks to kill and to be killed in the process. It is a ferocious force. It can be seen in the criminal who does not care what he destroys or even if he is caught. It can be a destructive energy that has parted company with any identifiable reality. Perhaps this is why no soldier comes away from a war untraumatized. They will, each of them, have felt the lawless murderer within, seen it in others, and been appalled. People who have used weapons, knowing that they intend to kill another human being, wanting to kill the other person, have crossed a line that may frighten them forever after. The terrible massacres that happen in wartime seem to be an expression of this. Lt. Calley and his company were not brutal men, yet at Mi Lai in Vietnam they killed everything in that village that breathed. Most men have not experienced anything like this, and yet plenty of men and women are drawn to activities that are self-destructive. Those who engage in unprotected sex and do not care what happens, or who drink quantities of alcohol and insist on driving – we don't have to go too far for examples. These are people in the grip of the Shadow, for the Shadow can emerge no matter what stage one is at. It is, however, at Warrior-Lover stage that it can be successfully confronted and tamed. The Lover aspect of this stage has to learn to accept and even to love the Shadow, so that its strength can be assimilated – and this is the greatest test the Lover has to face.

For women the experience will be a little different, since women fight our wars in smaller numbers than men, but it will be no less intense. Along with alcohol, drugs, gambling and other temptations to a self-destructive life, there may exist the desire to exhaust oneself for the sake of the children and be destroyed by the demands of the family. This may seem, at first sight, to be heroic, yet it is on occasions an essentially self-destructive urge that will destroy relationships and hurt family members. The woman who takes on three jobs, does everything for the family, and falls ill from a stress-related disease, may seem to be an heroic figure at first glance. But, in some cases, the family benefits not at all from this devoted behavior, not even in the long term, let alone the short run. Having the heroic provider collapse can be extremely frightening and can also spread a burden of guilt, doubt, and helplessness. Unconsciously the parent in this situation may be resentful of the weight she has to carry and may in fact be destroying herself and her family at the same time. Occasionally this erupts onto the front pages of our newspapers when we read about a woman murdering her children, or a man who shoots his family and burns down the family home.

What needs to be remembered here is that the energy of the Shadow can be used, indeed it has to be used, without giving in to the destructive aspect. Women can – and many women do – show magnificent determination in bringing up families under difficult circumstances.

The struggle with the Shadow is probably the single most important struggle any of us can ever undertake. In popular mythology this is the cowboys in white hats routing the bad guys in black hats. This is Luke Skywalker destroying the death star. Oversimplifications such as these are more misleading than they are helpful. The Shadow that exists in each of us is not there to be killed or annihilated; indeed it cannot be isolated in this way. The Shadow is perhaps best described as the enemy who is the exact mirror image of ourselves. Let me put this differently: I think that most people would agree that murderers should be punished and imprisoned. Yet which of us has not fantasized about murdering someone? I doubt that there is a single person on earth over the age of fifteen who hasn't felt like killing someone. In fact the only thing that stops some of us giving in to murderous and larcenous impulses is the law. So we cannot claim that we have nothing in common with murderers; we have. But to live within the law simply for fear of the sanctions it applies is not a moral act, it's a fearful act. It would be better if we were able to remove the legal framework from the equation and say that we do not do these things because they are repellent to our sense of what is right. That's the point at which we can say we have the Shadow under some sort of control. If we were all to work from that mind set we might indeed change the way our society works. We can only make such a statement when we have met the temptation to do wrong and turned it down. This is Gawain refusing the lady's sexual advances. This is Oedipus refusing his sons' offers of shelter which come with a moral price tag attached. This is Prince Hal rejecting Falstaff. Gawain's case is particularly rich, since the lady just doesn't seem to see anything wrong with her sexually provocative behavior, and because Gawain nearly gives in – he accepts the belt which he keeps unlawfully. We all of us could be tempted, and we all could fail, as the story makes abundantly clear.

We do not fight the Shadow so much as accept it and tame it. Perhaps this is what lies behind Jesus' statement of 'Love thine enemies.' (Matthew 5.44) If we treat our enemies with respect and respond to them lovingly (which may first involve vigorous actions to contain them) we can move towards peace rather than genocide. Anyone who has worked with convicts or offenders knows about this. Some really do need to be locked up for a long time, and some need to be contained while they get themselves sorted out. And yet they can't rehabilitate themselves unless they are treated as human beings first – human beings who have specific needs and who must be treated with care so that they can begin to change who they have been until this point. To act lovingly may mean to act sternly, but it also means that punishments are not levied in a mood of personal revenge, in anger, nor with a desire to hurt for hurting's sake. We call this justice: and it's exactly comparable to the way we have to deal with the Shadow. If one's enemies include oneself – the fear of the dark and anarchic promptings we all have – then we do indeed have to love our enemies, and without letting those impulses run our lives.

This is the stage at which the individual has enough sense of self and direction that she can take the responsibility of trying to heal the relationships with the parents that have been strained in Orphan and Pilgrim phases. This essential task leads to deeper self-awareness, and enriches the Warrior-Lover as she becomes a parent in turn. Since the Warrior-Lover is capable of deep unselfish love for both her children and her spouse, the relationships with the children as they grow can be some of the deepest and most intense. The Warrior-Lover's challenge is to know when the best form of love is, in fact, letting go of the loved one so he or she can grow in a way that is authentic. This is a paradox that every parent will face, for the parent who remains too forcibly the Warrior-Lover will eventually infantilize the child, the spouse, and even her own parents by fighting all their battles for them.

The Warrior-Lover at Warrior-Lover sub-stage is therefore also a nurturer, and since there isn't always a fight going on, this archetype can become a guardian of the standards of conduct. As such, the sub-stage may look at times like a conservative incarnation of the Orphan. She will live by society's accepted standards and protest only if they are violated. She will have friends, and committees, and meetings, and seem to blend in. Yet when the occasion arises, she will show her worth as a Warrior-Lover by standing up for what she knows to be important, and she will do it without a sense of ego-gratification. She won't do it for the applause, but because it's the right thing to do for the community. She will be a Warrior-Lover Monarch, working for the larger good.

The Warrior-Lover Monarch knows that there will always be another battle, and that the job is never over. Knowing this, he does not give up. This can be a figure of such deep courage that he is truly inspiring – a Magician indeed. In fact this is always part of the Monarch sub-stage, which we can describe as learning to take one's skills and pass them on to others so that, eventually, others will take on the struggle willingly and even surpass our own level of expertise. This is a form of love that has nothing to do with pride or ego fulfillment.

The Monarch takes the Warrior-Lover stage a step further, since the King and the Queen working together can balance might and mercy, love and war. Again, one can see this as the logical continuation of the Warrior-Lover phase, except expressed in a larger context.

The challenge for the Monarch is to take the just and effective action. Ego, vainglory, and self-love are the hallmarks of capricious rulers who do not usually last long. This is the Monarch Orphan, who feels that she is owed something. The Monarch has to be aware of this, refuse to be seduced by it, and use this information. This requires the questioning capacity of the Pilgrim and also the balance learned by the Warrior-Lover as decisions are made. So the true Monarch has to be aware of the earlier sub-stages and make use of them when necessary. This results in a Monarch who truly understands the other stages and who will feel confident enough, for example, to promote an egocentric Pilgrim in his administration, such as an ambitious and energetic leader. The Monarch will be able to see that such a person needs rewards to soothe his ego, and knows that if those rewards are denied, the fledgling leader may turn into a rebel or usurper. The Monarch doesn't just have to get the personal decisions right for herself, she has to do it for many others as well, knowing that they may be at different stages of awareness. In some ways the Monarch is always the nurturer of the next generation, even as she leads the present one. At this point we could say that the Monarch doesn't just move through the sub-stages in the way we have seen up until now. The Monarch instead, has to be fully aware of all those stages, able to access them all and not be swamped by any one viewpoint.

And here we have another point to consider – the Monarch may combine the two aspects of the king and queen, but he or she is always just one person, choosing to be a little sterner in response to a challenge or a little more compassionate when the situation demands it. Her decisions may be arrived at as a result of collaborative work, but the Monarch is the one who weighs the information and who elects one course of action over another. Clearly this requires a high degree of self-awareness, an almost limitless faith in one's judgment, as well as deep humility.

The relationship of the Monarch to his or her parents is therefore one of equality, respect, and even a little distance. They both have similar experience at this point. The Monarch doesn't want anything from anyone, except that they should be true to their highest selves. This is a contrast to the Warrior-Lover, who often wants the child or the parent to be like herself. The Warrior-Lover relationship is easier for the child, since it seems to say, 'be like me', whereas the Monarch asks that the child aspire to a higher, abstract level of achievement. The Warrior-Lover's tendency to expect the child to please her works well for younger children. The Monarch will tend to say that if the child does what the child feels is important and moral, then that is a pleasing course of action in the wider sense.

There are many examples of this within families. A child will tend to attach strongly to one parent or the other and attempt to be just like that parent. So the son of an engineer may find himself wanting to connect to his parent by showing an interest in mechanical things, and the two will share this to some extent. The Orphan phase child attaches to a Warrior phase parent. Soon, however, the child may want to develop an interest that diverges from the parent's areas of expertise. He may decide to become a dentist where the parent was fascinated by aeronautics. The wise Monarch parent will accept this and encourage the child's quest even if he has no idea what the child's pursuits add up to, simply because the right thing to do is to encourage people to grow in whatever direction feels authentic to them. The parent may have dreamed of a child who would follow in his footsteps. And it will be necessary to let go of that ego-based wish. The child may well choose a career that the parent cannot understand, as well as friends, hobbies, and even a spouse that the parent does not care for. But at that point the parent is not making the choices. The Monarch has to be tactful, open, honest, loving, and above all else has to be able to listen; and that's a hard task to fulfill.

We may wish to see the Monarch's path to the achievement of balance as one we all will face at some point. For if the Monarch has to balance the stereotypically 'masculine' and 'feminine' aspects, we can recognize that as the reconciling of the professional and the personal lives within the individual, bringing the whole self into harmony. We are more likely to know people whose lives are out of balance than those who have got it right, if only because the ones who are off-kilter are so much more noticeable. The man who spends all his time at the office, or on the golf course, might be an example of this, especially if he remains a stranger to his family. From our point of view, the Monarch has to be able to use this regal ability in every aspect of his or her life and not opt out of one aspect or another. The king never stopped being the king, according to European doctrine from about 1400 to 1900, and he also never stopped being the country he was king of. They were the same thing. The King of England was addressed simply as 'England' since he was the embodiment of the entire country. He spoke for it, he ruled it, he was it. This odd idea of the complete fusion of the private and the public persona is one way to illustrate what the Monarch can achieve. In more modern terms, this is the person who does not have to act a part, take on a role, or try and be superior to anyone. Such people have a natural dignity.

I was privileged some years ago to work with a pleasant, rotund woman who was very kindly. One day, she told me, she was looking out of her window and she saw some youths with knives waiting at the corner of an alley that ran past her yard. Without a moment's hesitation she walked round to where they were and asked them what they were doing. Something in her openness, perhaps, and her lack of fear, made the four young men pause. One of them declared in a loud voice that they 'were waiting there to kill somebody', which she told him was a silly idea. After a few moments of conversation they handed over their knives to her and went away, feeling as if they had been rather foolish, I don't doubt. It wasn't until the woman reached home again, safely, that she realized what she'd done, and wondered how she'd done it. We can achieve a quiet authority when we are simply ourselves, and it can be most impressive. Another example is the local policeman in my village in England when I was a boy. This overweight and unathletic constable, pedaling his bicycle one night on his rounds, saw a burglary in progress. He dismounted and found himself facing three burglars carrying loot and wrecking bars. He arrested all three without a struggle, even though he had no weapons, no radio, and only one set of handcuffs. Faced with the constable's absolute certainty about what was right they all caved in. He told them, he said, 'Don't be daft and come along quietly, now'. Sometimes the power of the Monarch comes out in the most unexpected places.

As the Monarch grows, he or she reaches closer to the level of the Magician.

The Magician's challenge is that having attained all this awareness, there is a tendency to close the mind. The Magician's task is to balance qualities, as the Monarch does, and yet to stay open and receptive – in fact he or she must embrace the qualities of the Innocent, find wonder in the ordinary, and trust, almost without reserve. This is not blind trust. Instead it is, perhaps, a faith in goodness. The experienced Warrior-Lover might be suspicious of others, as a self-protective move. The Magician is much more likely to encourage others to trust, be trusted, and to trust themselves, simply because the Magician trusts them. I've seen this a number of times in my work with disturbed adolescents. One young woman was talking to me about her childcare case-worker, and she said, with tears in her eyes, "He was the first person who ever had any confidence in me. He let me know that I wasn't a total screw up. He trusted me. It made all the difference." She went on to add that she had, at first, found it difficult to live up to that trust, that she had often disappointed her case-worker, but that whenever she did so she felt she'd also disappointed herself. She learned over time to trust herself and respect the trust of others. As a result she became far more than she had ever believed she could be. Most of us would acknowledge something similar to be true in our own lives, also. The times we are given a task to do and the more senior people trust us to do it – those are the times when we're likely to do a good job even if it's all new territory. Trust breeds trust, for the most part.

In the literature section we saw this sort of trust displayed when Hector's father goes to see Achilles, his son's killer, in order to ask for the corpse. Achilles is not a patient man and Hector had killed his best friend, which is why he's taking out his rage on Hector's corpse. Hector's father appears before his son's killer and, without reproach or condemnation, begs Achilles to do the decent thing – for Hector's soul will not be able to rest if he is not properly buried. The feeble, sorrowing old man is able to achieve what no one else could do – he brings out the compassionate and reverent aspects of Achilles' character. He does this largely because he trusts Achilles' innate goodness, putting himself totally at his mercy, and addressing him as a fellow mourner. This is the Magician in action.

There's a lovely piece of the New Testament that illustrates this. In it a Roman centurion comes to find Jesus to ask him to cure his servant. He hasn't brought the servant with him; he's left him at home. When asked about this he explains that as a soldier he gives orders and expects them to be carried out precisely, and he assumes Jesus operates the same way. Here is St. Matthew's version:

> And when Jesus was entered into Capernaum, there came to him a centurion, beseeching him, and saying, 'Lord my servant lieth at home sick of the palsy, grievously tormented.' And Jesus saith unto him, 'I will come and heal him.' The centurion answered and said, 'Lord I am not worthy that thou shouldest come under my roof: but speak the word only, and my servant shall be healed. For I am a man under authority, having soldiers under me, and I say to this man "Go," and he goeth; and to another "Come," and he

cometh; and to my servant, "Do this," and he doeth it.' When Jesus heard it he marveled and said to them that followed, "Verily I say unto you, I have not found so great faith, no, not in Israel." (8: 5-10)

You can imagine what the crowd thought – here is a Roman, one of the unpopular occupying troops, asking a favor, and he hasn't even brought the sick man with him. What sort of an idiot is this? Yet Jesus' reply is eloquent, because he responds to the man's unshakable trust. And the servant is cured. The New Testament calls this "faith" and the gospel of St. Matthew has Jesus frequently saying to the doubters around him "oh ye of little faith." The Magician nurtures faith, and trust, by giving it. The Magician's challenge is to give to everyone, not just the chosen few who will be properly grateful. The enemy centurion deserves the gifts because of the depth of his trust.

When we have absolute faith, total trust in what we are doing then something miraculous happens. Everything becomes very simple and we take on the empowerment that comes with clarity. Emmet Fox, the great Christian writer, called it being in tune with God's energy. If we can do that, then everything changes, even those things we thought were impossible. Fox makes this plain in many of his books; no matter what your beliefs you will find his writing illuminating. The point that needs to be made here is that when we have absolute unshakeable faith that we can do something that is not just about fuelling our own egos (the Centurion asks for his servant, not for himself, we notice) then changes can happen. Sometimes it feels as though they are miraculous. Here is an example. The labor agitators in the United States during the early years of the twentieth century campaigned at first because they were starving. Gradually more protesters joined their cause because they saw that exploitation was a national problem, far bigger than just the immediate needs of one small group. They were beaten, imprisoned, assassinated, machine-gunned, charged by cavalry; and each confrontation caused some to give up. Each confrontation caused others to become more dedicated. Eventually the labor laws were changed, and today the holiday of Labor Day marks symbolically the alteration of the way the country was run – an alteration that affects each and every one of us. Some people would call that just a boring fact of history. Others might see that series of events as the Magician spirit in action, changing what had seemed unchangeable. Perhaps the point that needs to be added is that most of us are so stuck in our ego concerns that it is only when situations become truly desperate, as in the case of the starving workers, that we can give up our old ways and move towards the Magician's phase. When we've nothing left to lose except our sense of what is right we become, paradoxically, extremely strong.

Every popular revolutionary movement has started from this place. The image that came from Tiananmen Square in Bejing, showing one lone man carrying a shopping bag standing in front of a whole column of tanks, causing them to stop, was pasted all over the newspapers in many countries. Bizarre, we say. Miraculous. Seen on video it seemed that the man with his bag of groceries was talking with the leading tank's driver, perhaps, who had only his narrow driving slit through which he could speak. What could that dialogue have been? It hardly matters. That was the power of the Magician at work.

And what better emblem for the Magician's struggle! Often we'll have to go out, alone, pitifully unequipped, to face our opponents who are behind walls of steel – actually or metaphorically. Perhaps we may be crushed. And perhaps we may be heard. When I saw those pictures from Tiananmen Square I was astonished – I still am whenever I think about them – because the human spirit in action is a very moving sight to behold.

And here we need to be careful, because the power that comes from this personal faith can very easily be misused. Blind faith is the trap that waits for the Magician Orphan. Lenin's Bolshevik revolution rocked the world, and yet at one point the Leninist party consisted of just three people, one of whom was Lenin himself. Lenin's vision, as we all know, was corrupted into the horror that became the Soviet Union, but it was essentially inadequate right from the first. Similarly the Nazis were, in 1922, just a few thugs clustered around Hitler, who probably was the only person who really had any belief in what he was doing at that time. Faith is necessary, but faith alone, unreceptive to the questioning the Pilgrim can provide, divorced from the sense of right the Warrior-Lover upholds, and alienated from the sense of humane balance the Monarch must strive for – that can only lead to disaster. In fact we seem to need all the archetypes working harmoniously within us if we are to reach Magician phase.

There are examples of this around us, in a less dramatic form, if we care to notice. These are the moments when people contact the Magician stage, even if only temporarily. I've heard creative writers speak about a version of this on many occasions. It is when they refer to stories that just came to them, fully formed, or when they speak of "just taking dictation" rather than writing. Sometimes writers say that the Muse took over; when this happens, it is as if the writing does itself, using the human being who just happens to be handy, pen at the ready. Poets and writers will tell you that for the Muse to arrive like this, one has first to spend a long time training oneself not to get in the way. One has to be ready, open, innocent, and to some extent fully prepared for the task. I think of this as a version of the 'faith' we have already observed. And then, if one is very fortunate, the magic happens. St. Matthew echoes this in Jesus' instructions to his disciples when he urges them:

'Take no thought how or what ye shall speak, for it shall be given you in that same hour what ye shall speak. For it is not ye that speak, but the Spirit of your Father which speaketh in you.' (10: 19-20).

Don't rehearse your life, he says, don't have all the answers memorized. Be open, be alert, and the words that need to be said will come to you. This may seem risky, and yet I've spoken with educators and substitute teachers who on many occasions have said that they've arrived in classrooms fully prepared for the day only to discover that the situation before them was too confused for them to be able to put their lesson plans in motion. The best course, they agree, is not to forge ahead regardless, but to take the time to listen and make what they can from the material in the room. And the words do come, as needed – but one has to have faith in what one is doing. Whether we call this following one's intuition, or experience, or the Muse, matters less than that it does happen. And when it does we are briefly in Magician mode.

Here is another example. In my work with writers I've used the expression, 'sometimes one has to get out of one's own way'. What this equates to is that very often when writers are blocked it's because they don't have faith in their own process and they're trying too hard to make the words come. The ego desire to achieve actually can prevent the successful continuation of their project. That's the time to stop trying to impress others, and concentrate on following the words to where they want to go. It's another way of having faith that the necessary words will arrive.

How these examples relate to the rest of one's life may not be obvious, so it's a good idea to consider them in terms of parenting. As a parent the Magician is sometimes hard to pin down, since she will love the child unquestioningly and be fascinated by all the child does. Yet the love may seem to be clouded by the slight sense of distance that we've already described as grandparental. The Magician parent may not be cheering at every softball game, but will be there when spiritually needed, a tad cool, even detached, but always paying attention. This parent will have total faith that the child will make right and meaningful choices within his or her capacity at the age the child has reached, and will allow the child to do so – and yet will keep a weather eye open, since the Magician is not a fool. Clearly, this is not the same as allowing the child to run rampant, which is simply neglect; it is instead an honoring of where the child is at that moment.

I was once introduced to an old lady who was remarkable because children of all ages seemed to adore her. After observing her and talking with her relatives I asked them what they thought her secret was. The reply that seemed to make the most sense was that she always took children absolutely seriously. Even their jokes were received with an understanding smile of amusement rather than indulgent laughter. There was no pseudo-parental pretended delight at the child's production of artwork, for instance; no extravagant over-praising for fear of hurting the child's sense of self-esteem. Phrased differently, we could say that her great talent was that she accepted the children wherever they were in their development, not judging and not expecting, but simply witnessing and honoring.

A larger example might be the Dalai Lama. When the Chinese invaded Tibet they forced him to flee and they smashed as many Buddhist temples as they could. As a Monarch most people felt he had been a manifest failure. He'd lost his kingdom. But since then he has toured the world bringing the lessons of peace, love and acceptance, and Buddhism is now stronger than ever before and treated with more respect than ever before. So who has the victory now? The Magician works in the realm of spirit, and like Jesus crucified, the failure becomes a success.

This is a broad schematic of what the different stages involve. In the literary material we've seen to some extent – and especially with Harry Potter – that within each stage, each individual has to go through the six sub-stages all over again at that level. So even the new Magician has to realize this is a role that demands the dependence of the Orphan; the further soul searching of the Pilgrim; the fierce, loving devotion to the task of the Warrior; and the more cerebral balance of the Monarch, before the Magician can meet herself and know the power that is at her command. That can only happen when he or she can be fully open, as a Magician who is also an Innocent, to trust and to love.

If these sub-stages seem to be difficult to recall and specify I will reassure you and point out that it is because they were never intended for this sort of analytic exposition. The six main stages will always be clearest, and that is exactly the point. A Warrior-Lover will be implicitly aware of the challenges that need to be faced, such as the loss of idealism, the wish to love and be loved, the need to question, and the need to face the self, but will probably not systematize these challenges in their respective terms of Innocent, Orphan, Pilgrim, and Warrior. They will just be challenges to be worked through. Having survived them and become proficient in all aspects of the Warrior-Lover's life she will transition to the level of Monarch, but for most of us we will not be able to spell out the exact moment we became proficient at something. We just know it's happened, usually after the event.

In this light, knowing about the stages can be extremely useful. For instance, from time to time I have found myself feeling as if I want someone to reassure me that I'm doing a good job. After a hard day at work, when it seems as if no one is noticing the effort I've put in, that's when that feeling tends to appear. When I was younger I'd look eagerly for approval from those I perceived as my seniors.

These days, if I'm wise, on such occasions I just tell myself that I'm feeling a bit like an Orphan today, and I must watch out that I don't let that take anything from away my competence. It reminds me that even though I can have moments of feeling like this, I am not necessarily condemned to remain at that point. I have choices.

Notes

1. Ofri, Danielle. *Singular Intimacies*. New York: Penguin, 2004.
2. Fox, Emmet. *Find and Use Your Inner Power*. New York: Harper, 1941.
3. For a concise history of labor disputes in the USA see: Zinn, Howard. *A People's History of the United States: 1492 – Present*. New York: Perennial, 2001, Chapter 15.

Chapter Nineteen

Identifying Stages of Development

O ne of the ways we can gauge where we might be on our spiritual journey is to consider how important material wealth is for us. Now, we all enjoy material comforts far superior to those experienced in most of the rest of the world, so one has to be sensitive in how one uses this. But consider someone who, for example, will not leave a dreadful marriage because of the financial hit that will have to be faced. There may be many good reasons to stay in such a situation – children and their welfare are frequently argued as being important. Yet it's worth making the observation that the Orphan needs physical wellbeing, and is likely to feel panicked by any threat to remove it. Even the most fully developed Monarch can slip back to Orphan level, at least temporarily, when faced with this sort situation.

When life sends us monetary challenges we may all slide back to this level. The point, of course, is not to get stuck there. So the Pilgrim, if she truly is a Pilgrim, may decide to leave a marriage or a job but will take only as much as she can easily carry, and only if the objects mean something to her. *These* possessions have value, but other possessions do not. The Warrior regards possessions as items to be used in order to get the job done, not as personally important. So a mother might fight for the physical means to keep her children decently housed. This can look like the Orphan at work, but what is important is the motivation behind the actions, which may well be those of the Warrior-Lover. We've all come across cases when one member in a divorced couple will use the children as an excuse to hurt the spouse financially. That sort of poorly-disguised egoism fools no one. The vengeful person who uses money as the weapon of choice is acting out of angry Orphan impulses, since money really matters to Orphans and they imagine it matters just as much to everyone else as well.

In understanding the Warrior-Lover it's worth considering that actual military men seem to feel that things, especially equipment, is not for treasuring. Like a tool kit, one uses the items, and when they break or wear out, they are thrown away. The task is what's important. This jeep is wrecked, find another. This gun is jammed, throw it away. It's not a sentimental attachment but about getting the job done. In World War II Stephen Ambrose records that members of the British glider brigades landed on D-Day and by a few weeks later many of them were carrying German submachine guns. These were not trophies. They were better guns than the British models, and so were pressed into immediate unsentimental service. The tale that bookends this one is that Goering, the Nazi head of the German air force, asked his pilots what they wanted to help them fight better, and his chief ace, Adolf Galland promptly replied that he wanted Spitfires (the British plane of the time). Goering was furious at the perceived anti-German attitude of his pilots. Galland himself couldn't understand why Goering took his comment so badly. After all, the British plane was better in many ways.

Here's a different example. In the early Anglo-Saxon tale *Beowulf*, we recall that Beowulf is given the sword Hrunting by Unferth. It's an historic sword, and has won many fights, and anyhow Unferth gave it to Beowulf in friendship after some initial rivalry. Unfortunately when Beowulf uses it to strike at Grendel's mother (a ferocious dragon) her hot black blood makes the sword melt. Beowulf doesn't stop to lament that Unferth will be upset at the loss of his famous sword. He immediately grabs another from the dragon's treasure and finishes the job. We hear no more about the loss of Hrunting. So why did the poet put in the episode at all? I suspect that the incident is there because Unferth's original sense of chagrin arises from ego-based rivalry with Beowulf, who is a stranger to Heorot. And who could blame Unferth? Here comes a stranger who says he'll solve all their problems, problems that Unferth himself has been unable to put right – no wonder he feels affronted! Beowulf is man enough to rise above the taunts Unferth throws at him. He doesn't want a squabble and his ego is not aroused. He just wants to kill the monster and get life at Heorot back to normal again. Material possessions are nice, but the task in hand is more important to the Warrior. Unferth's reconciliation with Beowulf, which is symbolized in his gift of the sword, is an indication that he has put his own ego-based sense of self aside and wishes to contribute to the solution.

The *Beowulf* poet is beautifully subtle here. Of course Beowulf prizes the sword; he carries it to the fight in preference to his own weapon. Yet it seems clear he values it for the spirit in which it was given, not for its extrinsic value. If the story of Beowulf has a message that was important for the Anglo-Saxons of the eighth century and is still important now it might be that ego-based pride may cause a man to seem courageous, but that in the end it will lead to feuds and destructive in-fighting. The real hero has to let go of ego. The true Warrior-Lover does not fight for rewards, fame, medals and adulation, but rather to establish peace.

The person who decides to sell everything and travel the world, or to move to a smaller house so she can raise the tuition money to take the college courses she's always wanted to, or who leaves a successful spouse and takes on poverty because it feels more authentic than a lifeless marriage – these are the people who know that money is a tool, not a destination. In contrast, for the Orphan, the money is the destination; at least for a while. But the Orphan always has a choice when these sorts of events offer her the chance to move forward.

Unfortunately many people in the world seem to act like Orphans and when they face challenges to their value systems they become passive Orphans, only able to see meaning in comforting, generally accepted situations. To them, any job is better than making one's own career. Any relationship, no matter how bad, is preferable to being – gasp! – alone. Look at how many children return home after college because they claim that rents are too high, living is too expensive ... and so on. Well, we can have some sympathy with that view, at least for a short while. Yet the timid Orphan will never really leave home, and so cannot become her own person. We take possession of ourselves when we decide to go ahead and be Pilgrims, taking a few risks, discovering what we really can do in the process. Remember – a real pilgrim takes only as much as can be conveniently carried as she heads off on her quest.

Unfortunately, the more home comforts we have the harder it may be to leave them behind. Many Orphans don't make the leap to Pilgrim. They fail not because they are stupid, or lack courage. They fail because they do not know that the relative discomforts of Pilgrim phase lead to the Warrior-Lover stage, and after that to the Monarch. They stay put because they do not know what's over the horizon, and no one is telling them that it's worth a little hard work to get there. In addition, even Monarch and Magician phase look, at first glance, very much like Orphan phase. The Monarch and Magician must live in houses, face troubles, and have to live within their incomes, just like everyone else. The added responsibilities they seem to have to shoulder don't seem to be recompensed in any obvious way, either.

Today we have an added dimension to consider. When the Orphan faces a crisis she cannot cope with, not knowing that this could be the impetus that will lead her to rethink who she is, she may seek help from her doctor who will probably prescribe various pills. In fact any time any of us face a situation we cannot fathom we are likely, even if only temporarily, to slip into Orphan mode. It is a sad fact that the help we may need is not always available in the most useful form. Our doctors and psychiatric caseworkers are interested in calming their patients down so they will accept a norm of anxiety and disappointment. The most cost effective method of doing that is with the correct pills. So a 'successful treatment' is someone who goes back to work, functioning at a reasonably effective level in the work place. And what can we expect when the company pays for health insurance? They want their people back, in place, no questions about it. One could say that their methods encourage Orphan thinking. Indeed, in giving some sort of chemical that relieves a feeling of distress many practitioners may be stalling any chance of self-reflection while removing pain. So the suffering person is not only encouraged back into a situation that may be partially to blame for the distress (a re-adoption) but she is also made to some extent dependent upon that particular chemical, which encourages her to be a doubly passive Orphan. Becoming dependent in this way can then cause the individual to feel as if she is personally inadequate to deal with life on a continuing basis. This represents a threefold passive Orphan helplessness.

One of my clients taught me an important lesson about this. I had assumed my task was to help her transition to a more meaningful line of work, since that was what she had initially asked for help in achieving. Yet when she went out on her own she did not go back to her dull but well-paid job, and she didn't take one just like it, either. In fact she sold almost all her possessions, and began taking classes not really caring whether or not she finished the Master's Degree requirements. Instead she studied because she wanted to know more about the topics concerned. She has not settled down to a placid suburban existence. The last I heard from her she was a spiritual pilgrim, fully engaged in her search for meaning, and in no danger of giving it up. I'm sure her health care insurer considered her time and money spent with me to be a waste, and from their point of view they would be right. If we're considering spiritual development and happiness, however, I'd respectfully disagree.

Under these circumstances we are unlikely to get health care workers who say the difficult but honest things that may need to said.

> A man came to him saying, 'What must I do to be saved?' And he answered, 'Take all you have, sell it, and give the money to the poor. Then follow me.' And the man went on his way sorrowing for he had great possessions. (Mark 10. 22)

Jesus' advice was pretty hard to act upon, too. Yet it may be a metaphor for exactly what we need to hear at certain points. The right advice that may be truly what we need to do might not be what we'd like to be told. Sometimes we just can't get to the new place in our life if we don't let go of the old way of living, but that does mean letting go. Completely. And that's frightening.

Some years ago, for example, I was observing a therapy group and one man kept saying that he didn't know how long he could stand the pressure at work, and if something didn't change soon he couldn't be held answerable for the consequences. I kept hoping the M.D. who was leading the group would say the brave thing, which would have been, "Go ahead and quit. You want to. You need to. It's OK. Take the risk." After all, this is America. The man wouldn't starve to death. Neither would his family. The words were never said.

Perhaps it's not fair to give that example with so little supporting detail. However, I think you can see how a perfectly decent person can wind up feeling trapped and helpless. A different example may serve to illustrate the point. Female bears, it is said, are doting and ferociously protective mothers. Yet, at a certain point, mother bear will turn on her cub and literally drive her offspring away, orphaning the cub, because that's what her instincts tell her to do. If the cub is to grow, it has to leave the mother's protection, and if left to decide that for itself the cub will choose the safe option every time. Many of us do the same thing; most of us can't change until we are forced to.

People don't change, don't grow, because they very often cannot imagine what the next stage may be and they don't feel any pressing need to find out. If we know in general terms what may be ahead of us, we can choose whether or not we wish to take on that challenge. We may decide not to. It's a free world, and that is a respectable choice. It only remains respectable, however, if we make the choice consciously.

Alas, our culture seems to have obliterated our awareness of those choices.

Partly that has to do with what the culture demands of us. It demands we become tax-paying citizens, with jobs and addresses. If you don't have these, you are probably crazy, most likely a criminal, and maybe also a political terrorist. These are persuasive reasons to stay politely ordinary. And if we do, as the culture requires, we get substantial rewards. A good job is generally recognized to be a mark of status, a reward in itself, no matter what added stress it may bring. Everyone will agree that it is a desirable thing even if we may have some secret doubts about the worth of what we are doing. And when we cling to the status value of what we do, rather than the intrinsic value we have for what we do, we are giving away our personal authenticity and signing up instead for reassurance from the crowd. If we only ever do what's popular, then we are no longer in charge of the decisions; others are.

In this section we've considered the pressures that keep many of us as Orphans, and we have done so in terms of how one can assess where others might be by external observation. The Orphan's world is a rich and complex one, and it is also the place at which most people get stuck at one time or another. And here it is necessary to spell out just how vital the Orphan's contribution is in our world. It is the diligent ones, working within the rules, who make our lives possible. The Orphan loves stability and will insist on a stable, meaningful world within which others can, if they wish, search for other meanings (as Pilgrims, for example). So we need to be absolutely clear; it is the *balanced Orphan* who is valuable for us all. The passive Orphan will always be discontented and despairing since validation only comes from outside sources, not from within. In fact, without the balanced Orphan to construct the world properly around us all, there would be no real possibility for the other stages to exist. Beowulf may already be a fighter, but the epic makes it quite clear that he has to be accepted into Heorot first – in a form of adoption – before he can set about helping to restore order. Without the stable world maintained by those who are Orphans there is little scope for anything else. To rephrase this we could say that our challenge is to know the Orphan's world, value it, love it – and yet not be confined by it when it becomes necessary to move into other stages. Remember, the successful Warrior-Lover will return home and accept the status quo, just as an Orphan will, and he'll respect it. Indeed, he will defend it, since that's the safe place out of which the next generation of Pilgrims and Warrior-Lovers and Monarchs will come.

Notes

1. Ambrose, Stephen. *Pegasus Bridge*. New York; Touchstone, 1985, p 149.
2. Galland, Adolf. *The First and the Last*. New York: Ballantine, 1967.

Chapter Twenty

Love and Creativity

Every child loves itself. A baby will cry and wail if it needs something, which is about as direct a way of loving itself as I can think of. And the child loves others: mother is loved with a ferocious energy that matches the child's self love.

At a certain point, we stop loving ourselves, and we moderate our love for others. Perhaps we encounter mean people, people who hate, and we resolve to be more guarded. We also start to make comparisons, from about the age of four onwards. We may decide that we're not as good as others at certain things. This is reality, and it's also depressing. I'm not as tall as Joey or as fast a runner as Laura. So we may attach ourselves to these two companions. What we admire in them is what we wish we had for ourselves, and we become Orphans looking for protection. Tall, athletically competent children are rarely short of friends. Yet even those children know they're not always perfect if only because their parents tell them so, and show them more abilities that the child has yet to learn. So we are likely to gain a realistic sense of our abilities and, in the process, we love ourselves less.

The challenge is to be realistic about who we are and yet to remain fully loving to ourselves.

The Orphan knows there is a better love, somewhere, and, as the Pilgrim, she goes looking for it. This is potentially a dangerous phase, as promiscuity is a real temptation. If I don't love myself, then the fact that lots of people want to have sex with me means I really am loveable, doesn't it? Well, at least it's a diversion for a while. And who hasn't been tempted into promiscuity? Our hormones are more insistent than almost anything else in our early years. Some young women become pregnant and have children because, they say, they want someone to love them. And that will be true for a while. The child will offer them total acceptance and absolute love to begin with. But if the parent has trouble loving herself then the child will know, at some level, and she will have trouble accepting that she is loveable, also. Children learn from their parents' attitudes, even if those attitudes are unspoken.

The task of learning to love oneself is a difficult one because we assume we have to earn the right to be loved. One of the things I admire about some religions, and especially some versions of Christianity, is that even though they tend to insist on codes of conduct, there is a deep sense that no matter what, we are loved by God. As Anne Lamott puts it, "God loves us exactly the way we are, and God loves us too much to let us stay like this." We are loveable *and* we have to get our act together anyhow. This is what the Pilgrim learns, and it is this determination to love oneself, and to put this knowledge into action, that makes the individual into a Warrior-Lover, because the old saying that one can't love anything unless one has first learned to love oneself just may be true. And it may be co-existent. As we learn to love ourselves, we discover that we already do love others; they love us back, and we feel more loveable. And so we grow to the point at which we can commit to real loving and caring for others.

The Monarch, as a ruler over a kingdom has to, loves all the subjects in the realm, even the unpleasant ones. They are entitled to help, human rights, and care. Even when they refuse the help extended to them, they should ideally be treated with humanity. Sometimes it is a necessary, and loving, act to imprison a wrongdoer. The larger population needs to be protected, and it in turn will protect the Monarch when the time comes. The king still has to be a judge, though. The Magician doesn't have to judge. Like the Innocent, the Magician loves others and is so unselfconscious that it seems almost a contradiction in terms to ask if he loves himself.

This brings us to the next part of our discussion, creativity.

As Innocents, we are all creative. Just spend a few moments watching toddlers and you'll see that for them the world is wondrous, a constant toy-box. In fact, toddlers routinely have to be told to put things down – as they find yet another piece of garbage that will become part of their play world. Perhaps this is where creativity first arises and meets its first challenge. Parents don't want their children picking up all sorts of debris and dirt. Who knows where it's been? Think of the risk of disease! That sharp object could poke out an eye. This is all very sensible and it may also destroy creativity. So parents buy nice bright hygienic plastic toys, in cheerful boxes, and they nourish the child's innate abilities in ways they can feel good about. "I'm a good parent," they seem to say. "I buy nice expensive toys that prove how good I am. My child's play will not be messy." Except that children's play is always messy. At least the plastic toys are easy to wipe clean, and to pick up, compared to the branches, the old cans, the bits of litter, and so on.

The child learns fast. So, socially sanctioned toys are much more acceptable? Before we know it, we've got a child who will only accept brand-name toys as advertised on TV. Why? Because if it has been advertised on TV, then the toy must be legitimate, and if everyone else is doing the same thing, then that must be OK, right? What has happened is that the child has moved from Innocent to timid Orphan, and has readily adopted the values that are promoted by the seemingly most powerful side.

Artist friends of mine have observed the same thing. In first grade, children are often wonderfully spontaneous in their drawing and artwork. But all too soon, they begin to want to do things "right", to draw "proper" pictures. And they labor to reproduce reality with photographic exactness. Often they do copy photographs. What happened to all that exuberant creativity? It got orphaned and it headed for the nearest safe space. Some people never leave that space; they live from catalogs that tell them what to buy, how to dress, how to decorate. They always color inside the lines. They adopt "creative" hobbies based more on following the rules than on pushing the boundaries. Pushing the boundaries becomes something one does only for gain, not for the exploration of a feeling. When I worked in the Massachusetts prisons, I saw men who had exercised a huge amount of creativity in the pursuit of crime, and I often wondered at the pity of it; all that energy, skill, and ingenuity wasted on acts that were essentially destructive, ego-based, and self-defeating.

The technician and the mechanic – they may be brilliant at what they do. Yet their creativity is being used within the boundaries of what the job involves. It is a muted creativity, perhaps. After all, not everyone wants to be some sort of inventor, striving for a new discovery. And yet, which of us does not feel a flash of pride, of satisfaction, when we discover a new skill for ourselves?

There are many people who are engaged on a regular basis in creative work, even if there is no discernable reward other than the act itself. Here is the situation in one man's words: "I used regularly to give up writing. I'd always say, "The pay is too poor," as an excuse, because I'd never made a dime from it. That was me allowing the outer world to determine the worth of what I did. Well, I'm still writing."

We don't do writing, or art, or sculpture, or drama, or whatever it is, because of the money or fame. We do it because every creative act reclaims one's soul. It frees us from that timid Orphan-state and it gives back the freedom we surrendered all those years ago.

And so we throw aside our hesitations. We create anyhow. For several months I had a press cutting (until it got swept out one day) which was the obituary of a local man, a mail delivery man as I recall. His great passion, however, was using old bathtubs, which he'd set up on end as enclosures for religious statues. He'd decorate the whole shrine with a mosaic of found objects – painted shards of pottery, broken glass, you name it. I'm sure the neighbors complained. Yet for him his art was deeply spiritual, and the images of saints were testimony to his faith.

Now, his bathtub Madonnas probably didn't deserve a place in the Metropolitan Museum, but it was clear he was a man who was not going to be kept down. He had made himself a Pilgrim – most people treated him as crazy – and this allowed him to wander freely in creative possibilities, a Warrior-Lover now moving towards the authentic expression of himself. He reminded me a little of Da Vinci, whose studio was said to be a revolting sight, even by the standards of the Renaissance, which was far more accustomed to dirt and filth than we are. Da Vinci's interest in anatomy meant there was usually some decaying animal lying about or, worse still, some decomposing human remains which he had been dissecting and drawing. There were no refrigerators to keep it all from stinking, of course. And there were chemical experiments, metallurgical experiments, as well as innovations in paints – all paints had to be hand-made, with assistants to grind the colored pigments and mix the medium. A promising paint was at one time constructed by using dozens of egg whites as a suspension for the pigment. A hot summer studio, devoid of fly screens, could be an unpleasant experience under those circumstances. Here was a creativity that didn't care about conventions.

Using our creativity allows us to love ourselves, our processes, no matter how messy it all may seem. Human beings seek out interesting work and are, on the whole, much happier when engaged in some form of activity than when sitting about doing nothing. Action, creative action, gives us a sense of personal agency without which we would feel lost. This is the most basic impulse of creativity.

When once one takes hold of one's creativity and agrees to use it, and take it seriously, one has to show it to others. That's the Warrior-Lover impulse. When one has achieved mastery of the medium, one is likely to be a Monarch. And yet, Magician status cannot be reached unless one has been able to retrieve that first stage, the Innocent. The Innocent hardly knows why he's creating. He just is; the energy of the world flows through him or her. The dancer becomes the dance; the painter becomes the vision. I suspect that little children really do not see any difference between their products and the vision that they are following, because they are still, imaginatively, at one with that perfect vision. All the other stages are about developing the courage to keep doing it, and the mastery of the techniques so that what emerges is the real thing – not an imitation, not second-hand art, but a true expression of something larger than the individual.

The Innocent is always there within us, ready to appear. We just have to allow the necessary space.

And this should tell us something about the whole process of the six stages. Ultimately, they are about developing creativity in its widest sense, and sharing it. When one reaches the Magician phase – if one does – all the previous stages are incorporated into it. So the Magician can use all that experience of all those struggles and render it for others, if she wishes. She can write about Orphanhood, or paint Warriorhood from a point of intimate awareness of that mental place.

We don't have to be artists in the conventional sense to use our creative energies. When we live our lives creatively we mobilize our experiences, our wisdom, in our daily activities. We bring love and imagination and empathy into our relationships, observing, wondering, and delighting in this complex business of being human. By contrast, if we choose to be rigid and treat everyone as exactly the same (and we can do that out of fear, or pride, or anger) we are not permitting our creativity to function.

Wayne Dyer, in *The Power of Intention* makes an important series of points about people at what we are calling the Magician phase. He suggests that the power to make things happen already exists in the universe, and our task is to try and connect with it. He quotes Carlos Casteneda: "Intent is a force that exists in the universe. When sorcerers (those who live of the Source) beckon intent, it comes to them and sets up the path for attainment, which means that sorcerers always accomplish what they set out to do."

He goes on to quote Patanjali from more than 2,000 years ago: "Dormant forces, faculties, and talents come alive, and you discover yourself to be a greater person by far than you ever dreamed yourself to be."

When we tap into those forces, we are not engaging the sort of bull-terrier determination that may serve a Warrior, or even a Monarch. In fact, we are doing the exact opposite. We are trying less hard. We're working with the world's energy, not against it.

A friend, a Japanese-style acupuncturist and energy healer, put it to me in a similar way. She said: "What I do is get people aligned with the Universe's energy so they can heal themselves. The energy comes through me, but it isn't me." One could discount her words, because she's not famous – except that she is the most extraordinary healer and except for the small detail that she is just one of several people who think and feel this way, all of whom are impressive in their record of healing. The proof of the pudding is in whether it tastes any good, and the proof of the validity of the idea is whether it causes change.

The question is not whether the energy exists. The question is how we are going to use it. It can be used in a variety of ways, some more useful than others. We can mobilize this energy for what we love. The man who works three jobs and juggles their demands so he can get to every Red Sox game each season has chosen to center his life around this love. He mobilizes all his energy for this, before anything else, every waking day. He is a miracle, in his own specialized way. Do I feel in awe of him? Yes. Do I want to use my energy the same way? Well, despite what my friends may want me to say, I'll have to answer No, for I have other loves. His energy is admirable, yet his creativity seems to be that of the Orphan, held within specific limits.

When we connect with our intentions, with our love, with those things which we have identified in Pilgrim stage as being important to us, then we become very hard to stop. Limited thinking drops away as possibilities take over. The Magician emerges at such times..

In the terms we've been considering, the Magician can be observed closer to home in the form of a grandparent, perhaps. This figure is not just grandma, but grandma who has lived life and has done so with full awareness. She's paid attention to what it means to be around people. With luck she's become an astute judge of herself and others. Now she sees that she's a part of a family that she loves and is devoted to. It is at the center of who she is. The family is in turn part of a community, and she sees that her contribution to its success depends upon her being aware of all those relationships happening at the same time; but none of this matters if she cannot bring that knowledge productively, creatively, into play.

Margaret Mead, the famous anthropologist, makes a wonderful comment upon her own experience as a grandmother in her memoir *Blackberry Winter*, in which she describes this same situation more poignantly. She writes with impressive awareness of what her role needs to be, and of how much consciousness it takes to seem to do less.

> I felt none of the much-trumpeted freedom from responsibility that grandparents are supposed to feel. Actually, it seems to me that the obligation to be a resource but not an interference is just as preoccupying as the attention one gives to one's own children. I think we do not allow sufficiently for the obligation we lay on grandparents to keep themselves out of the picture – not to interfere, not to spoil, not to insist, not to intrude – and if they are old and frail, to go and live apart in an old people's home (by whatever name it may be called) and to say that we are happy when, once in a great while, their children bring their grandchildren to visit them.

Her awareness sums up how what may seem to be an easy situation is, in fact, one that depends upon careful assessment of what is best for the family, not just for oneself. We all need to be adaptable. What worked for many years may not work forever.

Just similarly, the man who today writes the perfect seventeenth century sonnet will never be a truly successful communicator in the twenty-first century realm of poetry. The Magician has to be present and alert to what is going on each day, and cannot rely upon old mindsets or fossilized opinions. Yesterday's tactics may have worked brilliantly yesterday, but for today they may need to be adapted.

Grandma may no longer be the center of the family, but if she is vitally engaged in its life then she is more likely to be listened to. She must be in it but not swamped by it. The Magician who retreats to a lofty remote spot of outmoded expertise is no longer a real Magician.

In fact the Magician is not a stage one is ever permanently in, I suspect. If the cliché of the magician has her 'casting a spell' to make things happen, this can be seen as a metaphor for the way a Magician comes into being at the moment in which she makes her presence felt – and once she's made her move she goes back to being Grandma. Here we must remember that this is Grandma who is working as a true Monarch already. As we'll recall, the true Monarch is not the one who gives a lot of orders, but is the one who can bring out the best in others because she sees them as they can be in their best selves, and they know this. And they are able to give their best, out of love, trust, and loyalty. They do this freely, notice, even if it takes them some effort to do so.

Perhaps the Magician is not so much the artist as the work of art the creator is able, just at that moment, to bring into being. There are no casual masterpieces.

This brings us back to our starting point in this section, for the Magician can only use her considerable creative power within the realm of people, and to re-main within the world of imperfect, annoying, wonderful, exasperating humanity is, surely, an act of love. Love and trust go hand in hand, of course, but love seems to lead the way.

As we've already seen, this situation is described to some extent in the story of the Buddha, who refused the ultimate temptation. He was on the brink of achiev-ing Nirvana, which would have meant freedom from the world of mortal incarna-tion with its recurrent cycles of pain. Instead of leaving he decided to stay in this world and help bring others closer to Enlightenment. This was an act of love. It is echoed in the story of Jesus, who came back from the dead to instruct his disciples in what they had to do to become the fullest expressions of their potential. It's even echoed in the story of Moses, who could have stayed on the mountain with God, but instead he came down with the tablets of the law to try and work with a reluctant tribe, which had already started to worship the golden calf.

The way this can play out in our lives is perhaps somewhat unexpected. These days most of us will see death coming closer as we age, even if we don't know exactly when it will strike. If the Innocent's lesson is to discover how to leave home successfully, the Magician's final, best gift of love is to be able to die well. What does this mean? Even those who die in an untimely fashion can be seen to be dying well, if we know what to look for. I am sure that we've all been to funerals and funeral services that have moved us more than we had expected. Grief will be present, but there is also something else available for us in many cases. I can recall going to the funeral of a gentle, relatively modest man, and all of us present were astounded to see that not only was the chapel full, it was overflowing to the point that the outer doors had to remain open and people crammed the aisles. Talking with some of these people later I was surprised at how deeply this self-effacing man had managed to touch so many lives. That day I met people I'd only known slightly before, and as a result we became good friends, caring friends, from that point on. I'd like to think that in this death we had all been given a gift of magnificent proportions; we'd been given the gift of more love in our lives.

A second instance, very similar in many ways, occurred for me when I attended the memorial service of Mai Kramer, a person I had known through friends. She had broadcast a blues radio program throughout the Boston area for some twenty years. At the memorial people were asked if they had any words to say. A steady file of mourners spoke, and what was surprising was that so many said that they had never met Mai; they had only ever heard her radio program. Yet they had felt that they had made contact somehow with a vital, caring person, someone they trusted and felt was a friend, one who had showed them the beauties of the music she loved. Now, these people were not the damaged and deranged of this world; they were those who had successful lives and families. And they spoke about how when they were new to Boston, or at a low point in their lives, Mai's program had made a difference. This is the Magician at work, when we don't even know it.

And here is the point. You may have read this book and thought: Gracious, what a lot of stages to go through! And you'd be right. It all looks like rather hard work. The thing to remember is that we can move through the stages in many ways, but that this is not like a job in which one gathers a certain number of years of seniority and is then promoted. We can, any of us, move very rapidly through the stages when the situation prompts us. People can move from Orphan to Magician in the space of a few hours on their deathbeds, as they use their deaths not to bemoan their situation but to show love to others. It seems to come naturally. Which of us hasn't heard, or seen, an instance of a dying person who has held on until a certain relative arrives? I like to think that, on the whole, the dying person does that because he or she loves the relative, and wants to feel that love and give love as life ends. Remember, the Innocent who has achieved balance knows how to leave home properly, with love. And what is death if it isn't a leaving of home? Death is a loss, of course. But it can also be a gift to those left behind, and it can create more love.

That is the Magician at work. We are all capable of getting to that point. Getting there is good; better still, however, is taking the path we have been discussing, fully aware of where we are and what we need to do. That way we can bring more love and more understanding into the world as we move along. If the good death can be seen as a way to heal some of the rifts and sadnesses that happen in life, then the well-lived life can be seen as a way of attempting to make sure that there are fewer things to heal, and that those we touch are able to be happier, healthier, and more fulfilled throughout their lives. And they in turn will spread the happiness. Magical, really, isn't it?

Love seems to be the most important component. Without love nothing much can happen. As we've seen it is love that causes individuals at Innocent stage to be able to explore and attach. It is, therefore, the first motivator. Since the exploration that follows is a way of acting creatively on one's environment, we can perhaps say that without love there can be no real creativity, just as without creativity exploration cannot get far. As creativity grows it requires courage to keep it alive. Courage must always be kept aware of where it needs to be used, and that requires honesty, as well as the ability to listen. And each of these emotion-laden words, all of them abstractions, needs support from its fellows. These qualities all support each other, and they all grow and develop in each of the stages. So grandma's love will not be the same as the Innocent's love, but it will be rooted in it and connected to it. When we look at a tree in full leaf what do we see? Leaves, mostly, and a trunk; yet we know that the tree is its fruit, its leaves, its branches, its trunk, and the entire root system as well. When we consider the Magician, we must make ourselves aware of all that brought that situation to completion.

Notes

1. Lamott, Anne. *Traveling Mercies: Some Thoughts on Faith*. New York: Random, 1999, p.135.
2. Dyer, Wayne. *The Power of Intention*. Hay House, 2005.
3. Mead, Margaret. *Blackberry Winter*. Quoted in: *Modern American Memoirs*, ed. Dillard and Conley, New York: Harper, 1996, p.405.

Chapter Twenty One

Closing: Some Thoughts on Education

The six stages may seem like an adventure that only a few of us can ever embark on. I do not know if we can all complete it, but I do know we're all invited on the journey. What we do with that invitation is up to us. We can choose where we feel comfortable living our lives. Some people – perhaps most people – really do feel their greatest sense of contentment living as reasonably balanced Orphans. Doing this is a choice, and a worthy one; yet if people do not see that there could be other choices then they will feel stuck, unhappy, unfulfilled, and in despair. As a society we will quickly find ourselves in the company of discontented Orphans, and these are the figures who are mostly likely to become either passive Orphans, haunted by their desperate need to belong to something, or destructive, rejecting active Orphans. Neither is a healthy option. As I have already pointed out, the passive Orphan is easily manipulated by advertising, by trends, and by unscrupulous political leaders. These passive Orphans are the ones who will unhesitatingly fill the ranks of armies of all kinds and accept simplistic arguments that suggest that the enemy is the root of all their problems.

This failure to think critically may be due to poor education, or to deliberate mis-education. Unfortunately the United States does not at present have a very good record in terms of educating its citizens, and our prisons and juvenile facilities are full of offenders who are angry, alienated, and almost entirely without basic skills. Academic education and social education are not at their highest level, and they cost us dearly in terms of crime, poverty, and social dislocation. Whatever the reasons may be behind this failure to educate our citizens (and there have been many books written about this) a considerable number of the people of this country have few resources that can help them move out of angry Orphan status.

If people could be made aware that there are other options, other ways of being and that life could offer them more, then Orphans would be less easily manipulated, with fewer destructive results when those manipulations are used for immoral purposes.

If we are to entertain genuine hopes for peace in this world, for a lessening of violence on our streets and in our families, then it will be necessary to address the causal roots of violence. In a society that is truly dedicated to peace and to the valuing of its citizens, the situation of the passive Orphan would be one that would demand immediate attention, it seems clear. In the years ahead we will need a citizenry that can think, assess, and be concerned with practical ways of making our very complicated society function better. The six archetypal stages are therefore not just a personal obstacle course, but rather a possible key to understanding what it is that people need in order to reach genuine personal fulfillment; and that, surely is a step towards the achieving of an intelligent and lasting peace. That's a pretty good reason for paying attention to these stages.

As we've witnessed, the wisdom they have to convey to us is embodied in the great masterpieces of literature in our culture, the same literature that we routinely do not teach in our schools because it's seen as too demanding or too old fashioned. 'The Western Canon' – by which we mean the great masterpieces of the western world – was for a time a phrase used in our universities and colleges with sneering disdain. That viewpoint represented the triumph of trendy ignorance over real knowledge. If we take the time to read it, our literature can provide us with a world of delight, wonder, and psychological insights – and it can also tell us something about how to live, and do so in ways that are far more engaging than any textbook. But we have to be aware of what's been written before it can work its magic. That means not just reading it or turning it into movies and graphic novels. It means considering literature seriously, deeply, as a tool to help us become fully human. It means talking about these topics, reflecting on them in a careful and intelligent way, and becoming familiar with the stories that can give us what we need. It might mean we have to read these stories more than once, so they can work on us. Now that alone is a radical thought in a culture that is always reaching for the next bright toy. I have hopes, though, that this can happen. It already is happening whenever we see people lining up for a rock concert. The people who flock into those halls are going there to hear songs they already know, for the most part. They already repeat the words, sing along, and find meaning in the music through that repetition. They are looking for exactly the sustenance in art and music that I'm talking about. Unfortunately some of the messages they take away are not always of the finest, but the impulse they are responding to is the desire to find richness, direction, insight, and wisdom through art.

For if we are to use the guiding power of literature we'll have to be careful how we choose. It means our educators may have to reject the third-rate sensationalist fluff that so often passes for literature these days but is in fact just a waste of paper. If we recognize those tales for what they are, fun but vacuous, or sensational but essentially empty, we can make an important distinction that will help us to grow. For we cannot afford to feed ourselves on such material as is currently set before us by so much of the 'entertainment industry' – a name that explains exactly where the emphasis is for so many people who work within it – any more than we can expect to be healthy if we constantly feed ourselves on junk food. As a culture we are presently starving for real, substantial spiritual sustenance, and it's not going to come from reading the average mystery and detective novel, alas. That type of formulaic writing – or viewing experience – will appeal only to Orphans. Fortunately we still have the old tales. They can show us what we need to know. That is why the stories we have looked at in these pages, and many others like them, really are stories we need to know, and know at a deep level.